HOUGHTON MIFFLIN
ENGLISH

Shirley Haley-James   John Warren Stewig

Kenneth William Bierly
Jacqueline L. Chaparro
Helen Felsenthal
Norman A. Felsenthal
Michael C. Flanigan

Mary Mercer Krogness
Harry D. Laub
Nancy C. Millett
Paula J. Parris
Judy Griswold Parsons

Joy Harris Schlagal
Robert C. Schlagal
June Grant Shane
Helen J. Throckmorton

HOUGHTON MIFFLIN COMPANY · BOSTON
Atlanta · Dallas · Geneva, Illinois · Hopewell, New Jersey · Palo Alto · Toronto

Acknowledgments

"All the world is cold ..." by Buson, from *The Four Seasons: Japanese Haiku Second Series,* translated by Peter Beilenson, © 1958 by The Peter Pauper Press. Reprinted by permission.

"Before the End of Summer" (excerpt), by Grant Moss, Jr., © 1960, The New Yorker Magazine, Inc. Reprinted by permission.

"Charles" (excerpt), from *The Lottery* by Shirley Jackson. Copyright 1948, 1949 by Shirley Jackson, copyright renewed 1976 by Laurence Hyman, Barry Hyman, Mrs. Sarah Webster, and Mrs. Jerome Schnurer. Reprinted by permission of Farrar, Straus & Giroux, Inc.

"Dark They Were and Golden-Eyed" (excerpt), by Ray Bradbury. Copyright © 1949, © renewed 1977 by Ray Bradbury. Reprinted by permission of the Harold Matson Company, Inc.

"Daybreak on Avenue C" (excerpt), from *The Avenue Bearing the Initial of Christ into the New World,* by Galway Kinnel. Copyright © 1973 by Galway Kinnell. Reprinted by permission of Houghton Mifflin Company.

Dictionary excerpt, © 1977 Houghton Mifflin Company. Reprinted by permission from *The American Heritage School Dictionary.*

"Examination Day" (excerpt), by Henry Slesar. © 1966. HMH Publications, Inc. Reprinted by permission of Raines & Raines.

"Frog," from *Small Poems,* by Valerie Worth. Copyright © 1972 by Valerie Worth. Reprinted by permission of Farrar, Straus & Giroux, Inc., and Curtis Brown Ltd.

Haiku: "Now a spring rain falls," by Chiyo, from *More Cricket Songs: Japanese Haiku,* translated and copyright © 1971 by Harry Behn. Reprinted by permission of Harcourt Brace Jovanovich, Inc., and Curtis Brown Ltd.

Haiku: "That duck, bobbing up," by Joso, from *Cricket Songs: Japanese Haiku* translated and © 1964 by Harry Behn. Reprinted by permission of Harcourt Brace Jovanovich, Inc., and Curtis Brown Ltd.

Haiku: "A tree frog trilling," by Rogitsu, from *Haiku Harvest* translated by Peter Beilenson and Harry Behn. Copyright 1962. Reprinted by permission of Peter Pauper Press.

"Lost and Found," from *Think About It, You Might Learn Something,* by Robyn Supraner. Copyright © 1973 by Robyn Supraner. Reprinted by permission of Houghton Mifflin Company.

"Rivals" ("My Pal Pasha"), from *The Ghost and the Magic Saber,* by Glendon and Kathryn Swarthout. Copyright © 1963 by Glendon and Kathryn Swarthout. Reprinted by permission of Random House, Inc., and A. Watkins, Inc.

"The Scotty Who Knew Too Much," from *Fables for Our Time,* by James Thurber. (Harper & Row, 1940). Reprinted by permission of Mrs. James Thurber, and Hamish Hamilton Ltd.

"Steam Shovel," from *Upper Pasture,* by Charles Malam. Copyright 1930, © 1958 by Charles Malam. Reprinted by permission of Holt, Rinehart and Winston, Publishers.

(Acknowledgments continued on page 399)

Contents

The Sentence

1 | Kinds of Sentences

You know that a **sentence** is a group of words that expresses a complete thought. Each sentence begins with a capital letter. Sentences can perform four basic kinds of jobs.

Sentences can make statements. A sentence that makes a statement is a **declarative sentence**. It ends with a period.

> I bought a package of wrapping paper today.

Sentences can ask questions. A sentence that asks a question is an **interrogative sentence**. It ends with a question mark.

> What are you going to wrap?

Sentences can give commands or make requests. A sentence that gives a command or makes a request is an **imperative sentence**. It ends with a period.

> Help me tie this bow.

Sentences can also show excitement or strong feeling. A sentence that shows excitement or strong feeling is an **exclamatory sentence**. It ends with an exclamation mark.

> What a nice gift you gave me!   How bright the color is!

Try It Out

A. Tell whether each sentence is declarative, interrogative, imperative, or exclamatory.

1. The contest deadline is tomorrow.
2. How many pennies are in that bowl?
3. Write your answer in the box.
4. What an interesting guess you made!

B. Change each sentence above into a different kind. Tell what kind you made it. The first one has been done for you.

1. **Is the contest deadline tomorrow?**   interrogative

> ▸ A **sentence** expresses a complete thought.
> ▸ A **declarative sentence** makes a statement and ends with a period.
> ▸ An **interrogative sentence** asks a question and ends with a question mark.
> ▸ An **imperative sentence** gives a command or makes a request and ends with a period.
> ▸ An **exclamatory sentence** shows excitement or strong feeling and ends with an exclamation mark.

Written Practice

Copy each sentence. Add the correct punctuation, and tell what kind of sentence it is.

1. Will this first-aid kit fit in your backpack
2. How careless I was to forget my compass
3. Hiking boots help prevent blisters
4. Please give me the bug spray
5. Two pairs of socks will be enough for me
6. Did you pack a trail map and flashlight
7. Take this long-sleeved shirt with you
8. These snacks will give us extra energy
9. What fun this trip will be
10. Are you sure we have everything
11. Traveling on foot brings us closer to nature
12. What unusual birds I can spot with my field glasses
13. How gently that stream flows
14. Can we rest here for a while
15. May I have a drink of water
16. Hand me the canteen
17. Beyond the next hill, what a spectacular view we will have
18. Notice the majestic pines against the bright blue sky

- **Writing Sentences**   Write five sentences about a trip you have taken. Include each kind of sentence.

2 | Subjects and Predicates

Every sentence has two parts, the subject and the predicate. The **subject** tells who or what the sentence is about. The **predicate** tells what the subject does, is, has, or feels.

In some sentences, the subject is only one word.

Joanne / left.   Honesty / pays.

When the subject is more than one word, the main word, the word that names the subject, is called the **simple subject**.

Tall ships / raced.
The frisky brown puppy / leaped up at the noise.

The **simple predicate** is the main word or words that tell what the subject does or is. The simple predicate is always a verb.

Allen / is painting with oils.
The director / locked the dressing room door.

In most sentences, the simple subject and simple predicate are accompanied by words that tell more about them. The simple subject and all the words that tell more about it are known as the **complete subject**.

The green sneakers / are on sale.
Beaches with no surf / are better for small children.

The simple predicate (or the verb) and the words that tell more about it are known as the **complete predicate**.

The smallest problem / seems like a mountain today.
The garden / was filled with violets, tulips, and roses.

Try It Out

A. Give the simple subject and predicate in each sentence.

1. Yvette visited a toy shop last Saturday.
2. The short, freckled-faced girl took a bus to Elm Street.
3. The bus stopped in front of Behan's Joy of Toys Shop.
4. Friendly shoppers smiled at Yvette.
5. The long, narrow toy store bulged with customers.
6. Colored lights flashed on and off.
7. Stuffed lions stared at Yvette from one corner.
8. Monkeys hung from little swings.
9. Beautiful dolls with lifelike faces lined the shelves.
10. Children sat quietly at the tables in the reading room.

B. Give the complete subject and predicate in each sentence.

11. An entire army of toy soldiers stood at attention.
12. Radios featured sing-along microphones.
13. Two girls were working on a puzzle on the carpet.
14. Yvette wrote her name on an electronic chalkboard.
15. The friendly salespeople were wearing bright blue wigs.
16. A clerk in a clown costume wore a funny hat.
17. Loud music was blaring from six speakers on the wall.
18. Wide-eyed Yvette bought a stuffed animal for Ed.
19. The toy delighted Ed.
20. Yvette had a wonderful time at the toy shop.

- ▶ The **simple subject** in a sentence tells who or what the sentence is about.
- ▶ The **simple predicate**, the verb, tells what the subject is or does.
- ▶ The **complete subject** contains the simple subject and all the words that tell more about it.
- ▶ The **complete predicate** contains the simple predicate (the verb) and all the words that tell more about it.

Written Practice

A. Write each sentence. Draw a line between the complete subject and the complete predicate. The first one is done for you.

1. Nine-year-old Mike watched the train set.
   Nine-year-old Mike / watched the train set.
2. The tiny engine chugged along the tracks.
3. A trail of real steam floated into the air.
4. One part of the train disappeared inside a tunnel.
5. The child could hear the whistle.
6. The very last part of the train was painted red.
7. The train climbed slowly up and up.
8. Tracks spread out across a glass platform.
9. Mike could watch the whole train from below.
10. His eyes sparkled.

B. In the sentences above, underline the simple subject once and the simple predicate twice. The first one is done for you.

1. **Nine-year-old Mike watched the train set.**

- **Writing Sentences**   Use each word group below to create a sentence with a complete subject and a complete predicate.

   Example: boy sings   **The proud young boy sings a solo.**

   11. boat sank
   12. friend writes
   13. singer performs
   14. quarterback threw
   15. people need

   16. Alexander found
   17. light shines
   18. time flies
   19. Denver is
   20. soup boils

3 | Subjects in Imperative and Interrogative Sentences

Can you find the subject of these sentences?

IMPERATIVE: Call a taxi for me.
INTERROGATIVE: Did she buy the last orange?

In an imperative sentence like the first one above, the subject is not always stated. Usually the subject is understood to be *you*.

(You) Call a taxi for me.

In an interrogative sentence, you can find the subject by rearranging the question into a statement. Ask yourself who or what the verb talks about.

QUESTION: Did she buy the last orange?
STATEMENT: She did buy the last orange.

Who or what did the buying? The verb *did buy* refers to *she*, so *she* is the subject of the sentence.

Try It Out

Name the subject in each sentence below. Explain how you found your answer.

1. Deposit the correct change.
2. Did Paula find her scarf?
3. Please sit next to me.
4. Does the driver stop?
5. Are you coming with me?
6. Ask for help.
7. Watch that first step.
8. Can you make it?
9. Should we sit together?
10. Shall I call you?
11. Is the aisle crowded?
12. Take a seat.
13. Should I open a window?
14. Let the breeze in.
15. Breathe that fresh air.
16. Did Paula bring a book?
17. Show it to me.
18. Are you finished with it?
19. Do we get off soon?
20. Will someone direct us?
21. Can you read that sign?
22. Hold my bags for me.

> The subject of an imperative sentence is usually understood to be *you*.
>
> To find the subject of an interrogative sentence, rearrange the question into a statement. Then ask who or what the verb talks about.

Written Practice

A. Write the subject of each sentence.

1. Test the batteries first.
2. Does the car need water?
3. Please check the oil gauge.
4. Clean the rear window.
5. Will the helper wipe the mirror?
6. Do not fill the tank today.
7. Give me a half tank of gas.
8. Can we drive on an empty tank?
9. How much do I owe?
10. Put my change in this bank.

B. Write *interrogative* or *imperative* to name the kinds of sentences below. Then write each simple subject.

11. Buy your ticket at the box office.
12. Will you see a play or a musical?
13. Follow the usher to your seat.
14. Wait patiently for the first act.
15. Will the actors speak loudly?
16. Should I ask for a program?
17. Stretch your legs at intermission.
18. Does the curtain fall after the final act?

- **Writing Sentences** Write two imperative sentences and three interrogative sentences. Underline the subject of each one. Add *(You)* when you need to.

Subjects in Imperative and Interrogative Sentences 15

4 | Subjects in Sentences with *here* and *there*

When a sentence begins with the word *here* or *there*, the subject will not be either of these two words. You can find the simple subject of such a sentence by asking yourself, Who or what is here? or Who or what is there?

Here is our pizza. (*What is here?* Pizza.)
There is my favorite shirt. (*What is there?* Shirt.)

Try It Out

Read each sentence aloud. Then name each simple subject.

1. Here is my stop.
2. Here are my uncles.
3. There is Ted now.
4. There is the last row.
5. Here is Peter Pan.
6. There are the answers.

If a sentence begins with *here* or *there*, you can find the simple subject by asking either, Who or what is here? or Who or what is there?

Written Practice

Write the simple subject of each sentence.

1. There is a brand new bus.
2. Here is the express.
3. There are two new drivers.
4. Here is my fare.
5. There was no schedule.
6. There is a huge crowd.
7. Here are the last seats.
8. Here is a pillow.

• **Writing Sentences** Write five sentences. Begin some of them with *here* and others with *there*. Circle each simple subject.

5 | Compound Subjects and Predicates

Every sentence has at least one simple subject and predicate.

> The <u>children</u> in the band / <u>played</u> well.
> <u>Joan</u> / <u>listened</u>.

Some sentences have more than one subject. When a sentence has two or more subjects joined by *and* or *or*, the subject is called a **compound subject**.

> <u>Joan</u> and her <u>mother</u> / left.
> <u>Rain</u>, <u>sleet</u>, or <u>snow</u> / was predicted.

Some sentences have more than one predicate. When a sentence has two or more predicates joined by *and* or *or*, the predicate is called a **compound predicate**.

> The rain / <u>dripped</u>, <u>splashed</u>, or <u>bounced</u>.
> Water / <u>has leaked</u> into Joan's shoes and <u>soaked</u> her socks.

Notice that the connecting word *and* or *or* joins the parts of a compound subject or compound predicate.

Try It Out

Find the subject and predicate of each sentence. Tell which ones are compound.

1. <u>Joey</u> or <u>Iris</u> won the tennis match.
2. The <u>tennis instructor</u> watched both of them.
3. Two <u>judges</u> sat at the net and called the line shots.
4. <u>Joey</u> has a good serve and keeps his eye on the ball.
5. <u>Iris</u> can return the ball quickly and accurately.
6. <u>Iris</u> and <u>Joey</u> exchange a handshake at the net.
7. <u>Hard work</u>, talent, and luck make a tennis player great.
8. <u>Both</u> players enter and win major competitions.

> ▸ A **compound subject** has two or more subjects joined by a connecting word such as *and* or *or*.
> ▸ A **compound predicate** has two or more predicates joined by a connecting word such as *and* or *or*.

Written Practice

A. Write the compound subjects and the compound predicates in the sentences below. One sentence has neither.

1. Carla or Bert went on a fishing trip.   Carla   Bert
2. The wind stirred the sea and chilled the air.
3. The captain, the crew, and the passengers were ready.
4. The boat rocked and bobbed on the waves.
5. Live bait or flies were put on the fishing lines.
6. Carla caught a bass and two bluefish.
7. Bert cleaned the fish and put them on ice.
8. Nancy or Al ran the bait shop.
9. The sea and the wind became calm again.
10. They returned to the dock and carried home the catch.

B. Write *CS* if the sentence has a compound subject. Write *CP* if the sentence has a compound predicate. Then write the connecting word that joins each set of compound parts.

11. Joe took us to a museum and bought us lunch. CP   and
12. The menus had fancy lettering and looked like scrolls.
13. A salad, a sandwich, or hot soup was served.
14. Visitors toured the galleries or watched slides.
15. One guide wore a suit of armor and told dragon stories.
16. Ancient Greece or the Middle Ages was on the tour.
17. Work tools, jewels, and coins were under glass.

● **Writing Sentences**   Write three sentences with compound subjects. Write two sentences with compound predicates.

6 | Compound Sentences

The sentences you have studied so far have all been simple sentences. A simple sentence expresses one complete thought and has a subject and a predicate.

A <u>pencil</u> / is a modern writing tool.

Two simple sentences can be combined into one sentence. The new combined sentence is called a compound sentence.

SIMPLE SENTENCES: Ancient peoples had no alphabet.
They could draw signs and picture codes.

COMPOUND SENTENCE: Ancient peoples had no alphabet, but <u>they could draw signs and picture codes.</u>

SIMPLE SENTENCES: I studied the picture writing.
Jim read about the first alphabet.

COMPOUND SENTENCE: I studied the picture writing, and <u>Jim read about the first alphabet.</u>

SIMPLE SENTENCES: You can report on the printing press.
You can draw the Greek alphabet.

COMPOUND SENTENCE: <u>You can report on the printing press,</u> or you can draw the Greek alphabet.

A **compound sentence** contains two or more simple sentences that are related. Notice that the simple sentences are all joined by a connecting word—*and*, *but*, or *or*. A comma comes before the connecting word.

How do you decide which connecting word to use? Look at how the two simple sentences within the compound are related. If the simple sentences show a contrast or give different points of view, use *but*. Use *and* if the second simple sentence adds more information to the first. Finally, if the two simple sentences give a choice, use *or*.

Do not confuse a compound sentence with a simple sentence that has a compound predicate. Compound sentences always have a subject and a predicate on each side of the connecting word.

COMPOUND SENTENCE: The <u>letter</u> <u>was</u> wet, and some <u>words</u> <u>were</u> blurry.

COMPOUND PREDICATE: <u>Many</u> <u>scientists</u> <u>form</u> teams and <u>work</u> together.

Try It Out

A. Tell whether each sentence is compound or simple. Find the connecting word that joins the parts of each compound sentence. Then name the simple sentences that make up each compound sentence.

1. The pictures on cave walls communicate a story, but they are not made up of words.
2. Some pictures tell of hunting adventures, and others are just notes or reminders.
3. We do not always understand these pictures, but scientists still study them.
4. People wrote on clay surfaces, or chipped their message into stone.

B. Write compound sentences by joining each pair of simple sentences with a connecting word. Use commas correctly.

5. Pictures usually stand for things. A written letter stands for a sound.
6. Words were first written down five thousand years ago. We are still creating new words today.
7. Chisels were used for pencils. Stone was used for paper.

▸ A **compound sentence** contains two or more simple sentences that are related. The sentences are usually joined by a comma and a connecting word such as *and*, *or*, or *but*.

Written Practice

A. Copy only the compound sentences below. Underline the simple sentences that make up each compound.

1. The eagle is a strong bird, and it has a huge wing span.
2. It has small eyes but can see for miles.
3. The eagle may live in the Alaskan wilderness, or it may migrate to a warmer climate.
4. It is a powerful bird but cannot withstand the cold.
5. The eagle looks fierce, and it has a majestic quality.
6. It preys on salmon, or it looks for other animals.
7. Are most eagles owned by trainers, or do they fly free?
8. We admired the eagle, and it is now our national symbol.
9. The eagle represents power and courage, and harpy eagles are perhaps the most powerful of all.
10. Eagles can be found on coins and dollar bills, and the Great Seal of the United States also bears an eagle.

B. Combine each pair of sentences into a compound sentence by using a comma and *and,* *but,* or *or.*

11. We could play tennis. We could go to the movies.
12. I brought my key home. It is not in my pocket.
13. We played singles for an hour. Then we played doubles.
14. I used to like hockey. Now I prefer baseball.
15. Flo ran the fifty-yard dash. Jan jumped hurdles.
16. We could try out for the city team this year. Our school coach could ask us to begin workouts in the gym.
17. Marla will try out for the all-state team. She will go to a sports camp.
18. Well-known players will teach tennis. A major league player will give batting hints.
19. We can go for two weeks. We can spend the summer.
20. Mom will drive me there. Aunt Elise will bring me back.

- **Writing Sentences**   Think of a sport or game you enjoy. Write five compound sentences about it.

7 | Correcting Fragments and Run-ons

You know that a sentence is a group of words that contains a subject and a predicate and expresses a complete thought. A sentence begins with a capital letter and ends with a punctuation mark. Any group of words that does not form a sentence is called a sentence **fragment**. A sentence fragment does not express a complete thought. Which parts of these examples are fragments?

> My hand was on the phone. When it rang.
> I wanted to talk with you. About my dream.

The second part of each example is a sentence fragment. You can avoid sentence fragments by keeping the sentence parts together.

> My hand was on the phone when it rang.
> I wanted to talk with you about my dream.

You can also correct a fragment by expanding it into a sentence.

> My hand was on the phone. When it rang, I was startled.

Another kind of sentence error is run-on sentences. A **run-on sentence** strings together sentences that should be written separately. Run-on sentences are hard to read because you cannot tell where one thought ends and the next one begins. Read these run-on sentences.

> Uncle Frank is a writer he also is a puppeteer.
> Our family saw his show, everyone loved it.
> Addie designed the costumes, she moved the sets.

You can correct a run-on sentence by separating each thought into a sentence of its own. Use a capital letter at the beginning of each sentence and a punctuation mark at the end.

> Uncle Frank is a writer. He also is a puppeteer.
> Our family saw his show. Everyone loved it.
> Addie designed the costumes. She moved the sets.

You can also correct a run-on by writing a compound sentence.

> Uncle Frank is a writer, but he also is a puppeteer.
> Our family saw his show, and everyone loved it.

Another way to correct a run-on sentence is to use a compound subject or predicate.

> Addie designed the costumes and moved the sets.

Try It Out

A. Tell whether each item is a complete sentence or a fragment.

1. Three little boxes.
2. Because I am early.
3. Talking for two hours.
4. Can she go?
5. Quietly at midnight.

6. When it rings?
7. A scarf and gloves.
8. Watched this part.
9. Hold that nail steady.
10. Down the stairs!

B. Tell how you would correct these run-on sentences.

11. My dad used to work at a dirt track now he owns racing cars, he races sometimes.
12. I loved the track on Sunday I watched races from the pit.
13. Bikes stop at the pit for repairs Dad worked there.
14. Once I waved the checkered flag, they use flags to start and stop the race.
15. I want to be a mechanic I will be a good one, I would like to work in the pit at the track.
16. Janet Guthrie is my favorite racing car driver she did not win the Indy 500 she promotes safe driving.

▸ A sentence **fragment** is a group of words that does not express a complete thought.
▸ A **run-on sentence** strings together sentences that should be written separately.
Avoid fragments and run-ons in your writing.

Written Practice

A. Read each group of words. Write *S* if it is a complete sentence. Write *F* if it is only a sentence fragment.

1. A first-class marble contest.
2. Six of us entered.
3. The club champion and I. *S*
4. I had sixteen marbles. *S*
5. When it rolled into the ring. *F*
6. Do not hit that one. *S*
7. Because I need more practice. *F*
8. To my surprise, breaking into the lead. *F*
9. Forced me out of the competition. *F*
10. I lost. *S*

B. Rewrite these run-on sentences correctly.

11. Yesterday was an exciting day my teacher got married.
12. All of us in the class went, we sat together I sat next to Susan in the fifth row.
13. I wish you were there someone in the row in front of us began to cry.
14. First, Jamie cried and then Lou started and I cried, too.
15. You can probably guess what happened next the flower girls came in.
16. Chuck had hay fever he sneezed he could not stop.
17. The whole audience turned around the bride laughed the groom laughed.
18. Then Susan and I laughed and cried, Joe laughed and cried, too we all did.
19. It was the best wedding I had ever seen everyone agreed.
20. I am going to have lots of flowers when I get married they will be plastic.

- **Writing Sentences** Change the sentence fragments in exercise A into complete sentences. Begin each sentence with a capital letter and end it with a punctuation mark.

lend, borrow; let, leave

Do you know the difference in meaning between the verbs *lend* and *borrow*? Read this conversation.

May I <u>borrow</u> your hair dryer?
I will <u>lend</u> it to you for two days.

The person who borrows receives something. *Borrow* means "to take." The person who lends gives something. *Lend* means "to give."

Let and *leave* have different meanings, too. The verb *let* means "to allow." The verb *leave* means "to go away."

My brothers <u>let</u> me play football with them.
Tomorrow we <u>leave</u> for the Catskill Mountains.

Why are *let* and *leave* correct in the sentences above?

> *Borrow* means "to take." *Lend* means "to give."
> *Let* means "to allow." *Leave* means "to go away."

Practice

A. Choose a word from the parentheses to complete each sentence correctly.

1. Did I (let, leave) the dog go outside last night?
2. Please (leave, let) me go on the hay ride.
3. We (let, leave) for New York this afternoon.
4. (Let, Leave) the curtain fall after the first act.
5. (Lend, Borrow) me your bus pass.
6. I usually (leave, let) my house at six o'clock.

7. May I (lend, borrow) your brush?
8. Alda wants to (lend, borrow) five dollars from Katie.
9. Please (let, leave) me (borrow, lend) your mittens.
10. Ms. Rodriguez will (let, leave) José take piano lessons.
11. Do not (leave, let) the dough rise too high.
12. None of the neighbors has a mower that I can (lend, borrow).
13. If you need more chairs, (borrow, lend) some from us.
14. (Let, Leave) the adults (let, leave) after the children.

B. Write the word *borrow, lend, let,* or *leave* to complete each sentence.

15. Do you remember the flashlight you wanted to ____ from me?
16. Yes, you were going to ____ it to me, and I was going to ____ your hedge clipper.
17. Could you ____ me use it for a few days?
18. I promise not to ____ it out in the rain.
19. My sister-in-law and brother ____ my snowblower every winter.
20. Should you ____ them ____ it so often?
21. Why shouldn't I ____ it to them?
22. They might not ____ you have it back for a long time.
23. ____ me guess who else does the same thing.
24. I will ____ the flashlight on this table for you.

• **Writing Sentences** Write four sentences of your own, using *lend, borrow, let,* and *leave* correctly.

Our English Language

The English language is made from an international family of words. Many English words originally came from Spanish, French, Italian, and other European languages. Explorers brought back to England riches from all over the world. They also brought words from China, India, and Africa.

Early settlers in the United States found much that was new to them. As they named these new things, they borrowed words from Native Americans. Words like *chipmunk*, *moccasin*, and *succotash* became a part of the English language in this way.

The language of Spanish settlers mixed with that of English settlers. *Ranch*, *vanilla*, and *cafeteria* come from Spanish words.

Read these English words and the languages they come from.

silk (Baltic)   garage (French)   gorilla (Greek)
pretzel (German)   pajamas (Hindi)   piano (Italian)

Even today new words continue to be added to English. We still turn to Latin and Greek to name new ideas and discoveries, such as *phonograph* and *television*.

Practice

A. Look up these words. Write the language each word comes from. Write the meaning of each word.

1. skunk   **3.** jungle   **5.** banana   **7.** madras
2. rodeo   **4.** auction   **6.** violin   **8.** penguin

B. Look up *technology* and *interplanetary*. Write where each word comes from. Then write the meaning of each word.

- **Writing a Paragraph**   Write a paragraph telling how and why you think the English language will change in the future.

Review

- **Kinds of Sentences** *(pp. 9–10)*   Copy each sentence, adding the correct punctuation. Then write *declarative*, *interrogative*, *imperative*, or *exclamatory* to identify each sentence.

  1. Has a circus ever come to your town
  2. A small circus visited us in early June
  3. What a wonderful sight the parade was
  4. Our seats were in the front of the center ring
  5. Go to the circus when one comes to your town

- **Subjects and Predicates** *(pp. 11–13)*   Copy each sentence. Draw a line between the complete subject and the complete predicate. Underline simple subjects once, simple predicates twice.

  6. The girl next door collects posters.
  7. Her present collection includes twenty horse posters.
  8. One huge poster of the Beatles hangs on her door.
  9. Posters cover her bedroom walls.
  10. A cousin from Texas gave her a giant poster of a sunset.

- **Subjects in Imperative and Interrogative Sentences** *(pp. 14–15)*   Write the subject of each sentence.

  11. May we see your new dog?
  12. Step into the yard.
  13. Look at the doghouse.
  14. Would Jed like a puppy?
  15. Please hold the leash.
  16. Do collies fetch sticks?

- **Subjects in Sentences with *here* and *there*** *(p. 16)*   Write the subject of each sentence.

  17. Here is our playground.
  18. There is the tennis court.
  19. There is the slide.
  20. Here is the huge pool.
  21. There are the boats.
  22. Here are our friends.

- **Compound Subjects and Predicates** *(pp. 17–18)*   Write the compound subject or compound predicate of each sentence.

    23. Will Warner, Fran, or Joe rebuild the bicycle?
    24. They planned and sketched their new design.
    25. Orange paint or reflectors glow in the dark.
    26. Mirrors and a loud horn completed the accessories.

- **Compound Sentences** *(pp. 19-21)*   Combine each set of simple sentences into a compound sentence. Use the correct punctuation.

    27. We can stand on the hill. We can go down by the lake.
    28. The air is still cool. The sun is very warm.
    29. They had a picnic in the woods. They stayed until sunset.
    30. Nora borrowed a sled. One of the runners was broken.

- **Correcting Fragments and Run-ons** *(pp. 22-24)*   Read each item. If it is a complete sentence, write *C*. If it is a fragment, write *F*. If it is a run-on sentence, write *R*.

    31. In three minutes near the new public library.
    32. Last weekend was exciting my sister got married my brother came home from college.
    33. Should I leave?
    34. Our lawn was full of people everyone parked on the road and in the driveway.

    Change each fragment into a complete sentence. Write each run-on sentence correctly.

- **Using Words Correctly** *(pp. 25-26)*   Write the word in parentheses that correctly completes each sentence.

    35. Leah allowed me to (lend, borrow) her book from her.
    36. Can we (leave, let) for the country early tomorrow morning?
    37. Libraries (lend, borrow) people many books each day.
    38. Please (leave, let) me talk to my parents about it first.
    39. May I (borrow, lend) your sleeping bag?

Listening and Speaking

1 | Hearing or Listening?

Do you know the difference between hearing and listening? When your father asks, "Do you *hear* me?" and you reply, "I hear you, Dad," you are right. You have *heard* him, even though you might not have *listened* to what he said.

All day long you hear a combination of sounds—horns honking, people talking, dogs barking, and music playing. When you listen, however, you choose a certain sound and focus your attention on it. **Listening** is hearing with a purpose. When you listen to a class discussion, for example, your purpose is to understand what is being said, not just to hear the sounds of the words. Being an effective listener is not easy. Listening requires thinking, and thinking requires concentration. Sometimes we get a cue, or signal, to listen. Just when your thoughts are carrying you a million miles away, you hear your teacher's question, which snaps you out of a daydream.

One way to become an effective listener is to think about the sounds that you have just heard. Ask yourself these questions.

1. What is that sound? (fire alarm ringing, a cricket chirping, brakes screeching, a cat purring)
2. How might that sound affect me? (alert, calm, sadden, scare, anger)
3. What are the words being spoken? (words that instruct, praise, suggest, warn, scold, question)
4. How are the words being used? (context or situation)
5. How are the words being spoken? (quickly, slowly, softly, loudly)

Practice

Be perfectly quiet. Listen to all the sounds around you. Try to identify each sound and then concentrate on one sound. Ask yourself the questions above.

2 | How to Listen

Why is it important to be a good listener? Most of the time that you spend communicating comes through listening—not through reading, writing, or speaking. Consequently, a tremendous amount of your knowledge comes from listening.

Being a good listener is a skill you learn, and therefore, it takes some work. You must force yourself to listen even when you are not especially interested in what you are hearing. You must block out other sounds you hear. You must pay attention and concentrate on what you have chosen to listen to.

The following guidelines will help you listen better. Keep track of what you hear with the word *TRACK*.

T reminds you to **think.**

> Think about what you are listening to. Did you understand what the speaker said? If not, ask questions.

R reminds you to **review.**

> Think over what the speaker said. What are the main points? Do you remember them? If you do not remember them, find out what they are.

A reminds you to pay **attention.**

> Be alert when you listen. Actively listen to the points the speaker makes. Do you have something to add to the speaker's ideas? Do you have questions to ask?

C reminds you to **concentrate.**

> Block out any distractions, and do not let your mind wander to other subjects or to other sounds. Think about what you are listening to.

K reminds you to **keep up.**

> Keep your mind on what the speaker is saying. Keep your eyes on the speaker. Keep up with the points the speaker makes.

Practice

A. How much time do you spend listening as compared to reading, writing, and speaking? Make a chart that shows how much you listen, read, and write between the hours of 9:00 A.M. and 3:00 P.M. At the end of this time, you will know how much time you spent listening.

B. Pair off with another student. Each of you take five minutes to tell your partner something about yourself. You might tell something you have done or something you want to do. After both of you have finished, tell the class what your partner told you. See how well you listened.

C. Find out if you listen well.

1. Five students wait outside your classroom while your teacher reads a passage to the rest of the class.
2. Student A comes back into the room. Your teacher asks a student to repeat to Student A the passage he or she just heard.
3. Then Student B returns to the room, and Student A repeats the message.
4. Repeat step 3 with all five students who left the classroom. (Student B tells C; Student C tells D, and so forth)
5. After the last student has repeated what he or she heard, your teacher will reread the passage to the class.

3 | Listening Clues

You have been a detective who picks up sound clues since you were a baby. Although babies probably do not understand the meaning of most words they hear, they do understand how the words sound.

Without being aware of it, you, the listener, decide what someone is *really* saying to you. Not only do you listen to the words that are spoken, but you listen to how the speaker says the words. For example, when you say "Yes" in an even voice, it suggests that you agree about something. If you say "Yes?" with a slight rise in your voice, you are really saying, "What is it?" "What do you want?" "What do you mean?" or "I need more information."

Pitch, stress, and juncture determine the meaning of words people say.

Pitch

Pitch is the rise and fall of your voice, its highs and lows. Say the sentence, "It's snowing." Your voice sounds even. Say the same sentence as a question, "It's snowing?" Your voice rises suddenly, and the meaning of the sentence is changed. You are questioning if it is snowing. Now say, "It's snowing!" with excitement. Your voice rises gradually and falls, and the meaning of the sentence is changed again. This time you are excited about the snow.

Practice

Read each of the following sentences first as statements, then as questions, and last as exclamations. Pay attention to the way your voice rises and falls.

1. Harry has a new bike.
2. Wilma is a good soccer player.
3. That is a good book.

Stress

Stress is the amount of force or emphasis you put on a word. If you stress one word over another in a sentence, you can change the meaning of the sentence. Read how stress or emphasis changes the meaning of this sentence.

Will <u>you</u> dance with me now?	(This sentence is about the person.)
Will you <u>dance</u> with me now?	(This sentence is about the person's action—dance, not talk.)
Will you dance with me <u>now</u>?	(This sentence is about the time.)

Practice

A. Each sentence below has two possible meanings depending on which word you stress. Pair off with another student, and practice saying each sentence so that it has the meaning given in parentheses.

1. Are you going to the movies? (you, not someone else)
2. Jon liked the book I gave him. (the book, not something else)
3. Rita is a great skater. (Rita, not someone else)
4. Did you call your aunt? (your aunt, not someone else)

B. Pair off with another student. Say each sentence stressing a different word each time. How many different meanings did you discover?

5. Ted found his scarf yesterday.
6. Melissa went to a play last week.
7. Tom and Evelyn won the election.

Juncture

Juncture is the pauses in your speech. You pause to show that one thought is ending and another is beginning. You also pause to break up a list of words. Juncture or pausing is another way to show emphasis in your voice.

How is the meaning changed in these sentences by juncture or pausing?

Tony let the ball drop.
Tony, let the ball drop.

Marie George and Doug played basketball.
Marie, George, and Doug played basketball.

In the first pair of sentences, the first sentence tells you that Tony dropped the ball. In the second sentence, someone is telling Tony to let the ball drop. In the first sentence of the second pair, two people are playing basketball, Marie George and Doug. In the last sentence how many people are playing?

Practice

Practice saying each sentence in two or three different ways by changing juncture.

1. Can you hear Rebecca?
2. Christopher Robin and I are going to the movies.
3. Francine let the horse out of the corral.
4. Susan Robin and Elizabeth won the competition.
5. Did you see Andy?

4 | Listening for Main Ideas and Details

Main Ideas

When you listen to a speaker, if you focus only on the details, you will pick up some information, but not the main points. Listening for the main idea is the most important skill in understanding what you are listening to. As you listen, think about the single most important point the speaker is making. (Remember the *T* in TRACK.) Which idea would make a newspaper headline? Try to summarize the main idea into one sentence.

Imagine that you are listening to someone speak about Hawaii.

Hawaii is a collection of many large and small islands. Eight major islands make up the group, and Hawaii is the largest. Maui, Oahu, and Kauai are the next largest islands. The most populated and economically developed island is Oahu. Three other main islands are Kahoolawe, Lanai, and Nihau. There are over 100 small islands in the Hawaiian group. Many are so small that only birds inhabit them.

What is the main idea of the paragraph? If you said, "Hawaii has eight major islands," or "Hawaii has over 100 small islands," you were stating details. Remember, the **main idea** is the most important point and is usually the topic sentence of a paragraph. In this paragraph, the main idea is that Hawaii is a group of many large and small islands.

After you finish listening to a discussion or to someone speak, review the main ideas. (Remember the *R* in TRACK.) You might even write down the main ideas. Then you can write any details that you recall.

Practice

Listen while your teacher reads a paragraph to you. State the main idea in your own words.

Details

Details give supporting information and facts about the main idea of a paragraph. When you listen, notice what details the speaker uses. Details can be examples, descriptions, facts, comparisons, and contrasts.

Here is the talk Walter gave on peanuts. Listen for the main ideas and details.

> Peanuts produce different grades of oil that have a variety of uses. High-grade oil, for example, is used in foods. Low grades of peanut oil are used to oil machinery and as an ingredient in products such as soap, shampoo, and paint. This versatile oil is also used in making explosives.

What is the main idea of Walter's talk? Did you say, "Peanuts produce different grades of oil that have many uses"? Walter used four details to support his main idea. What are they?

Sometimes speakers use signal words that alert you to the details. (Remember the *K* in TRACK.) Examples of signal words are *for example, first, such as, then.* What signal words did Walter use in his talk?

Practice

Listen while your teacher reads a paragraph to you. What is the main idea of the paragraph? What details support the main idea? Do you remember any signal words?

5 | Listening to Remember

Have you ever been in this situation? You have been sent to the store to buy four items—paper towels, bananas, dog food, and milk. You get to the market, and all you remember are the milk and paper towels. People have a hard time remembering what they have heard and what they have learned. Sometimes they forget from one minute to the next. Listening to remember requires special skill, because you usually do not have a second chance to hear a talk or discussion.

Here are some guidelines to help you remember what you learn. They are based on information that is known about remembering.

1. You remember what you understand. If you do not understand something, ask that it be explained.
2. You remember something better if you review it when you learn it. After a discussion, try recalling the main points and important details. Go over the same information mentally about an hour later. Repeat the same process after a week and after a month.
3. Your mind wanders more during the middle of a learning time. You naturally remember more of what you hear from the beginning and end of a class discussion or a talk. Therefore, you must concentrate harder during the middle of a class discussion or other listening situation.
4. You tend to remember things that are unusual—a mental picture that is ridiculous, moving, and colorful is easier to remember. Form a strong mental picture, therefore, of what you are hearing.

Practice

Your teacher will read you a list of words. When your teacher finishes, write down as many words as you can remember. How many words did you remember?

6 | How Well Do You Speak?

Listening and speaking go together like a hand and a glove. If you learn to be a good listener, you will probably learn to be a good speaker. Good listeners let others talk, and they listen attentively. Good listeners stay on track with a speaker. Good speakers do not take over conversations so that others cannot participate. Good speakers say things clearly so that their main points are easy to understand.

How effectively do you speak? Here is a checklist to guide you in your speaking skills.

1. Do you speak clearly? Do you pronounce syllables distinctly and put endings on your words? Do you pronounce words correctly? If you run your words together or mispronounce words, you will not be understood.

2. Do you speak loudly enough without shouting? Loud talkers can be irritating to listeners, and very soft speakers can hardly be heard.

3. Do you speak at the correct speed? If you speak too fast, you will be hard to understand. If you speak too slowly, it will be hard to pay attention to you.

4. Do you look at the people you are talking to? If you look around instead of at someone you are talking to, that person will be less interested in what you are saying.

5. Do you choose words that work for particular situations and people? Each speaking situation is slightly different, and the language you use should show the difference. When you speak with a friend, for example, it is likely that you speak differently from how you speak with people you hardly know.

6. Do you interrupt people who are talking? People do not like interruptions when they are speaking. If you must speak, excuse yourself for interrupting.

7. Do you use many "filler" words such as *er, ah,* and *um*? Such words make you sound unsure of what you are saying and harder to pay attention to.

8. Do you use feeling and expression in your voice? Remember pitch, stress, and juncture. How you say something affects what you mean. Say the sentence, "I am tired" calmly then angrily. Calmly, these words sound like a statement of fact. Angrily, they seem to mean, "Leave me alone."

9. Do you move your body and face when you speak? Body language and facial expression add a lot to what you say. When people are excited, they often move around. They may tap their feet or move their hands more than usual. People's faces almost always show just how they are feeling.

10. Do you think before you speak? Thinking out loud leaves you little time to organize your thoughts. If your thoughts are not organized, your words or message will be unclear.

Practice

A. In the sentences below, two words are underlined. Choose the correct words and say them correctly.

1. When you travel north are you heading toward the <u>artic</u> or <u>arctic</u>?
2. Would you <u>ask</u> or <u>ax</u> a question?
3. Do lions <u>escape</u> or <u>excape</u> from the zoo?
4. Did you take a <u>pitcher</u> or a <u>picture</u> with your camera?
5. Did you find a good book in the <u>library</u> or <u>liberry</u>?

B. Get together with three or four students. Take turns saying each of the following sentences in each of these ways: glad, sad, mad, and scared.

6. Did you really mean that?
7. Where do you think they went?
8. I want to leave now.

7 | Using the Telephone

How well do you communicate on the telephone? Talking on the telephone is an everyday experience that requires listening and speaking. Follow these guidelines for using the telephone.

1. When you call someone, do you start the conversation by identifying yourself to the person who answers the phone? "Hello, this is Beverly Jamison." If you know the person well, you may give just your first name. It is important to identify yourself on the telephone because your voice is not always recognizable.

2. If the person you are calling is not there, do you leave a brief and clear message? Leave your full name and telephone number, and tell the message briefly, in an orderly way. Thank the listener for taking the message. Henry called his mother at her office and left this message for her.

> Please tell Mrs. Jacobs that her son Henry called. I am at my friend Jeff's house. The number is 459-8629. Please ask her to call me as soon as she can.

3. If you are taking a message for someone, do you write it down? It is important to write down a message because you might forget it, or you might not be there to give it to the person when he or she returns. If you take a message for someone, it is important to include all the necessary information. The person taking the message for Henry wrote this message for his mother.

> Mrs. Jacobs, your son Henry called. He is at Jeff's house, 459-8629. Please call him soon. 3:20 Stan.

Did you notice that Stan wrote the time of the call and his name? He did that so Mrs. Jacobs would know when the call was received and who left the message. That way if she had a question about the message, she would know who to ask.

4. Have you ever called a business or friend who has a telephone answering machine? After you dial the number, you hear a recorded message that might sound like this: "Hello, this is Harvey Simons. I'm sorry that I can't answer the phone just now. When you hear the tone, please leave your name, number, the time of the call, and your message. I'll get back to you as soon as I can. Thank you."

Do not panic and hang up! Think before you speak. Then clearly say your complete name and telephone number, if the person might not know it. Tell what time you are calling, and briefly tell why you are calling. Here is the message Joni left for her friend Wendy.

Hi, Wendy. This is Joni Webster. My number is 265-1378, and it's 3:30. I was calling about our math homework. I don't understand some of it. Please call me back. Thanks.

5. What do you do if you reach the wrong number? Do you apologize to the person you reached? Do you tell the number that you meant to dial? If the person says you reached a different number, excuse yourself for bothering the listener and hang up. Then carefully redial the number. If you dialed the number correctly and reached the wrong person, do not keep dialing the same number. Look up the number.

Practice

Pair off with a classmate. Take turns being the caller and the receiver. If you make mistakes, point them out to each other.

1. The veterinarian calls to say that you can pick up your dog after 4:00. You take the message for your parents.
2. Call the Thousand and One Kites store to ask about the price of a diving kite. You get a recorded message saying the manager is out of the store, but to please leave your name and number and your message.
3. Call a famous person to ask her or him to speak to your school. A secretary answers the phone.

8 | Making Introductions

Introducing one person to another is a necessary speaking and social skill that requires practice. When you introduce people, say each person's name and something about the person. Do the same when you introduce yourself to someone. Knowing something about another person makes it easier for people to start a conversation. It is especially helpful to mention common interests the people have.

Read what happened when Angella met Stacie and George at the bus stop.

ANGELLA: Hi, I'm Angella Franklin. I just moved here from Canada. Is this the right place for the school bus?

STACIE: Hi, Angella. Yes, it is. I'm Stacie Kelly, and this is George Davio. We're in the sixth grade. Are you?

ANGELLA: Hi, George. Hi, Stacie. Yes, I am. Maybe we have the same teacher.

GEORGE: We have Ms. Kurtz this year. You moved here from Canada, you said. I visited British Columbia last summer with my family. It's really beautiful. Where in Canada are you from?

When you introduce a young person to an adult, say the adult's name first.

KAYE: Hello, Uncle Ed. This is my friend Daisy Virella. Daisy, this is my uncle, Mr. Siniski, who runs the card shop on Main Street.

DAISY: Hi, Mr. Siniski. I've bought cards in your store many times.

What if you cannot remember the name of the person you are introducing? Do not feel embarrassed. Simply say, "I'm sorry, but your name has slipped my mind."

When someone is introduced to you, repeat the person's name. That way you are more likely to remember it. If you did not hear the person's name when the introduction was made, ask the person to repeat it. Say, "I'm sorry, but I didn't hear your name. Will you please repeat it?"

Practice

Form a group with two other students. Practice introducing one another using the situations below. Follow these guidelines.

1. Look at the people you are introducing.
2. Say each person's name that you introduce.
3. Tell something about each person.
4. When someone is introduced to you, repeat the person's name.
5. Introduce yourself, if no one else does.

A. Yvonne Cook just moved to your neighborhood from Venezuela. She played flute in her school band.

B. Ms. Harvey, the principal of your school, plays the piano.

C. Mr. Akhbari plays many instruments and is the director of the school band and chorus.

D. Stephan Thomas lives next door to you and traveled to Kenya last year.

9 | Giving a Talk

Giving a talk or a speech might bring butterflies to your stomach, make your knees knock and your palms moist, and give you a dry mouth. People who normally have no trouble talking, often search for words when they are speaking in front of an audience.

How can you overcome your nervousness and be a good speaker? Remembering these five P's should help—Prepare, Plan, and Practice, Practice, Practice.

Prepare

1. Choose a topic that is interesting to *you.*
2. Choose a topic that you can research if necessary.
3. If appropriate, add humorous or interesting details or personal stories that will keep your audience interested.

Plan

1. Be sure that you know exactly what you want to say. Make notes or an outline on note cards or slips of paper that you can look at during your talk. Write only key words on your cards that will help you recall your main points and details. You do not want to read your speech.
2. If you are using illustrations or pictures, be sure they are large enough for your audience to see.
3. Ask your family or friends to set aside some time for you to practice your talk in front of them.

Practice

1. Find a quiet place to practice your talk out loud.
2. Read over your notes until you have them almost memorized. Then practice your talk by just glancing at your note cards occasionally. Find the key word, and look up again as you continue with your talk.
3. Practice in front of a mirror so you can see how you look. Your hands are busy with your note cards, but how are you

standing? Are you rocking back and forth? Are you pacing like a caged lion? Try standing with your feet slightly apart so that you are comfortable. If you feel yourself getting tense, take a deep breath, and relax.

4. Listen to yourself as you practice out loud. Are you talking loudly enough without shouting? Are you stressing your main points and details? Let your voice show your feelings. Look at one or two spots while you practice. When you give your talk, replace these spots with actual people.

5. Practice in front of your family and friends. Time yourself. If you are over or under your time limit, speed up or slow down or change the length of your talk. Practice using your illustrations. Ask for comments when you finish.

If you follow the five P's, you will feel confident in front of your audience. You will know that your talk is interesting and that your presentation is strong. Try to enjoy yourself.

Practice

Write notes or a short outline for a five-minute talk on one of the following topics, or choose one of your own.

a strange pet I would like to own
my favorite activity
somewhere I would like to visit

10 | Group Discussions

Conversations and discussions are different from one another. In conversations, people talk about several topics or subjects. What is talked about is not decided ahead of time; instead, the conversation unfolds spontaneously. One person mentions something that sparks an idea or memory in another participant, and the conversation shifts to something else.

In discussions, people usually share information and opinions about one topic or problem in order to decide something. The subject of the discussion is decided beforehand, and the participants stick to that topic.

Here is a discussion that took place in Mr. Tong's class. The group was planning a picnic.

EVE: We have to decide if we will bring our own food or collect money and buy it.

ROGER: I vote for bringing our own food. Then we will each get to eat what we like.

FRAN: I agree with Roger.

GROUP: Me, too.

STU: We also have to decide where to have the picnic.

KIM: What about Echo Lake?

MR. TONG: What about it, Kim?

KIM: Well, it was great there for last year's picnic. Let's have it there again.

SUSAN: Echo Lake is nice, but there's also Miller's Glen. Its playing fields are better than Echo Lake's. What do you think, Mark?

MARK: Susan's right about the fields, but Echo Lake is within walking distance. We would need transportation to Miller's Glen.

ANDY: What about the food?

AMY: Oh, Andy. Weren't you listening? We already decided that we would bring our own.

MR. TONG: Is everyone agreed then about Echo Lake and bringing your own food? Good. Then, it seems that you have solved the two main problems—the place and the food.

What was the purpose of the discussion? Did each speaker keep to the topic? How do you know that the participants listened to one another? Who did not? What do you think would have occurred if everyone had not agreed about the place and the food?

Follow these guidelines for taking part in discussions.

1. Know the topic or purpose of the discussion.
2. Move the discussion along by making helpful comments that stick to the topic or by asking appropriate questions.
3. Listen carefully to what others say.
4. If you disagree about something, say so, but be polite.
5. If you do not understand something, say so.
6. Help others take part by asking them questions.
7. Try to reach a decision.

Practice

Form a group with five or six classmates to have a ten-minute discussion. Decide on a topic, or choose one of the topics below.

How can your class raise money for a worthy charity?
What can you do to improve your local park?
Whom will you ask to be a speaker on Career Day?

3 Nouns

1 | Recognizing Nouns

A **noun** is a word that names a person, place, thing, or idea.

The <u>girl</u> was called <u>Nina</u>.   The <u>doorbell</u> buzzed.
<u>Denver</u> is in <u>Colorado</u>.   <u>Kindness</u> is often rewarded.

The nouns in the sentences on the left name a person or a place. The noun in the first sentence on the right names a thing. The noun in the last sentence names an idea. When a noun names an idea, it is naming something that cannot be touched, like *time, excitement*, or *winter*.

A noun can be made up of more than one word.

Has the <u>drive-in</u> closed?   <u>Ms. Ruiz</u> climbed <u>Pikes Peak</u>.

Try It Out

Find the nouns in these sentences.

1. Is winter approaching?
2. A dove is a sign of peace.
3. Our troubles are over.
4. Ann skis in Vermont.
5. My dad loves his new bike.
6. Seattle had a heavy rainfall.

> ▶ A **noun** names a person, place, thing, or idea.

Written Practice

List the nouns you find in this paragraph.

Kites have been used for centuries. Benjamin Franklin flew a kite and a key in a thunderstorm. He found that lightning and electricity are the same thing. Kites record temperatures, humidity, and the velocity of the wind.

• **Writing Sentences** Write five sentences, describing something you have done recently. Circle each noun.

2 | Singular and Plural Nouns

A noun that names one person, place, thing, or idea is a **singular noun**. A noun that names more than one person, place, thing, or idea is a **plural noun**. The singular form is usually different from the plural. In most cases, singular nouns can be changed to plural by adding -*s*.

truck – trucks   plant – plants   letter – letters   noise – noises

Many nouns, however, have irregular plural forms. The chart below shows you how to form the plurals of these nouns.

Singular Ending	Plural Form	Example
-s	add -*es*	Thomas – Thomases
-ss		boss – bosses
-ch		porch – porches
-sh		bush – bushes
-x		fox – foxes
-z		waltz – waltzes
-o	add -*es*	potato – potatoes
		veto – vetoes
		echo – echoes
	(some add -*s*)	(Eskimo – Eskimos)
		(solo – solos)
consonant + y	change *y* to *i* and add -*es*	baby – babies
		party – parties
		country – countries
vowel + y	add -*s*	day – days
		turkey – turkeys
-f or -fe	change *f* to *v* and add -*es*	wolf – wolves
		scarf – scarves
		life – lives

Some nouns remain the same in the singular and plural.

moose – moose   salmon – salmon

Other nouns are spelled differently in the plural.

child – children   woman – women
man – men   goose – geese

Use your dictionary to check for correct plurals.

Try It Out

A. For each pair of words in parentheses, choose the correct plural form.

1. Put the (boxs, boxes) on those two (shelfs, shelves).
2. The new (puppies, puppys) have sharp (tooths, teeth).
3. The gardener weeded the berry (patchs, patches) and planted (tomatos, tomatoes).
4. Loggers use (axes, axs) to cut (tree, trees).
5. The (moose, mooses) heard (echos, echoes) from the distant canyon.

B. Give the plural form of each noun.

6. dancer   11. scarf
7. apple   12. dress
8. policy   13. lake
9. tornado   14. donkey
10. watch   15. wish

To form the plural of a regular noun, add -s.
To form the plural of most nouns ending in -s, -ss, -ch, -sh, -x, -z, and -o, add -es.
To form the plural of a noun ending in a consonant and -y, change the y to i and add -es.
To form the plural of a noun ending in -f or -fe, change the f to v and add -es.

Written Practice

A. For each of the following nouns, write *singular*, *plural*, or *singular and plural*.

1. goose
2. moose
3. women
4. classes
5. glass
6. deer
7. lilies
8. oxen

B. Write the plural form of each noun.

9. knife
10. opera
11. couch
12. county
13. monkey
14. soprano
15. cross
16. style
17. mouse
18. nursery
19. envelope
20. hero
21. calf
22. stereo
23. mix
24. zero

C. Write the sentences, using the plural form of each noun in parentheses.

25. Today ____ have ____ of ____. (plastic, thousand, use)
26. Most ____ and ____ use plastic ____. (family, business, product)
27. ____, ____, and even ____ can be made of plastic. (Box, shelf, scarf)
28. ____ make plastic by combining carbon with other ____. (Chemist, element)
29. Now, most ____ have ____ that make plastic ____. (country, factory, item)
30. Almost all ____ for ____ contain some plastic ____. (toy, child, part)
31. Many clothes for ____ and ____ are made with plastic. (man, woman)
32. Most of us will be using plastic ____ every day of our ____. (object, life)

- **Writing Sentences** Use the plural form of the following words in sentences of your own.

33. valley
34. moss
35. marsh
36. leaf
37. potato
38. piano
39. torch
40. flash

3 | Common and Proper Nouns

Some nouns name a particular person, place, thing, or idea. These are called **proper nouns**. A proper noun begins with a capital letter. Nouns that do not name a particular person, place, thing, or idea are called **common nouns**.

Look at the lists of common and proper nouns below.

Common Nouns	Proper Nouns
city	Baltimore
girl	Amy
ocean	Atlantic Ocean
train	Super Chief
month	July

A proper noun may be made up of more than one word. Only the important words in a proper noun begin with a capital letter.

Gulf of Mexico   Statue of Liberty   Tower of London

Try It Out

Find the nouns in these sentences. Tell whether each noun is common or proper.

1. Edward White was the first astronaut to walk in space.
2. His suit weighed thirty-one pounds.
3. The astronaut practiced in an airtight chamber for hours.
4. Astronaut White walked in space above California.
5. The astronaut did not want to return to the spacecraft.
6. His command pilot convinced White to come inside.
7. The spacecraft orbited Earth before the flight ended.
8. A crew and ship waited in the Atlantic Ocean.
9. Doctors gave the astronauts medical tests.
10. Their journey in space was a success.

> ▶ A **common noun** names any person, place, thing, or idea.
> ▶ A **proper noun** names a particular person, place, thing, or idea.
>
> A proper noun always begins with a capital letter.

Written Practice

A. Write each common noun in the sentences below.

1. Juan and Francie decided to start a newspaper.
2. A friend wanted to be a reporter.
3. Francie wrote a story about a boy who built his own boat.
4. Juan took a picture of a new baby at the hospital.
5. Many people bought space to advertise their businesses.
6. Copies were sold at the school, drugstore, and market.
7. The manager of the hotel ordered one hundred papers.
8. The last page was full of jokes, riddles, and cartoons.
9. Uncle Ted liked the editorial about honesty.
10. Francie and Juan were proud owners.

B. Copy each proper noun. Beside it, write the common noun that matches it best.

11.	Egypt	**a.**	skater
12.	Thursday	**b.**	island
13.	Longs Peak	**c.**	mountain
14.	Bermuda	**d.**	day
15.	Peggy Fleming	**e.**	country
16.	Mercury	**f.**	continent
17.	Africa	**g.**	month
18.	Alabama	**h.**	state
19.	Jackie Robinson	**i.**	planet
20.	July	**j.**	baseball player

- **Writing Sentences**   Write a sentence for each pair of common and proper nouns in exercise B.

4 | Possessive Nouns

Nouns can show ownership, or possession. A **possessive noun** names who or what owns something. Read these sentences. Notice the underlined words.

Here is the trophy <u>that belongs to the school</u>.
We can put it in the <u>window of Ms. Newall</u>.

To form the possessive of most singular nouns, add an apostrophe and an -*s* ('s). Now read the sentences below. Which words are possessive nouns? How can you tell?

Here is the school's trophy.
We can put it in Ms. Newall's window.

To form the possessive of a plural noun that already ends in -*s*, add only an apostrophe (').

market of the farmers = <u>farmers'</u> market
club of officers = <u>officers'</u> club
pictures of the babies = <u>babies'</u> pictures
den of wolves = <u>wolves'</u> den

You know that all plural nouns do not end in -*s*. To form the possessive of a plural noun that does not end in -*s*, add an apostrophe and an -*s* ('s).

uniforms belonging to children = <u>children's</u> uniforms
cage belonging to mice = <u>mice's</u> cage

Do not confuse plural nouns (the Joneses) with singular possessive nouns (Thomas's bike) or plural possessive nouns (the Dillons' cat). Look at these sentences.

Bea Lewis's drum needs tuning.
All the Lewises played in a concert.
The Lewises' instruments are heavy.

Which sentence has a singular possessive noun? Which sentence has a plural possessive noun? Which sentence has a plural noun?

Try It Out.

A. Complete each sentence with the possessive form of the noun in parentheses. Tell whether the possessive ends in *'s* or *s'*.

1. ____ dream was to become a doctor. (Elizabeth Blackwell)
2. ____ applications to medical schools were not welcome. (Women)
3. After many months, one of ____ hospitals accepted her. (New York)
4. Her hard work and persistence gained her ____ respect. (professors)
5. Elizabeth Blackwell was this ____ first woman doctor. (country)

B. Fill in the blank by giving the possessive form of the noun in parentheses. Tell whether the possessive ends in *'s* or *s'*.

6. ____ car (Mr. Douglas)
7. ____ toys (children)
8. the ____ apartment (Perkinses)
9. the ____ webbed feet (goose)
10. a ____ meeting (parents)

▶ A **possessive noun** shows ownership.
To form the possessive of most singular nouns, add *'s*.
To form the possessive of a plural noun that ends in *-s*, add *'*.
To form the possessive of a plural noun that does not end in *-s*, add *'s*.

Written Practice

A. Rewrite each group of words, using a possessive noun. The first one has been done for you.

1. club of bowlers
   bowlers' club
2. dish belonging to the cat
3. croaks of frogs
4. odor of the skunk
5. log of the ship
6. tentacles of the octopus
7. desk of Nicholas
8. convention of fruit growers
9. health of Becky
10. pencil belonging to Lani

B. Write the possessive form of each noun in parentheses.

11. Please pass ____ strawberries. (Helen)
12. The children eat Sunday dinner at a family ____ house. (member)
13. Alan especially likes ____ famous chili. (Lucas)
14. The children dressed in both their ____ old clothes. (grandparents)
15. Grandmother set up a special ____ table. (children)
16. The adults and children listened to ____ story about her fishing trip. (Aunt Augusta)
17. After dinner Helen filled the ____ dish with leftover scraps. (dog)
18. Three of the ____ friends washed and dried the dishes. (children)
19. The family watched ____ slides of her trip to California. (Stephanie)
20. Next week dinner will be at the ____ house. (Williamses)

- **Writing Sentences**   Write five sentences, using singular possessive nouns from exercise B.

5 | Appositives

An **appositive** is a word or a group of words that tells more about the noun it follows.

Robin, our class president, planned the party.

Appositives can help you improve your writing. Use an appositive to combine two choppy sentences into one.

Our summer party was a barbecue. It was great fun.
Our summer party, a barbecue, was great fun.

Notice that appositives are usually set off from the rest of the sentence by commas.

Mr. McLean, Robin's father, furnished the chicken.
The party had a theme, careers.

Try It Out

A. Combine each pair of sentences into a single sentence with an appositive.

   1. Annie is my partner. She is building a new barn.
   2. Mrs. Scott is Ken's mother. She is also my teacher.
   3. My picture is in the local paper. The paper is the *Tribune*.
   4. Harry is a disc jockey. Harry played the record I requested.
   5. We're having my favorite soup. It is cream of tomato.

B. Use each noun and appositive in a sentence. Then tell where you would place the commas.

   6. Paulette the fastest runner
   7. my barber a talkative person
   8. last Thursday my birthday
   9. Cal's terrier Ruffles
   10. Frisbee match an exciting event

> ▸ An **appositive** is a word or a group of words that tells more about the noun it follows.
>
> An appositive is usually set off from the rest of the sentence by commas.

Written Practice

A. Combine each pair of sentences into a single sentence with an appositive. Use commas to set off the appositives.

1. Primo is my Italian pen pal. Primo sings in the opera.
2. Primo's father is a singer. Primo's father drives a taxi.
3. An opera is a play with special music. An opera was in town.
4. Arias are my favorite part of an opera. Arias are solos.
5. Primo's brother is a teenager. Primo's brother wants to sing in the opera.
6. Italy is the home of opera. Italy is famous for its singers.
7. Its most famous singers are its tenors. Tenors are men who sing the highest male part.
8. I have a record of Caruso. Caruso was an opera star.

B. Use the words below to form appositives that will complete these sentences. Write each sentence.

orange	Mrs. Adams	Will's Market
a gray stray	a music teacher	Monday

9. Our bus driver, ____, won a safety award.
10. I found this cat, ____, on our porch.
11. I take lessons from Mr. Cord, ____.
12. On my lucky day, ____, I won a radio.
13. Lyn brought along her favorite juice, ____.
14. Another store, ____, opened today.

• **Writing Sentences** Write five sentences, using a different appositive in each sentence.

6 Using Words Correctly

rise, raise, teach, learn

The words *rise* and *raise* are often confused. The meaning of each word will be clear when you understand the difference between them.

Rise means "to get up or go up."

>Dan and Louis rise before dawn.
>The dough will rise slowly.

Raise means "to move something up, to increase something, or to grow something."

>Students raise their hands.
>Farmers raise corn here.
>Stuart will raise his babysitting fee.

When deciding whether to use *rise* or *raise*, ask yourself, Raise what? If your answer names a thing, use *raise*. If the question has no answer, use *rise*.

Teach and *learn* are also verbs whose meanings are related but different.

Teach means "to give instruction."

John can teach puppetry.   Alice will teach kindergarten.

Learn means "to receive instruction."

We learn how to be funny.   Children learn a lot.

Use *rise* when you mean "to get up or go up."
Use *raise* when you mean "to move something up, to increase something, or to grow something."
Use *teach* when you mean "to give instruction."
Use *learn* when you mean "to receive instruction."

Practice

A. Choose the correct word in parentheses.

1. Sarah (rises, raises) early to feed the chickens.
2. She (rises, raises) Cornish hens on a farm in Virginia.
3. Her neighbors (rise, raise) corn and wheat.
4. The chickens come when Sarah (rises, raises) her hand.
5. Next year her family will (rise, raise) their prices.

B. Complete each sentence with either *teach* or *learn*. Write the sentences.

6. Shari can ____ how to grass ski this weekend.
7. Her uncle will ____ her in his back yard.
8. Next summer she will ____ her brother.
9. He is going to ____ snow skiing at a resort.
10. Shari will ____ to snow ski next winter.

C. Write the correct word in parentheses to complete each sentence.

11. Harriet Quimby can (learn, teach) to fly a plane.
12. A pilot will (learn, teach) Harriet every morning.
13. She would (rise, raise) eagerly to go for a lesson.
14. It was thrilling to feel the plane (rise, raise).
15. Do parents (raise, rise) their children with these ideas?
16. Harriet Quimby did (learn, teach) to fly easily.
17. How did the neighbors (teach, learn) of her lessons?
18. She will (learn, teach) to fly over water.
19. A contest may (raise, rise) concern for her safety.
20. Harriet and her teacher (raise, rise) to loud applause from the audience when she receives her award.

- **Writing Sentences** Use a form of *rise, raise, teach,* or *learn* correctly in four sentences of your own.

Synonyms and Antonyms

Speech and writing can be very dull if you use the same words over and over again. Being aware of synonyms can help make your writing more interesting. **Synonyms** are words that have similar meanings. Synonyms can help you add variety to your writing and speaking. Read the sentences below. Which word has been overused?

> I spent a quiet day at home.
> Our noisy neighbors were unusually quiet.
> Even the garbage truck was quiet.

Now read the sentences below. The synonyms for *quiet* have been underlined.

> I spent a <u>peaceful</u> day at home.
> Our noisy neighbors were unusually <u>silent</u>.
> Even the garbage truck was <u>still</u>.

Antonyms are words that have opposite meanings. The antonyms in the following sentences are underlined.

> Our performance <u>pleased</u> the audience.
> Our performance <u>disturbed</u> the audience.

▸ **Synonyms** are words that have similar meanings.
▸ **Antonyms** are words that have opposite meanings.

Practice

A. Use the words below as synonyms for the underlined words.

activities   program   quit   view
furious   started   tales   weary

1. Joe's family stopped watching television for a month.
2. At first Joe felt bored and angry.
3. Then his family began doing things together.
4. They played video games, read, and told stories.
5. Now Joe is content to see only one show a week.

B. Choose the antonym for the underlined word.

6. Ann enjoys carving animals out of soap. (likes, dislikes)
7. First, she spreads out a huge sheet of paper. (enormous, tiny)
8. She uses a dark pencil to outline the shape. (heavy, light)
9. Then Ann carefully cuts away the excess soap. (recklessly, cautiously)
10. Finally, her sculpture appears! (materializes, vanishes)

C. For each word below, write a synonym and an antonym.

11. anger   14. finish   17. remember
12. ask   15. friend   18. dull
13. fall   16. lose   19. defrost

D. Rewrite the following sentences, replacing the underlined words with synonyms. Try to use more exact synonyms.

21. Colorado has many things.
22. Red sandstone rocks are found near Colorado Springs.
23. A train climbs to the top of Pikes Peak.
24. Rocky Mountain National Park is great.

• **Writing Sentences**   Choose five words from exercise C. Write five sentences, using a word and its antonym in the same sentence.

Review

- **Recognizing Nouns** *(p. 51)* Write the nouns below.

    1. This drive-in belongs to Al and his family.
    2. Al works behind the counter in the summer and on holidays.
    3. At night he sweeps the floor and washes the tables.
    4. His mother greets the guests and counts the money.
    5. Next year Al will open a diner in Virginia.

- **Singular and Plural Nouns** *(pp. 52–54)* Write the plural form of the nouns in parentheses.

    6. Our city ____ have many ____. (park, bench)
    7. Sometimes ____ hide in the ____. (fox, bush)
    8. You can hear ____ from the band's ____. (echo, waltz)
    9. Sometimes we hold ____ on our ____. (party, porch)
    10. We have no ____ in these ____. (tornado, county)

- **Common and Proper Nouns** *(pp. 55–56)* Write each noun. Underline each common noun once and each proper noun twice.

    11. Linda fishes in Lake Geneva on weekends.
    12. Mother tied the fishhook to the line.
    13. Many people catch trout, catfish, and bass here.
    14. Linda and her family live in Indiana.
    15. Jim Dobbs sells tackle from his van.

- **Possessive Nouns** *(pp. 57–59)* Write the possessive form of the nouns in parentheses.

    16. A ____ career choice can often change. (person)
    17. Good salespeople know all their ____ names. (customers)
    18. An aircraft ____ job is very exact. (mechanic)
    19. Several ____ groups have career workshops. (women)
    20. All of the ____ children became farmers. (Curtises)

- **Appositives** *(pp. 60–61)* Rewrite each pair of sentences into a single sentence containing an appositive. Punctuate it correctly.

21. The Simpsons are our neighbors. They walk all of their dogs every day.
22. Pepper barks every morning at nine. Their dog is Pepper.
23. Pepper is a small dog. He has a very loud bark.
24. Teresa is my oldest sister. Sometimes she walks with Pepper.
25. Pepper's favorite toy is worn and faded. It is an old baby blanket.
26. Pepper's bed is a little basket with a cushion inside. It is next to the sofa.
27. Pepper is a very friendly dog. He always tries to jump on the sofa to play.

- **Using Words Correctly** *(pp. 62–63)* Write the word in parentheses that best fits each sentence.

28. Suddenly the students (raise, rise) their voices.
29. The teacher (rises, raises) from her seat and (rises, raises) the window to let the bee escape.
30. The students decide to (teach, learn) about bees.
31. Michael wants to (teach, learn) the class how bees make honey.

- **Building Vocabulary** *(pp. 64–65)* Write a synonym and an antonym for each underlined word in these sentences.

32. Paul enjoys difficult roles in plays.
33. The auditorium is crowded.
34. The end of the play is funny.
35. The actors were excited about performing.
36. The audience looked happy as they left the theater.
37. Paul's voice sounded strong and clear.
38. The people in the last row could hear every syllable.
39. The critics said he made a difficult role look easy.
40. The costumes designed by Mr. and Mrs. Dalton were great.

Maintain

- **Kinds of Sentences** *(pp. 9–10)* Copy each sentence. Label it *declarative, interrogative, imperative,* or *exclamatory.* Add the correct punctuation marks.

  1. Where did I put my glasses
  2. I took them off to swim
  3. How cold that water is
  4. Will you swim with me

- **Subjects and Predicates** *(pp. 11–18)* Copy these sentences. Draw a line between the complete subject and complete predicate. Underline simple subjects once, simple predicates twice.

  5. Roses blossomed first.
  6. Susan washes the dishes.
  7. My father loves animals.
  8. This copper pan shines.

  Write the simple subject of each sentence below.

  9. Here is the pretty dress.
  10. Did Leah like the movie?
  11. There is my office.
  12. Hold onto the railing.

  Write the compound subjects and predicates in these sentences.

  13. Terry and Fran walked their bikes and talked in the park.
  14. Three children and two dogs ran down the path.
  15. The riders petted and dismounted their weary horses.
  16. Sue waved to her friends and ran down the street.
  17. The children laughed at the clown and hissed the villain.

- **Compound Sentences** *(pp. 19–21)* Combine each pair of sentences into a compound sentence by using a comma and *and, but,* or *or.*

  18. My big sister goes to college. She comes home on weekends.
  19. We took her desk out. I built in some bookcases.
  20. Should I paint them white? Does this stain look better?
  21. She reads mostly mysteries. I like biographies.

- **Fragments and Run-ons** *(pp. 22-24)*   Make a sentence from each fragment. Rewrite each run-on sentence correctly.

  22. Before I came home yesterday afternoon.
  23. Hold the ladder, I will change the bulb.
  24. May I watch should I wait outside?
  25. Three paint brushes and a can of blue paint.

- **Common and Proper Nouns and Plural Nouns** *(pp. 51-56)* Write and label the common and proper nouns in the sentences below. Then write the plural form of each common noun.

  26. Mary Ann sat on her front porch.
  27. Her cousin from New York was visiting the family.
  28. A report on the radio warned of a tornado in the desert.

- **Possessive Nouns** *(pp. 57-59)*   Write the possessive form of each underlined noun.

  29. apartment of <u>Ms. Thomas</u>
  30. truck of the <u>plumber</u>
  31. careers of the <u>men</u>
  32. endings of <u>stories</u>

- **Appositives** *(pp. 60-61)*   Use an appositive to combine each pair of sentences.

  33. Karen runs her own business. Karen is a house painter.
  34. Karen's partner helps. Karen's partner is her brother.
  35. They painted our house red. Red is a very popular color.

- **Using Words Correctly** *(pp. 25-26, 62-63)*   Choose the correct word in parentheses for each sentence.

  36. The temperature (rises, raises) above ninety.
  37. I must (learn, teach) to think cool thoughts in hot weather.
  38. You can (let, leave) your jacket behind tomorrow.
  39. Next winter I'll (lend, borrow) it from you again.

- **Building Vocabulary** *(pp. 64-65)*   Write a synonym and an antonym for each of the following words.

  40. go   41. rise   42. cry   43. peace   44. build

Writing a Paragraph

1 | Main Idea of a Paragraph

A paragraph is a group of sentences that tell about one main idea. The first line of a paragraph is always indented.

Look at a page in a book or magazine. Each time you see a line indented, you know that a new idea is being discussed. Grouping sentences into paragraphs makes it easier for a writer to organize the ideas in a story or article. It also makes it easier for a reader to understand them.

Not every group of sentences is a paragraph. In order for it to be a paragraph, there must be one main idea. Even though the group of sentences below is indented, it does not form a paragraph. Can you tell why?

My older sister has a part-time job at the laundromat. Everyone in our family saves quarters for laundry day because the machines at the laundromat take only quarters. Next door to the laundromat is a bakery that sells delicious bread and rolls.

All the sentences above have something to do with a laundromat, but they are not a paragraph. There is no one main idea. Each sentence could be part of a separate paragraph. Now read this group of sentences.

Laundry day is a family affair at our house. Everyone pitches in. We all save quarters, since the machines at the laundromat take only quarters. My little brother is in charge of carrying the quarters in a jar. My mother and I carry the baskets of laundry. If there's enough for a third basket, my older brother has to come, too. Sometimes we have so much laundry that my older sister has to come and pick us up in her car.

- Is this group of sentences a paragraph? Why?
- Is the paragraph indented?
- Does it tell about only one main idea?
- What is the main idea?

Every sentence in a paragraph should tell about the main idea. The main idea of the paragraph below is how to make and eat a sandwich. The underlined sentence does not belong. Tell why.

Making a sandwich is almost as easy as eating one. First, take two pieces of bread, and spread them with butter. Then put some slices of cheese on one of the pieces of bread. Next, add lettuce, slices of tomato or onion, and bean sprouts. <u>My mom hates bean sprouts, and I always have to remind her to buy them.</u> Carefully lay the other slice of bread on top of your structure. Now eat very slowly, enjoying every bite.

Practice

Read the two groups of sentences below. Then answer the four questions that follow.

Before you even begin to look for an after-school job, there are several things you should consider. First, think about your experience and your skills. What do you know how to do that someone would pay you to do? You should also think about how many hours a week you want to work. Remember that this is time taken away from your other activities. I spend a lot of time playing my guitar. Finally, think about how you can get to a job—by bus, by bicycle, or by foot—and how far you are willing to travel.

It is difficult for a young person to find a job when many adults are out of work. A job can provide you with spending money, but it can also take time away from your sports and hobbies. A part-time job can sometimes give a young person ideas about the kind of work he or she might like to do as an adult. Yard work is excellent exercise.

1. Which group of sentences is a paragraph?
2. What is the main idea of the paragraph?
3. Is there any sentence in the paragraph that does not belong?
4. Why is the other group of sentences not a paragraph?

2 | Topic Sentences and Supporting Details

Often a paragraph contains a sentence that tells what the main idea of the paragraph is. This is called the **topic sentence.** The other sentences give **supporting details** about the main idea. The topic sentence is underlined in the paragraph below.

<u>Porpoises and other members of the whale family hear very well, even though they have no visible ears.</u> All that can be seen of their ears are tiny holes in the backs of their heads, but porpoises can hear the gentlest movement of water. Drop a marble into its tank, and the porpoise will hear it and find it.

- What two points does the topic sentence make?
- What details support the statement made in the topic sentence?

Although the topic sentence is often the first sentence in a paragraph, it does not have to be first. It can come anywhere in the paragraph. Read the following paragraph.

Jane and her mother picked me up at five o'clock. By the time we got to the lake, the sun was just starting to come up. Softly the calm waters reflected the sky's pink glow. We packed the boat with our lunches and fishing gear, then pushed off into the lake. Jane's mother showed us how to put the bait on the hooks. Then we waited for the fish to bite. How surprised I was that I caught the biggest fish! In spite of having to get up early, I really enjoyed my first fishing trip.

- What is the topic sentence of this paragraph?
- What main idea does it state?
- What supporting details are given in the other sentences?

Practice

A. Read the paragraph below. Tell which is the topic sentence. Tell how you made your choice.

An elephant trumpets in the distance. The screeching of monkeys fills the trees above. Shaking the earth, a lion's roar silences the chattering of the smaller animals. The sounds of the jungle are as varied as the creatures that live there.

B. Read the paragraph below, and decide what the main idea is. Write a topic sentence stating that main idea.

Unlike a dog, a cat does not have to be walked a couple of times a day. It is quite happy to snooze in your apartment all day long without constant attention. When you come home, the cat does not jump all over you in slobbering enthusiasm as Fido does. A soft purr, much easier on the ears than the dog's frantic yapping, is the dignified cat's only greeting.

C. For each topic sentence below, make up two or three sentences that give supporting details. The first one is done for you as an example.

1. **Topic Sentence:** Last night we gave my mother a surprise birthday party.
   Supporting Details: I made her favorite dinner and had it ready when she came home from work. We put presents on the table and then hid behind the sofa. Grandmother and Grandfather came to help us celebrate.
2. **Topic Sentence:** I saw the strangest thing on the way to school today!
3. **Topic Sentence:** That's how I learned to skate (*or* ___).
4. **Topic Sentence:** Our town provides many after-school activities for young people.
5. **Topic Sentence:** You can keep your bike (*or* ___) in good condition by following a maintenance schedule.

3 | Order in Paragraphs

The order of the sentences in your paragraphs depends on your topic. If you are writing about an event, you usually order your paragraphs by time. You start with what happened first, and then tell what happened after that, in order.

If you are explaining how to do something, you put your sentences in step-by-step order. Certain order words, such as the ones underlined below, will help make your steps clear.

The <u>first</u> thing I do when I set my alarm clock is decide what time I have to get up. <u>Then</u> I find the knob that sets the alarm hand. Usually, the first knob I turn changes the time instead. <u>Then</u> I have to reset this knob correctly, or my alarm will not ring at the proper time. <u>After</u> I have found the right knob and set my alarm, I have to find out whether the bell really works. Therefore, my <u>next</u> step is to set the time hands for the time I want to get up. If the bell rings, I know the alarm works. <u>Then</u> I reset the time hands. <u>Finally</u> I pull out the alarm knob. <u>After that</u>, I fall asleep. I have earned it.

Practice

Write a paragraph, using these sentences and putting them in step-by-step order. Add order words to make your paragraph clear.

Washing your face is a simple process.
Rinse the soap out of your washcloth.
Make the washcloth fairly wet.
Rub the soapy washcloth over your chin, cheeks, and forehead.
Either use the wet washcloth to wipe the soap off your face, or splash your face with clear water until it is rinsed.
Don't forget to wash the end of your nose.
Rub the washcloth over a bar of soap.

4 | Getting Started

When did you last explain to someone how to find your house or how to play a game? Did your listener understand you right away, or did the person have to ask questions such as "Exactly how many?" or "How far?" or "What kind?" in order to get you to be more exact?

To give instructions well, it is important to make your details exact. The sentence *Fold a piece of paper* is not exact. A person trying to follow that instruction might wonder, "Should I fold the paper in half? in thirds? Should I fold it the long way or the short way?" Read the two sentences below.

> Write your name on the paper.
> Write your full name in ink in the upper right-hand corner of your paper.

- Which sentence is more exact? Why?

Practice

Turn to a classmate who sits near you. Without using your hands, explain step-by-step exactly how shoelaces can be crossed, looped, and tied. Have your listener try to follow the instructions as they are given. Then work together to improve the instructions.

Steps for Writing Instructions Here are the steps for writing a paragraph of instructions. You will follow these steps to write your own paragraph.

Step One   Choose a topic.
Step Two   Write your paragraph.
Step Three   Revise your paragraph.
Step Four   Proofread your paragraph.
Step Five   Make a final copy to share.

5 | Step One
Choose a Topic

Think of some topics that you would like to explain and that someone else would enjoy knowing about.

Here is the list of topics Andrea made.

figure skating

running a movie projector

making puppets

cutting someone's hair

grooming a horse

making a drawing

Andrea looked over her list. She decided that it would be better to show someone how to figure skate or cut hair, rather than to write instructions. To explain how to run a movie projector would mean making complicated diagrams.

Andrea thought about the rest of her topics. She asked herself which she really wanted to write about. Andrea decided to explain how to make a drawing, using simple geometric shapes. She made a list of the steps to make sure she had them in order.

Assignment
- **Make a List**
- **Make Notes**
- **Choose a Topic**

A. Make a list of topics for your paragraph of instructions. Here are some questions to ask yourself.

1. What have I learned to do lately?
2. What do I know how to do that many people do not?
3. What have I explained well to someone lately?
4. What would someone else like to find out how to do?

B. Circle two ideas that appeal to you most. List the steps for both of them briefly. Are your steps in the correct order?

C. Decide on one topic, and circle it on your paper.

6 | Step Two
Write Your Paragraph

Andrea used her list of steps as a guide while she wrote her first draft. She did not worry about making mistakes in spelling and punctuation. She would have time to correct them later. Try to follow Andrea's instructions.

Andrea's first draft

Get out a pencil and a piece of paper. ~~Make a~~ In the middle of your paper, draw a rectangle. Draw a small square beside the rektangle at the lower rite corner. Now draw a circle under the rectangle and then draw a small triangle inside the circle. Next, draw two small circles that look like eyes inside the big circle. Draw an upside down triangle direckly under the first triangle. Draw another small square on the other side of the rectangle.

- Does Andrea's paragraph have a topic sentence? If not, what topic sentence can you suggest for her paragraph?
- Do all of the sentences keep to the topic?
- Are the sentences in step-by-step order?
- What order words did Andrea use?
- Are any of the steps unclear? If so, which ones? Why?

Practice

After you and your classmates have followed Andrea's instructions, compare drawings. Did everyone interpret Andrea's instructions in the same way? Can you decide what the drawing is supposed to look like? What does Andrea need to do to improve her instructions?

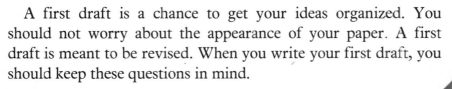

A first draft is a chance to get your ideas organized. You should not worry about the appearance of your paper. A first draft is meant to be revised. When you write your first draft, you should keep these questions in mind.

1. Am I telling enough?
2. Am I telling the steps in order?
3. Are my instructions clear and exact?

Assignment • Write Your First Draft

Use your list of steps as a guide to writing your first draft. Do not worry about spelling, punctuation, capitalization, or handwriting. Think about what you want to say, and find the words to say it. You may want to skip every other line. You may need the extra space if you want to make changes later.

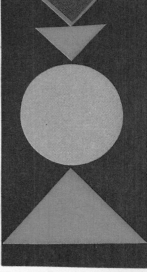

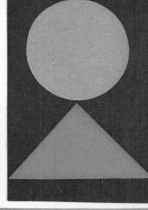

7 | Step Three
Revise Your Paragraph

Andrea knew what her drawing was supposed to look like. She wondered, however, whether someone following her instructions would come up with the same drawing. She tried to read her instructions over as if she were seeing them for the first time.

When she did this, Andrea saw some things that needed to be changed. She realized that one step was out of order. She circled that sentence and drew an arrow to show where it belonged. She thought of a few more details that should be added to make the instructions clearer. She wrote these new words above the lines and used a caret (∧) to show where they should go. She realized that her paragraph had no topic sentence. She thought of one that sounded good and wrote it at the end of her paragraph. Finally, she noticed that she had not indented the paragraph, and she marked a paragraph symbol (¶) at the beginning as a reminder.

After you have read over your writing and made some changes, it is a good idea to find out how your paper sounds to someone else. When you read it over yourself, you know what you mean. When someone else listens to the paragraph, he or she will hear only what is written on the paper.

Andrea read her paper to James. James got out a pencil and followed the instructions as she read them. When Andrea finished, James said, "I like the idea. It's supposed to be a face under something, right?"

"Yes," said Andrea, "under a tall hat."

"Oh," said James, "I think I drew my rectangle the wrong way. You need to say if it should be standing up or lying flat."

"Thanks," said Andrea, "I wouldn't have noticed that. Is there anything else?"

"I didn't know exactly where to put the little squares," said James. "Maybe if you said *beside* the rectangle or *against* it or something like that, it would help."

Andrea and James talked some more about her instructions. Then Andrea made more changes in her first draft.

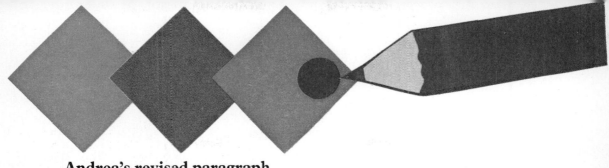

Andrea's revised paragraph

^A Get out a pencil and a piece of paper. ~~Make a~~ In the middle of your paper, draw a ^tall rectangle. Draw a small square beside the rektangle ^and touching it at the lower rite ^outside corner. Now draw a circle ^about the size of a nickel under the rectangle ^and touching it and then draw a small triangle ^in the middle of inside the circle. Next, draw two small circles that look like eyes inside the big circle. Draw an upside down triangle direckly under the first triangle. Draw ^a matching another small square on the other side of the rectangle. Do you see a funny picture.

- What symbol did Andrea put at the beginning of her paragraph? Why?
- What details did she add?
- Where did she write the new words? What symbol did she use to show where they should go?
- How did she change the order of her steps?
- Why does this change improve Andrea's instructions?
- Why is the topic sentence at the end of her paragraph?

Assignment
- **Revise Your Paragraph**
- **Discuss Your Paragraph**

A. Read your draft with a critical eye. Ask yourself these questions.

1. Are all the steps in the correct order?
2. Have all the important steps been included?
3. Are my instructions exact?
4. Would they be easy to follow?

B. Revise your draft. Cross out words or sentences that do not belong. Add details by writing words above the lines, as Andrea did.

C. Read your instructions to someone—a classmate or your teacher. Ask your listener to keep these questions in mind.

1. Are all the steps in order?
2. Is there anything else that should be included?
3. Is there anything that should be left out?
4. Are the instructions exact? Is there anything I do not understand?

Discuss your listener's reactions and suggestions. Then make any further changes that you think would make your instructions better.

8 | Step Four
Proofread Your Paragraph

Now you are ready to proofread your paper. When you proofread, you check your spelling, capitalization, and punctuation.

Because she had made so many changes, Andrea decided to copy her paper over. Then she proofread it, using a dictionary to check the spelling of any words she was unsure of.

Andrea's paragraph after proofreading

> Get out a pencil and a piece of paper. In the middle of your paper, draw a tall rectangle. Draw a small square beside the rectangle and touching it at the lower right rite outside corner. Draw a matching square on the other side. Now draw a circle about the size of a nickel under the rectangle and touching it and then draw a small triangle in the middle of the circle. Next, draw two small circles that look like eyes inside the big circle. Draw an upside down triangle directly under the first triangle. Do you see a funny picture?

- What misspelled words did Andrea correct?
- Where did she add or change punctuation? Why?
- What other corrections did she make? Why?

Practice

Here is the first paragraph of a set of instructions. Proofread it, and find twelve errors. Use a dictionary to help with spelling. Copy the paragraph correctly on your paper.

Do you no how to tame a flea. your first step is to find a flea That is ready to settle down. Intervue your pupil the flea to find out what it likes you will probably want to use the fleas favrite things as rewards.

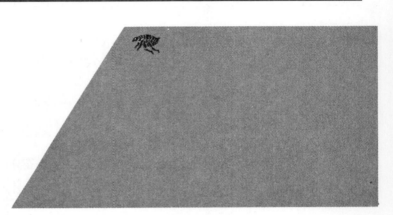

Assignment • Proofread Your Paragraph

Proofread your paper. Ask yourself these questions.

1. Is the paragraph indented?
2. Have I spelled all the words correctly?

Grammar skills checklist

3. Have I corrected my run-on sentences or sentence fragments?
4. Does every sentence begin with a capital letter and end with the correct punctuation mark?
5. Have I used a comma and a connecting word to join the parts of my compound sentences?
6. Have I used apostrophes to write possessive nouns correctly?
7. Have I used commas to set off appositives?

9 | Step Five
Make a Final Copy

Andrea copied her paragraph of instructions over neatly. Then she wrote a title, *Make a Surprise Picture*, at the top.

As a final check on the correctness of her instructions, Andrea followed the steps and made a drawing on a clean sheet of paper the same size as the paper on which she had copied her paragraph. Then she put the writing paper on top of the drawing and fastened them with a row of staples across the top. She made a crease in the top sheet, just below the staples, so that it could flip up. Then she pasted the bottom sheet to a piece of heavy cardboard. Finally, she added one sentence below her paragraph: *Lift up after you've finished!*

After Andrea's friends read her instructions and followed them, they could flip up the top sheet to see if their drawings matched hers. Andrea's classmates liked her idea so much that many of them wrote directions for different kinds of drawings and made flip-up charts, too. They enjoyed trying out each other's instructions. Maybe your class would enjoy it, too!

Assignment
- **Make a Final Copy**
- **Share Your Instructions**

A. Copy your paragraph over neatly.
B. Think of a good title, and write it above the paragraph. Be sure to capitalize the first word and every important word of your title. (Page 358 in the Handbook will help you.)
C. Check your paper to be sure you have copied correctly.
D. Think of a special way to share your instructions.

- You can make a tape recording.
- You can make a poster to illustrate your instructions.
- You can exchange instructions with your friends or classmates, as Andrea's class did. Provide a way for people to check that they followed the instructions correctly.
- Someone can act out your instructions as you read them.

Verbs

1 | Action Verbs and Being Verbs

You know that a **verb** is a word that shows action.

The car <u>swerved</u> dangerously. It <u>collided</u> with a truck.

Some verbs do not show action. They show a state of being. A **being verb** tells what something is or how someone feels or how something seems.

The drivers <u>are</u> safe. They <u>feel</u> relieved.

The most common being verb is the verb *be* itself in all its forms: *am, is, are, was, were, will be, have been,* and *had been.*

Here are more examples of action verbs and being verbs.

Action Verbs	**Being Verbs**
I <u>found</u> it on the beach.	I <u>became</u> more curious.
It <u>puzzled</u> me at first.	It <u>looked</u> like a white disk.
I <u>took</u> it into the house.	It <u>felt</u> wet and prickly.
I <u>studied</u> it carefully.	It <u>seemed</u> delicate.
I <u>held</u> it in my hand.	It <u>was</u> a sand dollar.

Try It Out

A. Find the verb in each sentence, and tell whether it is an action verb or a being verb.

1. We found a poster of a sand dollar.
2. A sand dollar is a type of sea urchin.
3. Sand dollars live on the sandy ocean floor.
4. Sometimes they float onto the beach with the tide.
5. Sand dollars are wonderful souvenirs.
6. A sand dollar looks like a silver dollar.
7. A five-point star is on the top surface.
8. Tiny movable spines cover a sand dollar's body.
9. The creatures crawl through the sand on their spines.

B. Complete these sentences with an action verb or a being verb. Tell which kind of verb you used.

10. Jamie ____ out of the pear tree.
11. Election Day ____ quiet at the polls.
12. Yesterday I ____ better about my work.
13. May we ____ on your minibike?
14. The thick black smoke ____ from the chimney.
15. Where ____ the fire?
16. The runner ____ tired and collapsed.
17. The narrator ____ from a script.
18. Have you ____ this book?

> ▶ A **verb** can show action or a state of being.

Written Practice

Write the verb in each sentence. Beside it, write *action verb* or *being verb*.

1. Marian Anderson became a great American concert singer.
2. She joined a choir at the age of six.
3. Her friends raised money for her singing lessons.
4. Mary Patterson, Giuseppe Boghetti, and Agnes Reifsnyder taught her everything about voice control.
5. Young Marian won a singing contest in New York City.
6. After that, she sang in concerts all over the world.
7. She was the first black member of the New York Metropolitan Opera Company.
8. Her modesty and charm attracted people to her.
9. In 1958 President Eisenhower appointed Ms. Anderson to a post in the United Nations.
10. Marian Anderson's career seemed full and rewarding.

• **Writing a Paragraph**   Write a short paragraph about someone you admire. Write *action* or *being* above each verb you use.

2 | Direct Objects

Often an action verb is followed by a word that tells who or what receives the action.

Fran <u>made</u> the **basket**.   Lou <u>finished</u> his **book**.

The word that tells who or what receives the action is called the **direct object**. To find the direct object in a sentence, first find the verb. Then ask who or what receives the action.

Study these sentences in which the action verbs are underlined and the direct objects are in dark type.

Jeremy <u>designed</u> a model **plane**. *(Jeremy designed what?)*
Ann <u>programmed</u> the **computer**. *(Ann programmed what?)*
That music <u>annoys</u> **Ray**. *(That music annoys whom?)*

In some sentences, the direct object is compound.

I <u>need</u> oil **paints** and a **brush** for my hobby.
(I need what for my hobby?)

Try It Out

A. Use direct objects to complete these sentences.

1. Last weekend we took a ＿＿ to the airport.
2. We watched the ＿＿ in the terminal.
3. A huge jet touched the ＿＿.
4. We ate ＿＿ in the airport restaurant.
5. We bought ＿＿ and ＿＿ in the gift shop.

B. Find the action verb and the direct object in each sentence.

6. We watched an aardvark at the zoo.
7. The aardvark eats termites or ants.
8. It digs a very large burrow.
9. An aardvark pushes dirt aside with great ease.
10. Its long pointed nose pokes the ground for food.

> ► The **direct object** receives the action of the verb. Some direct objects are compound.
>
> To find the direct object, find the action verb, and ask who or what receives the action.

Written Practice

A. Write the action verb and the direct object in each sentence.

1. Sir Francis Drake planned his voyage around the world.
2. His skill and courage helped England.
3. Queen Elizabeth I encouraged Drake.
4. Drake had no formal education.
5. He treated the members of his crew well.
6. He won their respect and loyalty.
7. Drake commanded three ships at once.
8. Two smaller ships carried the supplies.
9. Only Drake knew their real destination.
10. They visited many port cities in South America.
11. The crew bought spices at the Molucca Islands.
12. Then they crossed the Indian Ocean.
13. Soon the British people greeted the weary sailors.
14. The queen praised the captain and the entire crew.
15. Drake's adventures sparked the interest of everyone.

B. Write the direct object in each sentence. Beside it, write *direct object* or *compound direct object*.

16. Queen Elizabeth I knighted Drake.
17. The queen admired explorers and navigators.
18. She also encouraged authors and artists.
19. Elizabeth enjoyed their talent and energy.
20. She ruled England for many years.

• **Writing Sentences**   Write five sentences about something you made. In each one, use a direct object, and underline it.

3 | Linking Verbs

You know that being verbs are different from action verbs. Being verbs tell what the subject is or feels or seems like, not what the subject does. Being verbs are also called **linking verbs** because they link the subject of the sentence with a word that tells more about it. Study these common linking verbs.

is	be	taste
am	being	smell
are	been	feel
was	look	become
were	appear	seem

Mr. Wong <u>is</u> the principal. He <u>seems</u> very kind.

In the first sentence, the word *principal* is a noun linked to the subject. It is a predicate noun. A **predicate noun** is a noun that follows a linking verb and names the same person or thing as the subject.

Sometimes the word that follows a linking verb describes the subject instead of naming it. Then it is called a **predicate adjective**. In the second example, *kind* is a predicate adjective. It describes the subject *He* (Mr. Wong).

Study these examples of predicate nouns and predicate adjectives. The linking verbs are underlined. The predicate nouns and adjectives are in dark type.

Predicate Nouns
Mr. Hoey <u>was</u> our **leader**.
He <u>is</u> a **painter**.
We <u>became</u> close **friends**.

Predicate Adjectives
Ms. Hill <u>is</u> **friendly**.
She <u>seems</u> **shy** to strangers.
They <u>feel</u> **uncomfortable**.

Try It Out

A. Give a predicate noun or a predicate adjective to complete each sentence. Then tell which kind you used.

1. Our school looks ____.
2. The best part is the ____.
3. The new books seem ____.
4. This kitchen smells ____.
5. The food tastes ____.
6. The gym became a ____.

B. Find the subject and the linking verb in each of the sentences you completed above.

- ▶ A **linking verb** joins the subject with a related noun or adjective in the predicate.
- ▶ A **predicate noun** is a noun that follows a linking verb and names the same person or thing as the subject.
- ▶ A **predicate adjective** is an adjective that follows a linking verb and describes the subject.

Written Practice

Copy each sentence. Underline the linking verb, and draw an arrow from the subject to the predicate noun or adjective.

1. Five tribes were once famous in upper New York State.
2. These tribes were all Iroquois.
3. The Mohawks were one tribe in this group.
4. The Mohawks and the Oneidas had been enemies for years.
5. The chances for peace looked remote.
6. Hiawatha was a powerful chief.
7. He felt unhappy with the tribal warfare.
8. Peace was Hiawatha's goal.
9. Soon these Iroquois became a famous league.
10. Their constitution has been a model to other governments.

- **Writing Sentences**   Write five sentences, using linking verbs. Label predicate nouns *PN* and predicate adjectives *PA*.

4 | Main Verbs and Auxiliaries

Some verbs are composed of only one word.

> Kenneth <u>walked</u> home.

Sometimes several words together make up the verb.

> I <u>will be going</u> home soon, too.

A verb that is made up of more than one word is called a **verb phrase**. The last word in a verb phrase is the **main verb**. The other verbs are called **auxiliaries** or **helping verbs**.

Study these common auxiliary verbs.

am	were	do	had	will	would
is	be	did	can	shall	should
are	being	have	may	could	
was	been	has	must	might	

In the following sentences, the auxiliaries are in dark type, and the verb phrases are underlined.

> He **has** <u>skated</u> home. He **could have** <u>jogged</u> instead.
> The door **had been** <u>locked</u>. He **did** <u>take</u> his key.

Sometimes the auxiliary verb in one sentence can be used as the main verb in another. Be sure to read the whole sentence before you identify a main verb and its auxiliaries.

AUXILIARY: I **am** <u>waiting</u> here. Bob **has** <u>taken</u> it.
MAIN VERB: I <u>am</u> late. Jane <u>has</u> a new coat.

Questions are almost always formed with auxiliary verbs. In questions, the main verb and its auxiliaries are often separated by the subject.

> **Should** we <u>leave</u> now? **Will** the show <u>start</u> early?
> **Has** the box office <u>opened</u>? **Did** you <u>see</u> the sign?

Auxiliary verbs are also used to form contractions. As you know, a **contraction** is a word formed by combining two words and shortening them. An apostrophe takes the place of the letter or letters that have been left out. The contractions below are formed by combining a pronoun and an auxiliary verb.

we**'re** going = we **are** going   you**'ll** see = you **will** see
they**'ve** run = they **have** run   I**'m** coming = I **am** coming

Pronouns are never part of a verb phrase, even when they are written in a contraction. In the first example above, *we* is a pronoun. It is not part of the verb phrase *'re going*. What are the verb phrases in the three other examples?

Another kind of contraction combines an auxiliary verb with the word *not*. Notice in the examples below that *not* and its contracted form *n't* are never part of a verb phrase. The first verb phrase is *had gone*. What are the other verb phrases?

hadn't gone = had not gone   isn't going = is not going
wouldn't be = would not be   didn't like = did not like

Try It Out

Find the verb phrase in each of these sentences. Then tell which words are main verbs and which are auxiliaries.

1. Before 1803 the land between the Missouri River and the Rocky Mountains was owned by France.
2. By 1803 this land had been purchased by the United States.
3. This territory must be explored.
4. The leaders of this expedition should be selected carefully.
5. Meriwether Lewis and William Clark were chosen by President Thomas Jefferson in 1803.
6. Would this journey be dangerous?
7. A route to the Pacific Ocean would open new areas for United States fur trade.
8. The travelers didn't have a good map of the territory.
9. By 1805 they had become the first explorers in Idaho.
10. I'll write my history report on this expedition.

> ▸ A **verb phrase** is made up of one or more auxiliary verbs plus a main verb.
> ▸ The **main verb** is the last word in a verb phrase.
> ▸ **Auxiliary verbs** are helping verbs. They can be used to form contractions.

Written Practice

Write the verb phrases from the following sentences. Then underline the auxiliaries once and the main verbs twice.

1. Have you heard of the Shoshone princess Sacajawea?
2. She may have saved the Lewis and Clark expedition.
3. Sacajawea was born in Idaho in 1787.
4. She had been kidnapped from her tribe as a child.
5. In 1805 her French husband, Charbonneau, was hired as a guide for Lewis and Clark.
6. Sacajawea wouldn't stay behind.
7. Could the party cross the Rocky Mountains on foot?
8. Horses were needed for this part of the trip.
9. Only the Shoshone could supply them.
10. The Shoshone didn't trust strangers.
11. Sacajawea must have arranged for a horse trade.
12. Finally the mountains were crossed.
13. The pioneers had returned to St. Louis by September 1806.
14. Their 8,000-mile journey did last for more than two years.
15. Perhaps you've seen Sacajawea's memorial in Cheyenne, Wyoming.

● **Writing a Paragraph**   Write a short paragraph about some historical event. Underline each auxiliary verb once and each main verb twice.

Main Verbs and Auxiliaries   95

5 | Verb Tenses

The **tense** of a verb tells when the action or state of being takes place. "Tense" comes from a Latin word for *time*. The words *past*, *present*, and *future* all refer to time. They are also the names of some verb tenses.

The **present tense** tells that something is happening now.

The soloist arrives. The dancers perform outdoors.

The **past tense** tells that something has already happened. Usually the past tense of a verb is formed by adding *-ed*.

We stayed late. The audience applauded.

The **future tense** tells that something is going to happen. The future is usually formed with the auxiliary verb *shall* or *will*.

We shall be late. He will wait for you.

Try It Out

A. Tell whether the tense of each underlined verb is past, present, or future.

1. Olympic Games occur every four years.
2. The Olympics started thousands of years ago in ancient Greece.
3. Our modern Olympics developed from festivals in honor of local heroes.
4. Thousands of people will attend the next Olympic Games.
5. The International Olympic Committee governs the Olympic events.

B. Give the present, past, and future tenses for each of the following verbs.

6. laugh	**8.** tie	**10.** skate
7. spill	**9.** calculate	**11.** believe

> ▸ The **tense** of a verb tells when the action or state of being takes place.
> ▸ The **present tense** tells that something is happening now.
> ▸ The **past tense** tells that something has already happened.
> ▸ The **future tense** tells that something is going to happen.

Written Practice

A. To complete each sentence, write the correct form of the verb in parentheses.

1. Last year my family ____ an old house. (purchase)
2. At first we ____ on it a little at a time. (work)
3. My parents ____ our attic last week. (insulate)
4. In a few months, we ____ a back porch. (add)
5. Last Sunday we ____ friends to a painting party. (invite)
6. In six hours, we ____ seven rooms. (paint)
7. Then we ____ on the grill. (cook)
8. Tomorrow I ____ windows and screens. (wash)
9. Soon the house ____ a new roof and shutters. (need)
10. Next summer we ____ a vacation from our house. (take)

B. Copy this chart, filling in the past and future tenses.

Present Tense	Past Tense	Future Tense
push		
plant		
subtract		
rent		
move		

● **Writing a Paragraph**   Write a short paragraph, describing a project you have worked on. Use verbs in the present, past, and future tenses. Underline each verb. Label its tense.

6 | Principal Parts of Verbs

Every verb has basic forms called **principal parts**. All verb tenses are formed from these principal parts. Three principal parts are the verb itself, the past, and the past participle. The **verb** itself is used to write the present tense. Both the **past** and the **past participle** are used to show that something has already happened. Read the principal parts of these verbs.

Verb	Past	Past Participle
work	worked	(has, have, had) worked
play	played	(has, have, had) played
like	liked	(has, have, had) liked
begin	began	(has, have, had) begun
fly	flew	(has, have, had) flown
choose	chose	(has, have, had) chosen

When both the past and the past participle are formed by adding -d or -ed to the verb, it is called a **regular verb**. *Work* is a regular verb. What other verbs on the chart are regular?

Notice how the spelling of the principal parts of some verbs changes. Whenever the past and the past participle of a verb are not formed simply by adding -d or -ed, the verb is called an **irregular verb**. *Begin* is an irregular verb. Name the others on the chart.

Try It Out

A. Give the past and the past participle forms of the following regular verbs.

1. walk	**4.** pick	**7.** park	**10.** dress
2. hike	**5.** laugh	**8.** climb	**11.** dance
3. taste	**6.** open	**9.** wait	**12.** ask

B. Tell whether the main verb in each of the sentences below is regular or irregular.

13. People have watched birds for thousands of years.
14. Many scientists studied the secret of flight.
15. No one had found the answer until 1903.
16. Orville and Wilbur Wright changed the world.

▸ The **principal parts**, or basic forms, of a verb include the verb itself, the past, and the past participle.
▸ When the past and the past participle of a verb are formed by adding *-d* or *-ed*, the verb is **regular**.
▸ When the past and the past participle are formed in some other way, the verb is **irregular**.

Written Practice

Write the verb in each of these sentences. Beside it, write *regular* or *irregular*.

1. In 1927 a man surprised the entire world.
2. He did something entirely new.
3. Charles A. Lindbergh completed the first solo airplane flight across the Atlantic Ocean.
4. He flew nonstop from New York City to Paris, France.
5. During the flight, Lindbergh met many challenges.
6. Severe storms lashed his small plane.
7. Again and again, he fought against drowsiness.
8. More than once, ice formed on the wings of the plane.
9. Finally, after thirty-three hours and thirty minutes in the air, Lindbergh saw the Paris airfield.
10. He told the story in the book *The Spirit of St. Louis*.

• **Writing Sentences** Write five sentences about flying. Then write *R* above the regular verbs you have used and *IR* above the irregular verbs.

7 | Irregular Verbs

You probably already know the principal parts of most irregular verbs just from hearing them used. However, in most cases, it is difficult to find two irregular verbs that are formed alike. The best way to learn the correct principal parts of any irregular verb is to memorize them. The chart below lists some of the most common irregular verbs. Read these principal parts over to yourself until you are sure that you know them.

Verb	Past	Past Participle
blow	blew	(has, have, had) blown
choose	chose	(has, have, had) chosen
do	did	(has, have, had) done
drive	drove	(has, have, had) driven
freeze	froze	(has, have, had) frozen
lend	lent	(has, have, had) lent
ring	rang	(has, have, had) rung
speak	spoke	(has, have, had) spoken
steal	stole	(has, have, had) stolen
swim	swam	(has, have, had) swum
take	took	(has, have, had) taken
tear	tore	(has, have, had) torn
throw	threw	(has, have, had) thrown
write	wrote	(has, have, had) written

Try It Out

A. Without looking back at the chart, see whether you can give the principal parts of the following verbs.

1. speak	**4.** throw	**7.** write	**10.** do
2. blow	**5.** tear	**8.** take	**11.** swim
3. ring	**6.** drive	**9.** steal	**12.** lend

B. Use a word in parentheses to complete each sentence.

13. Our art class had (did, done) a mural.
14. I (spoke, spoken) to the manager about my damaged shirt.
15. Matthew Webb (swam, swum) the English Channel.
16. Who (drove, driven) north to see the fall foliage?
17. The fountains have (froze, frozen) into ice sculptures.

> The principal parts of many verbs are irregular. The best way to learn the principal parts of an irregular verb is to memorize them.

Written Practice

A. Write the past and past participle for each verb. Use a dictionary if you need help.

1. eat 3. know 5. ride 7. bring
2. go 4. shrink 6. come 8. swim

B. Complete each pair of sentences, using the past or the past participle form of the verb in parentheses.

9. Perhaps you have ____ some famous paintings by Grandma Moses. We ____ some at a museum. (see)
10. Grandma Moses ____ her first oil painting at age sixty-seven. She had ____ her life as a farmer. (begin)
11. Grandma Moses ____ pictures with charcoal as a child. She has ____ scenes from her childhood on a farm. (draw)
12. She has ____ the art world by surprise. Grandma Moses never ____ an art lesson. (take)
13. Grandma Moses ____ about her life and her painting. Scholars have ____ about her primitive art. (write)

• **Writing Sentences** Choose five irregular verbs. Use the past or the past participle of each verb in a sentence.

8 | Subject-Verb Agreement

A verb and its subject must agree. You use agreement automatically every time you say "I think" rather than "I thinks." If the subject is singular, the verb must also be singular.

I like books. **You** like books. **Mom** likes books.

If the subject is a singular noun (*Mom*) or the pronoun *he, she,* or *it,* the present tense verb agrees by ending in -*s* (*likes*).

If the subject is plural, the verb must also be plural. In the sentence below, *grandparents,* a plural subject, agrees with the present tense verb *read.* Does this plural verb form end in -*s*?

My **grandparents** read cookbooks.

When the parts of a compound subject are joined with *and,* the verb is always plural.

Horses, boxing, and **Mexico** are my favorite topics.

When *or, either . . . or,* or *neither . . . nor* is used to connect the parts of a compound subject, the verb is sometimes singular and sometimes plural.

Either **weekdays** or **weekends** are good times for books.
Neither **television** nor **radio** is as exciting as a book.

In the first sentence, because both parts of the compound subject are plural, the verb is plural (*are*). In the second sentence, both parts of the subject are singular. This compound subject agrees with the singular verb *is.*

What happens when one part of a compound subject is singular and one part is plural?

Neither **Theodore** nor his **dogs** like wet weather.
Neither the **dogs** nor **Theodore** likes wet weather.

Which part of the subject does the verb agree with in each sentence above? It agrees with the subject closer to the verb.

Try It Out

Choose a verb in parentheses to complete each sentence.

1. City libraries and the school library (is, are) helpful.
2. Our encyclopedia (has, have) an article on metallic alloys.
3. Our library (contain, contains) eight sets of encyclopedias.
4. Either this library or the city libraries (is, are) open.
5. Mrs. Kay or my dad (is, are) going to order books by mail.

The subject of a sentence must agree with its verb.

If the parts of a compound subject are joined by *and,* use a plural verb.

If the parts of a compound subject are joined by *or, either . . . or,* or *neither . . . nor,* the verb agrees with the part of the subject that is closer to it.

Written Practice

Write each sentence, choosing the correct verb or verb phrase from the parentheses.

1. Either books or magazines (is, are) excellent references.
2. These chapters and this article (seem, seems) interesting.
3. The first automobile (was built, were built) in 1769.
4. Cars (was called, were called) horseless carriages.
5. Neither steam cars nor electric cars (was, were) fast.
6. Either Benz or Daimler (deserves, deserve) credit for the first commercially successful car.
7. Ford, Olds, and Winton (was, were) early competitors.
8. Neither tolls nor a speed limit (was used, were used) at first.
9. Neither cars nor roads now (look, looks) like those of 1900.

- **Writing a Paragraph** Write a short paragraph about your favorite way of traveling. Include examples of *either . . . or* and *neither . . . nor* as connectors in compound subjects.

9 Using Words Correctly

sit, set; lie, lay

The verbs *sit* and *lie* mean "to rest or recline." The verbs *set* and *lay* mean "to put or place an object."

I <u>sit</u> in the barber chair. I <u>set</u> the bowl on the tray.
I <u>lie</u> on the blanket. I <u>lay</u> the book on the table.

To decide which verb to use, ask yourself what the subject is doing. If the subject is placing an object somewhere, use *set* or *lay*. If the subject is resting, use *sit* or *lie*.

Use the verbs *sit* and *lie* when referring to a resting position.
Use the verbs *set* and *lay* to mean putting an object somewhere.

Practice

A. Choose a word in parentheses to complete each sentence.

1. (Set, Sit) the ball here.
2. Please (sit, set) by me.
3. (Lie, Lay) that jar down.
4. Don't (lie, lay) on that.

B. Write the word from the parentheses that completes each sentence correctly.

5. I often (sit, set) by the kitchen window.
6. A sparrow (lays, lies) on a mound of leaves.
7. Dad will help me (sit, set) its leg in a splint.
8. Now the sparrow (lays, lies) on a soft cushion.
9. I will (lie, lay) it next to my bed tonight.
10. Soon we can (sit, set) it on the windowsill.

- **Writing Sentences**   Use *sit*, *set*, *lay*, and *lie* correctly in four sentences of your own.

Roots, Prefixes, Suffixes

The **root**, or main part, of each word below is underlined. When a prefix or suffix or both are added, the word's meaning changes.

re<u>charge</u>   <u>taste</u>ful   un<u>employ</u>ment

A **prefix** is a word part added before the root.

Prefix	Meaning	Example
un-, dis-, in-	not	unhappy
ex-	out of	export
pre-, pro-	before, for	preheat

A **suffix** is a word part added after the root word.

Suffix	Meaning	Example
-able	capable of	profitable
-er, -or	one who does	farmer
-ment	state or condition of	enjoyment

> ▸ The **root** is the main part of a word.
> ▸ A **prefix** is a word part added before the root.
> ▸ A **suffix** is a word part added after the root.

Practice

Add a prefix, a suffix, or both to each word. Write as many new words as you can. Use the examples on this page to help you.

1. view   3. act   5. claim   7. count   9. cover
2. correct   4. change   6. press   8. favor   10. govern

- **Writing Sentences**   Write a sentence for each word you wrote.

Review

- **Action Verbs and Being Verbs** *(pp. 87–88)* Write the verbs below. Label each one *action verb* or *being verb*.

  1. Yesterday we visited a computer science center.
  2. There was a room full of computer terminals.
  3. One computer's voice seemed almost human.
  4. Another computer asked us questions about our career plans.
  5. We wrote computer programs on punch cards.

- **Direct Objects** *(pp. 89–90)* Write the action verb and its direct object in each of these sentences.

  6. Carla requested information from the National Park Service.
  7. She received a booklet on parks and reservations.
  8. A cowboy discovered Carlsbad Caverns in 1901.
  9. The Mammoth Cave in Kentucky attracts visitors.

- **Linking Verbs** *(pp. 91–92)* Write each linking verb and its predicate noun or predicate adjective. Label each predicate noun *PN* and each predicate adjective *PA*.

  10. Ann is a newspaper carrier.
  11. She feels proud of her job.
  12. Her route is Main Street.
  13. The streets are hilly.
  14. The papers become heavy.
  15. Her pouch is an old feedbag.

- **Main Verbs and Auxiliaries** *(pp. 93–95)* Write the verb phrase in each sentence. Underline the auxiliary verbs once and the main verbs twice.

  16. Don Quixote had read many adventure books.
  17. He wouldn't listen to his friends' warnings.
  18. He did consider himself a brave knight.
  19. His old plow horse had been given a special name.
  20. Don Quixote and his horse would conquer the giants.

- **Verb Tenses** *(pp. 96–97)* Write the correct form of the verb in parentheses for each sentence.

   21. Last week Maggie ____ her first trophy in a rodeo. (earn)
   22. Tomorrow Maggie's brother ____ in bull riding. (compete)
   23. Next weekend her family ____ to another rodeo. (travel)
   24. Now Maggie ____ for the next rodeo. (practice)

- **Principal Parts of Verbs** *(pp. 98–99)* Copy the verbs below. Label each one *R* for regular or *IR* for irregular.

   25. Aaron did many things.
   26. He flew in an airplane.
   27. Last year he built toy cars.
   28. Friends teased him.
   29. He laughed with them.
   30. Aaron became famous.

- **Irregular Verbs** *(pp. 100–101)* Write the past participle of each irregular verb in exercises 25–30 above.

- **Subject-Verb Agreement** *(pp. 102–103)* Write the verb in parentheses that agrees with the subject of the sentence.

   31. Charlotte and her brother (take, takes) swimming lessons.
   32. Either the teacher or the lifeguards (watch, watches) them.
   33. Neither her brothers nor Charlotte (has, have) won an event.
   34. The competition (is, are) very strong.

- **Using Words Correctly** *(p. 104)* Write the word that best fits in each sentence.

   35. Did you (sit, set) here?
   36. (Lie, Lay) that coat there.
   37. (Sit, Set) the plant down.
   38. Maybe I'll (lie, lay) down.

- **Building Vocabulary** *(p. 105)* Write every word containing a prefix or suffix in these sentences.

   39. Our gym teacher will explain the new health chart.
   40. The class learns a comfortable way to exhale.
   41. We have a portable piano for our accompaniment.
   42. A news reporter wrote about our unusual classes.
   43. I disagree with your statement about proper nourishment.

Writing a Descriptive Paragraph

1 | Using Your Senses

All of your senses—seeing, hearing, touching, tasting, and smelling—constantly bring you information. Much of it you hardly notice. At other times, after a thunderstorm, for example, your senses suddenly come alive. You hear thunder rumbling in the distance; the air smells fresh and feels cool and damp on your skin; colors have a different, deeper, look.

Decide which of the five senses these lines of poetry refer to.

All the world is cold . . .
   My fishing-line is trembling
In the autumn wind.   *–Buson*

     . . . A broom
Swishes over the sidewalk like feet through leaves.
     –Galway Kinnell

     . . . the strong crust
of friendly bread; and many-tasting food;
Rainbows, and the blue bitter smoke of wood.
     –Rupert Brooke

Now concentrate on *your* five senses.

Practice

A. Look at an object near you. Pretend you have never seen it before. Write four details that describe how it looks.

B. Be perfectly quiet. Now write down every sound you hear.

C. Think of a place that wakes up your sense of smell—a kitchen, a forest, a zoo. List all the smells you can remember.

D. List four things near you, and write one word to describe the way each one feels to the touch.

E. Think of foods that have opposite tastes, such as vinegar and honey. List two other food pairs with opposite tastes.

2 | Using Exact Words

Read these sentences to see the difference exact words make.

My dog has short legs, long ears, and long brown fur.
My dog has stubby legs, floppy ears, and silky reddish fur.

Exact words like the ones in the second sentence present a more precise picture of what is being described. Can you hear traffic? What words describe what it sounds like? Does it *roar* or *whisper*? Are there *chugs, whines,* or *rumbles*?

If you touch your desk top, does it feel *even*? Other words can describe the texture—*satiny, glassy, smooth, slick, polished.* Does one of these words describe more exactly the way your desk top feels?

- When you walk down the street, do you *rush* or *stroll*? Is there another word that tells more exactly how you walk?
- Is a thin person you know *skinny* or *slim*?
- *Nice* is a general word that does not tell much. Try to go through the next three days without using the word *nice.* Find one or two or three words to replace it.

Another way to make your word pictures sharper and more interesting is by using comparisons. An elephant's skin is grayish and dried and cracked. What does it remind you of? Could you say the elephant's skin looks like a dried-up mud puddle?

Practice

Rewrite each sentence. Use words that are more exact, or make up comparisons. Try to make a picture with your words.

1. The chair was very old.
2. The building was tall.
3. His clothes are colorful.
4. A noise startled me.
5. Her shoes pinch.
6. A flower bud opened.

3 | Choosing Details

To write a good description, you will need to select just a few of the many possible details. Which details should you choose? It depends on your purpose. If you want to describe how your brand new jeans feel, include details about their texture. Let your reader see their "newness." You would not need details about belt loops or washing instructions. Read these sentences.

> Roger wore his brown felt hat tilted slightly to the side.
> Roger's brown felt hat was size 7¼ and was made in Chicago by the Brimm Brothers.

Both sentences have details. Which sentence tells only facts about the hat itself? Which one not only tells you about the hat but also shows you something about its owner? Each sentence uses details to suit a different purpose.

In the same way, when you write about a person, you will not need to describe every detail of that person's appearance. Look for striking features: freckles, a turned-up nose, dark eyes, hair the color of wheat. Next, think of a detail or two that reveals not only the person but also her or his personality. For example, describe how the person moves—at a brisk pace or a slow saunter.

If your purpose is to show that person at a moment of anxiety, you could include details about how the person paces back and forth, takes short breaths, checks his or her watch, or taps nervously on the desk. Details such as these give a clear, uncluttered picture of what your subject acts like at that particular moment.

Practice

Look at the picture on page 108. If you were writing a description, which details would you include? Since your readers cannot see the picture, try to create a mental picture for them. Decide on just a few important details, and list them.

4 | Getting Started

When you write a description, in a sense, you become a photographer. You choose when to snap the shutter and how much to include in each shot. You can take an action shot, for example, by describing a swimming pool full of people. If you stand back a little, your picture will create a general impression of what the pool is like on a busy day. If you step up closer, you can focus in on one part of the total picture—perhaps the expression on a child's face when he or she discovers how cold the water is.

No matter what kind of description you choose, you go through a selection process. You do not show everything. You tailor your description to create a single impression. Every detail you choose fits your purpose. Furthermore, your description comes alive for your reader through details. By using your five senses, you create a picture that seems real and believable. Finally, you adjust the focus on your camera. You choose exact words rather than "blurry" ones. Then your reader will see a clear image and begin to enjoy it.

Practice

Think of a place you like to be. Then pretend that you are a photographer. View it from two different angles—one at a distance, the other close up. List details for each one.

Steps for Writing a Description   Here are the steps for writing a description. You will follow these steps to write your own description.

Step One   Choose a topic.
Step Two   Write your description.
Step Three   Revise your description.
Step Four   Proofread your description.
Step Five   Make a final copy to share.

5 | Step One
Choose a Topic

Would you like to write about a person, a place, or a thing? Your choice will be easier to make if you consider only those subjects that you can look at before you write your description.

Conrad thought of several ideas for his description. He wrote them down, so he could think about them carefully.

my uncle's restaurant   *my oldest sister*
my room at home   *a campfire*
Grandfather's farm   *my model ship*

Conrad liked all these ideas. When he looked back over his list, he decided that it would be more interesting to choose something smaller than a restaurant or a farm. He wanted to concentrate on making an exact, sharp picture.

He decided to write about either his room at home or a campfire. He tried out each of these topics by making a list of details about it. Doing this made him see that he really wanted to write about the campfire. Besides, he was going to the woods with his dad that weekend, and there he could think about his description in front of a real campfire.

Assignment
- **Make a List**
- **Make Notes**
- **Choose a Topic**

A. List at least two people, at least two places, and at least two things that you would enjoy describing. Remember, the more ideas you list, the better your selection for a topic.
B. Pick the two ideas from your list that you would most like to write about. List several details about each one. Include details from as many senses as you can.
C. Look at your two sets of details and decide on your final topic. Circle your final choice.

6 | Step Two
Write Your Description

In a first draft, the important thing is to get your ideas down on paper. Remember that you are creating a word picture. Use words that help your reader imagine what you see, hear, feel, taste, and smell. Color your picture with details and exact words.

When Conrad wrote his first draft, he used his list of details about the campfire as a guide. He did make some mistakes in his first draft, but he did not worry about them at this point. There would be time to correct them later.

Conrad's first draft

> The flames of the campfire were high.
> The fire snapped and crackeled.
> There were tall trees all around.
> There was an owl hooting. There
> ~~was~~ The moon was hugh and
> full. The smoke smelled good.

- How many senses did Conrad use?
- Which words could Conrad replace with more exact ones?

Assignment • Write Your First Draft

Write a first draft. Here are some things to keep in mind.

1. For an object, describe its size, shape, color, texture, and use.
2. For people, show what they are like and how they look.
3. For a place, tell how it looks, sounds, smells, and feels.

7 | Step Three
Revise Your Description

Conrad read over his description. He saw dull words such as *good* that he could change to more exact ones. He also noticed that he had not written details about how the fire smelled.

Then Conrad read his paper to Luis. Luis said, "It's such a short paragraph. Did you forget something?" Conrad realized that he could tell more about the trees. Finally, Luis pointed out that two sentences began with *there were* or *there was*. This made the description sound dull.

Here are the changes Conrad made in his description.

Conrad's revised description

> The *high* flames of the campfire were ~~high~~.
> The fire snapped and crackeled.
> There were *pine* tall trees *circled the clearing,* all around.
> There was an owl hooting *hooted far away*. ~~There~~
> ~~was~~ *in the sky above the clearing, the* The moon was hugh *High* and
> full. The smoke smelled *sharps in the* ~~good~~.
> *chilly air. It mixed with the smell of pine needels.*

- Which two sentences did Conrad make into one sentence?
- Which sentence replaced *There were tall trees all around*?
- What detail did Conrad add about the moon?
- What did he write instead of *good* in the sentence about the smoke?
- Which of his senses did he use in the sentence he added?

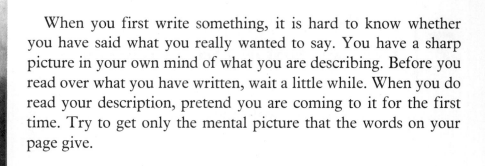

When you first write something, it is hard to know whether you have said what you really wanted to say. You have a sharp picture in your own mind of what you are describing. Before you read over what you have written, wait a little while. When you do read your description, pretend you are coming to it for the first time. Try to get only the mental picture that the words on your page give.

Assignment

- **Revise Your Description**
- **Discuss Your Description**

A. Read over your description. Ask yourself these questions about it.

    1. How many of my senses have I used? Could I use more?

    2. What sharp sensory words have I used? Which words could I replace with more exact ones?

    3. What details could I add to make my word picture sharper?

B. Make changes in your description. Cross out dull words, and write your new words above them. Add details.

C. Read your description to someone else—a classmate or your teacher. Ask your listener whether your description gives a sharp picture. If your listener has good suggestions for changes, use them.

8 | Step Four
Proofread Your Description

Now you are ready to proofread your description. In this step, you will correct any mistakes you made in spelling, capitalization, punctuation, and grammar.

Conrad realized that all his changes had made his paper hard to read. He copied his description over; then he proofread it. He used a dictionary whenever he was unsure of the spelling of a word.

At this point, Conrad had time to think of a title for his paragraph. He wrote it at the top of his paper and used capital letters to begin the first word, the last word, and each important word.

Conrad's description after proofreading

An Evening by the Campfire

The high flames of the campfire
snapped and crackled. Tall pine
trees circled the clearing; *a*n owl
hooted far away. High in the sky
above the clearing, the moon was
huge
hugh and full. The smoke smelled
sharp in the chilly air. It mixed
needles.
with the smell of pine needels.

- Which words did Conrad correct for spelling?
- How did Conrad correct his run-on sentence?

Practice

Proofread this description. You should find five errors. Look up any words you are unsure of. Then copy the description correctly on your paper.

The fishing pier sticks out into the bay a long way. The boards are rouf and you can see water thru the cracks. Waves splash against the poles underneath. There are salty sea smells and fishey smells from the bate.

Assignment • **Proofread Your Description**

Proofread your description. Ask yourself these questions.

1. Have I indented my paragraph or paragraphs?
2. Are all the words spelled correctly?
3. Have I looked up any word I am unsure about?

--- **Grammar skills checklist** ---

4. Have I corrected any run-on sentences or sentence fragments?
5. Have I used a comma and a connecting word to join the parts of compound sentences?
6. Have I used apostrophes to write possessive nouns correctly?
7. Does the subject of each sentence agree with its verb?

9 | Step Five
Make a Final Copy

Conrad took a clean piece of paper and copied his description in his best handwriting. He was ready to share it now, but he wanted to make it look special first.

He thought about drawing an illustration of the campfire scene, but then he had an idea he liked better.

First, he glued his paper onto a larger piece of dark blue construction paper. Then he cut a pine-tree shape out of dark green paper and glued it to one side. He glued a circle of aluminum foil near the top of the tree to be the full moon. Finally he cut flame shapes out of yellow and orange paper and glued them to the other side.

When he had finished, his description was in the center of a frame that fitted the subject. It looked like this.

Assignment

- **Make a Final Copy**
- **Share Your Description**

A. Copy your description in your best handwriting.
B. Check your description again to make sure you have not left out anything or made any other copying errors.
C. Think of a special way to share your description.

- You can make a frame for your description the way Conrad did.
- You can make a booklet with photographs or your own sketches.

Pronouns

1 | Pronouns and Antecedents

Read the following conversation.

BILL: Bill wants a sandwich.
TAMMY: When does Bill want a sandwich?
BILL: Now. Is Tammy hungry, too?
TAMMY: Yes. Will Tammy and Bill get the sandwiches now?

As you can see, our language would sound very strange if we could not use words like *I*, *you*, *we*, and *me*. These words are pronouns. A **pronoun** is a word that takes the place of a noun. Pronouns keep us from having to repeat the same noun again and again.

In order for a pronoun to make sense, you must be able to tell which noun it replaces. The noun that a pronoun refers to is called the **antecedent**. Now read the same conversation with pronouns.

BILL: I want a sandwich.
TAMMY: When do you want it?
BILL: Now. Are you hungry, too?
TAMMY: Yes. Will we get the sandwiches now?

I
you
he
she
it
we
you
they

Notice which pronouns from the list at the right replaced the nouns in the conversation above. You know that when Bill uses the pronoun *I*, he is referring to himself. The pronoun *I* replaces the noun *Bill*. You see that the pronoun *it* refers back to the noun *sandwich*. Therefore, *sandwich* is the antecedent of *it*.

In each of the following sentences, an arrow goes from the pronoun to the antecedent. Notice that a pronoun can have more than one antecedent.

James owns an ax, but he needs a log splitter.

Clyde and **Carol** closed the windows before they left.

George left his **bike** out in the rain, and it rusted.

The antecedent does not have to be in the same sentence as the pronoun. Read these sentences.

Brian and Cecil wrote a cookbook. Cecil illustrated <u>it</u>. <u>They</u> tested the recipes on their friends.

The antecedent of *it* in the second sentence is *cookbook*. What is the antecedent of *They* in the last sentence?

If a pronoun does not have a clear antecedent, a sentence can be confusing. In the sentence below, does *he* have an antecedent?

INCORRECT: Ted and Sam were swimming, and <u>he</u> went out too far.

Does *he* refer to Ted or to Sam? The sentence does not tell. You could rewrite the sentence in two ways to make it clear.

CORRECT: Ted was swimming, and he went out too far.
CORRECT: Ted and Sam were swimming, and Ted went out too far.

Try It Out

A. Replace the underlined part of each sentence with a pronoun.

1. <u>Nancy</u> walked fast.
2. <u>Tom and Wendy</u> walked home.
3. The book is <u>Vern's</u>.
4. <u>Bruce</u> answered the door.
5. <u>Ruth</u> has the racket.
6. <u>The players</u> left early.
7. <u>The bus driver</u> forgot the map.
8. <u>Telephone wires</u> were down.
9. <u>The road</u> was bumpy.
10. <u>Ted, June, and I</u> gave directions.

B. Name each pronoun in the following sentences, and tell what its antecedent is.

11. The fans rose and cheered when they saw the touchdown.
12. The seats are too far from the field. They are uncomfortable, too.
13. Judy knows the cheers. She yells from the stands.
14. Danny bought Judy a sandwich and an apple. He bought juice for her, too.
15. The musicians played our school song. Then they played some marches.

▸ A **pronoun** is a word that takes the place of a noun.
▸ The **antecedent** of a pronoun is the noun or nouns that a pronoun refers to.
Every pronoun should have a clear antecedent.

Written Practice

Copy all the pronouns from the following paragraph. Beside each pronoun, write its antecedent.

I am named Henry. I live in a treehouse. The story started when Joey and I found a tree. We climbed the special tree every day. It is very tall and has thick branches. Joey wanted to make a treehouse. He thought the tree was perfect. Joey and I started work. We built the treehouse in two days. It was beautiful. A sleeping bag and a chair are in the treehouse. They fill it. Mother says I have to pay rent. Is she serious?

• **Writing a Paragraph**   Write a short paragraph about something you have done with someone else. Underline the pronouns when you have finished. Does each pronoun you underlined have a clear antecedent?

2 | Pronouns as Subjects and Objects

Pronouns do the same jobs in sentences as the nouns they replace. A pronoun can be the subject of a sentence.

Phil Phillips hit the ball.	I hit the ball.
Suellen Cox finished first.	She finished first.

When a pronoun receives the action of the verb, it is a direct object. The underlined pronouns are direct objects.

Kim saw Phil Phillips.	Kim saw me.
Dad knows Suellen Cox.	Dad knows her.

The chart shows how most pronouns change their forms according to their use. Which pronouns do not change their forms?

Subject Pronouns	Object Pronouns
I	me
you	you
he	him
she	her
it	it
we	us
they	them

Try It Out

A. Are these underlined pronouns subjects or objects?

1. We built a new porch on our house.
2. Uncle Lou planned and designed it.
3. Mom bought the cedar boards and hauled them home.
4. She stacked them by the fireplace.
5. Now you can enjoy the porch, too.

B. Complete each sentence with a subject or an object pronoun. Tell which kind you used.

6. (We, Us) like cherry tomatoes.
7. Dad planted (them, they) in a window box.
8. (I, Me) noticed the first ripe tomatoes.
9. Gloria picked (they, them) from the vine.
10. (Us, We) enjoyed (they, them).
11. (They, Them) will last all summer.

A pronoun can be the subject of a sentence.
A pronoun can be a direct object.
The subject pronouns are *I, he, she, we,* and *they.*
The object pronouns are *me, him, her, us,* and *them.*
You and *it* can be either subjects or objects.

Written Practice

Choose the correct pronoun to complete each sentence. Write *S* beside the pronoun if it is used as a subject and *O* if it is a direct object.

1. (I, Me) earn money in the fall.
2. (I, Me) rake leaves and pile (they, them).
3. My friend Dennis helps (I, me).
4. (We, Us) put ads in the local newspaper.
5. I write the ads, and Dennis illustrates (them, they).
6. (He, Him) carries the equipment.
7. (I, Me) make a pile, and he helps (I, me).
8. Sometimes (we, us) jump into the pile.
9. The leaves scratch and tickle (we, us).
10. (We, Us) share the profits.

- **Writing Sentences**   Write a sentence for each pronoun.

11. she	**13.** we	**15.** them	**17.** they
12. you (plural)	**14.** him	**16.** us	**18.** me

3 | Possessive Pronouns

You have seen how pronouns change their forms to show which jobs they perform in sentences. A pronoun also changes its form when it shows ownership. A pronoun that shows ownership is called a **possessive pronoun**. Study the list below.

Possessive Pronouns

my	her	its	mine	hers	ours
your	his	our	yours	his	theirs
		their			

Any pronoun in the first three columns can come before a noun. Notice how possessive pronouns are used in these sentences.

This is <u>my</u> **mug**.   <u>Your</u> **mug** is on <u>their</u> **shelf**.
<u>Its</u> **handle** is broken.   <u>Her</u> **mug** is near <u>his</u> **mug**.

The possessive pronouns in the last three columns can stand alone in sentences. Read these two sentences.

The prize is <u>ours</u>, not <u>yours</u> or <u>theirs</u>.
The house was <u>his</u> and <u>hers</u>.

Be careful to distinguish between possessive pronouns and contractions. The pairs below are often confused.

<u>its</u> and <u>it's</u>   (it's = it is)
<u>their</u> and <u>they're</u>   (they're = they are)
<u>your</u> and <u>you're</u>   (you're = you are)
<u>whose</u> and <u>who's</u>   (who's = who is)

A possessive pronoun never has an apostrophe. Contractions have apostrophes to show that a letter or letters are missing. Study how these possessive pronouns and contractions are used.

<u>It's</u> time for the tree to shed <u>its</u> leaves.
<u>You're</u> wearing <u>your</u> glasses on <u>your</u> head.
<u>Who's</u> helping the family <u>whose</u> house burnt down?

Try It Out

A. Use a correct possessive pronoun to complete each sentence.

1. A glove that belongs to me is ____.
2. A house that belongs to us is ____.
3. A dog that belongs to them is ____.
4. A paw that belongs to a lion is ____.
5. A memory that belongs to you is ____.

B. Complete each sentence with a word from the parentheses.

6. (Your, You're) assignment is better than (my, mine).
7. (My, Mine) assignment looks longer than (her, hers).
8. (They're, Their) work looks better than (our, ours).
9. (Who's, Whose) deciding (who's, whose) work is best?
10. Did the boys finish (their, theirs)?

> ▸ A **possessive pronoun** is a pronoun that shows ownership.

Written Practice

Write the word that correctly completes each sentence.

1. The snake has already shed (it's, its) skin this season.
2. (Whose, Who's) batteries are these?
3. Do you know where (your, you're) friends are?
4. (Whose, Who's) lunch was left on that desk?
5. (Your, You're) skates are too tight, aren't they?
6. This brand new camp stove is all (our's, ours).
7. I'll paint mine, and you paint (your, yours).
8. Somehow I knew that case was (her, hers).
9. (Your, You're) umbrella is not as old as (my, mine).
10. Can this entire building be (their's, theirs)?

- **Writing Sentences**   Write five sentences, using at least five of the possessive pronouns from the list on page 126.

4 | Pronouns After Linking Verbs

You have learned that a linking verb joins the subject of the sentence to a predicate noun or a predicate adjective. A linking verb can also join the subject to a pronoun.

The champions were <u>they</u>.   My aunt is <u>she</u>.

The pronoun *they* in the first sentence is in the subject form and refers to the subject *champions*. Pronouns that follow linking verbs are always in the subject form. What form is *she* in the second sentence?

Sometimes more than one pronoun follows a linking verb.

Our class officers were <u>she</u> and <u>I</u>.

Try It Out

A. Tell whether the pronoun after each linking verb is used correctly. If it is incorrect, replace it with the correct pronoun.

1. The bank teller is her.
2. The cheerleaders were they in red uniforms.
3. It was him on the phone.
4. The best swimmers are her and the coach.
5. The baby in the photo is I.
6. The winners were them and us.

B. Choose the correct pronoun to complete these sentences.

7. It was (them, they) who found the boat.
8. It was (I, me) who saw the wreck.
9. The rescuers were (we, us).
10. The bravest ones were (her, she) and (him, he).
11. The heroes are (they, them).

Use the subject form for pronouns that follow linking verbs.

Written Practice

A. Write these sentences, using a pronoun for the words in parentheses. The first one has been done for you.

1. The most talented artist in our class is ____. (a boy)
   The most talented artist in our class is he.
2. The telephone installer was ____. (a woman)
3. It was ____ who found your sweater. (a man)
4. Our class's newest student is ____. (a girl)
5. The people we met were ____. (a man and a woman)
6. It was ____ who rang your doorbell. (two people)

B. Write each sentence, choosing the correct pronoun from those in parentheses.

7. It was (she, her) who planted those flowers.
8. It was (I, me) who planted the roses.
9. The gardeners with the most creative landscaping ideas are (him, he) and (her, she).
10. That is (he, him) now.
11. Our friends are (they, them).
12. The woman who is hoeing is (her, she).
13. I am (she, her).
14. The man who planted the garden was (him, he).
15. That man is (me, I).
16. The members of the garden club are (they, them).

- **Writing Sentences** Write six sentences, using each of these pronouns after a linking verb.

  17. he   20. you
  18. I   21. she
  19. they   22. we

5 | Compound Subjects and Objects

A compound subject is two or more simple subjects joined by *and* or *or*. Use the subject form for any pronoun in a compound subject. When you want to include yourself as part of a compound subject, use the pronoun *I*. It is polite to mention yourself last.

INCORRECT: Pam and me took a walk.
INCORRECT: I and Pam took a walk.
  CORRECT: Pam and I took a walk.

To check the pronoun you chose, use it alone with the verb. For example, drop the words *Pam and*. Does *I took a walk* make sense? Does *Me took a walk*?

Use the object form for any pronoun in a compound object. Again, it is polite to mention yourself last.

INCORRECT: The dog followed Veronica and I.
INCORRECT: The dog followed me and Veronica.
  CORRECT: The dog followed Veronica and me.

Check your choice by asking yourself which pronoun fits if it is used alone. Drop *Veronica and*. Does *The dog followed I* make sense? Does *The dog followed me*?

Try It Out

A. Choose the correct pronoun to complete each sentence.

1. You and (me, I) will fix this radio.
2. I will help you and (him, he).
3. Alex and (I, me) will take the back off.
4. The electricity did not shock you and (me, I).
5. He and (I, me) will buy a new battery.

B. Tell which compound subjects and objects are correct.

6. (Kelly and I, Me and Kelly) took the road test.
7. Everyone on the bus heard (Al and she, Al and her).
8. (You and me, You and I) play on the same team.
9. Valerie coached (her and them, she and them).
10. (I and Tony, Tony and I) are the team mascots.

> When you include yourself as part of a compound subject or object, it is always polite to mention yourself last.
> A pronoun in a compound subject must be a subject pronoun.
> A pronoun in a compound object must be an object pronoun.

Written Practice

Choose the correct compound subjects and objects from the parentheses. Write each sentence.

1. Joe called (Kate and me, Kate and I) on the phone.
2. (She and I, I and her) both answered.
3. He asked (me and her, her and me) for help.
4. (Her and me, She and I) could not find the number.
5. A radio station called (Dad or me, me or Dad).
6. (Him and I, He and I) were not at home.
7. That night Mrs. Chase visited (him and I, him and me).
8. (Her and Sue, She and Sue) knew the answer.
9. They told (Dad and me, Dad and I) about it.
10. I invited (her and Sue, she and Sue) to come back.

- **Writing Sentences**   Write five sentences about an experience you shared with a friend. Use pronouns in compound subjects and in compound objects in your sentences.

Who, Whom

The pronoun *who* has one form when used as a subject (*who*) and another form when used as an object (*whom*). In informal spoken English, *who* may be used as either a subject pronoun or an object pronoun. In written English, however, you must use the correct form.

Who is the correct form for the subject of a sentence.

> Who is the best candidate?
> Who ate the cucumber?

The pronoun *whom* is the correct form for the direct object.

> Whom did you believe? (*You did believe* whom?)
> Whom has Barry chosen? (*Barry has chosen* whom?)

Notice that each question has been rearranged in parentheses. By placing *whom* after the verb, you can check that it works as a direct object and that *whom*, not *who*, is the correct form.

> The pronoun *who* is the correct form to use as subject.
> The pronoun *whom* is the correct form for direct object.

Practice

A. Choose the correct pronoun to complete each sentence. You can check your answer by rearranging the sentence.

1. (Who, Whom) did you see at the store?
2. (Who, Whom) loads the produce?
3. (Who, Whom) will she ask for the crates?
4. (Who, Whom) manages the store for Bobbie?
5. (Who, Whom) will drive you home after work?
6. (Who, Whom) are you calling?
7. (Who, Whom) did you see at the party?
8. (Who, Whom) will you take skating?

B. Write *who* or *whom* to complete each sentence.

9. ＿＿ turned out the light?
10. ＿＿ do you trust?
11. ＿＿ ordered the fishing pole?
12. ＿＿ will you contact at the newspaper?
13. ＿＿ wants to go to the movie with me?
14. ＿＿ can answer this question?
15. ＿＿ will we ask for another glass of water?
16. ＿＿ do you believe?

C. Write the correct form of *who* for each sentence. Then write *S* or *O* to tell whether it is a subject or object form.

17. (Who, Whom) owns that red skateboard?
18. (Who, Whom) did you race last Tuesday?
19. (Who, Whom) should I tell about your surprise?
20. (Who, Whom) wrote me that thank-you note?
21. (Who, Whom) did the teacher help?
22. (Who, Whom) brought you flowers?
23. (Who, Whom) did she invite to the concert?
24. (Who, Whom) has a minibike?

• **Writing Sentences** Write five sentences of your own, using *who* or *whom* correctly in each one.

7 Building Vocabulary

Idioms

You use idioms every day, and yet you may not know what they are. An **idiom** is an expression that has a meaning different from the meaning of its separate words. The idiom in the sentence below is underlined.

Matthew is <u>a chip off the old block</u>.

If you look at each word in the idiom separately, the meaning is simply, "a small piece off a large piece of wood." However, Matthew is not a small piece of wood! To find the meaning of the idiom, consider all the words together as one expression. This idiom means that Matthew is "just like his parent."

Read the paragraph below. The idioms are underlined.

Our language is full of idioms. <u>Take my word for it</u>. Whether it is <u>raining cats and dogs</u> outside, or whether you are <u>on your last leg</u>, idioms are <u>right under your nose</u>. People who are <u>trying to make ends meet</u> or who <u>step on someone's toes</u> use idioms. Even people who live <u>in the lap of luxury</u> or who are <u>burning their candles at both ends</u> use idioms. So you must <u>put up with it</u>.

You are probably familiar with all of these idioms plus hundreds of others. The expression *Take my word for it* means "Accept this as the truth." *Raining cats and dogs* means "raining heavily, pouring." What do the other idioms in the paragraph above mean? If you are not sure, you can look up the idiom in a dictionary.

▶ An **idiom** is an expression that has a meaning different from the meaning of its separate words.

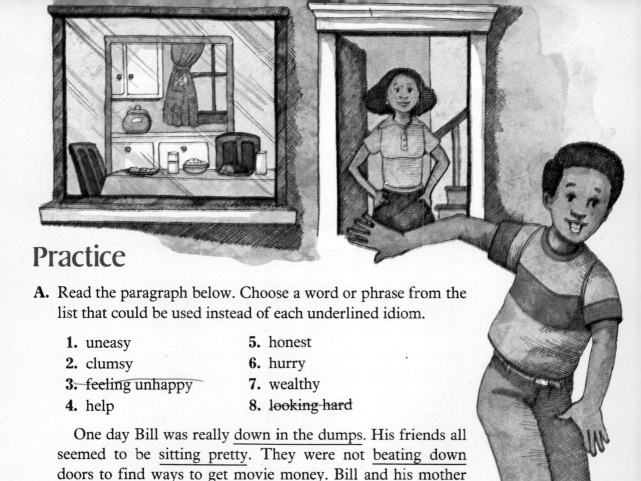

Practice

A. Read the paragraph below. Choose a word or phrase from the list that could be used instead of each underlined idiom.

1. uneasy
2. clumsy
3. feeling unhappy
4. help
5. honest
6. hurry
7. wealthy
8. looking hard

One day Bill was really <u>down in the dumps</u>. His friends all seemed to be <u>sitting pretty</u>. They were not <u>beating down doors</u> to find ways to get movie money. Bill and his mother had a <u>heart-to-heart talk</u> about it. Bill's mother promised to pay him if he would <u>lend her a hand</u> in the kitchen. <u>Bill was all thumbs</u>, but he agreed. When his mom took the first bite of his meat loaf, he was <u>on pins and needles</u>. She loved it. "Here," she said as she gave him the money. "<u>Step on it</u>, or you'll be late."

B. Write the meaning of these idioms. Use your dictionary for help.

9. put your foot down
10. for a song
11. turn over a new leaf
12. live it up
13. fly off the handle
14. under the weather

- **Writing Sentences** Start your own book of idioms. List as many as you can in one week. Write a sentence for each idiom. Then choose one of your idioms, and illustrate it.

Review

- **Pronouns and Antecedents** *(pp. 121–123)* Copy each pronoun, and write its antecedent after it.

  1. Rose was pleased with the pigeons. They returned to the cages faster than she had expected.
  2. She raises carrier pigeons on the roof of the apartment building where she lives.
  3. They are trained to deliver messages.
  4. Rose rolls up the message she has written and ties it to the leg of one of the pigeons.
  5. She watches them fly sixty miles an hour to deliver her messages safely and inexpensively.

- **Pronouns as Subjects and Objects** *(pp. 124–125)* Write each pronoun in these sentences. Label each one either *S* for subject or *O* for object.

  6. Today we cleaned the entire house.
  7. Dad and I dusted and polished the furniture.
  8. Next, Kay washed the curtains and hung them.
  9. I washed the kitchen floor and waxed it.
  10. Dad took us out for pizza afterwards.

- **Possessive Pronouns** *(pp. 126–127)* Write the word in parentheses that best completes each sentence.

  11. I'm glad you let me use (your, you're) telescope.
  12. (Its, It's) lens is very clear and powerful.
  13. (Who's, Whose) telescope shall we use to watch the moon eclipse?
  14. I'll bring (mine, my), and you can bring (your, yours), to (their, they're) observatory.
  15. I wish we could combine (their, they're) power.

- **Pronouns After Linking Verbs** *(pp. 128-129)* Write the correct pronoun to complete these sentences.

  16. The first person to bowl will be (she, her).
  17. Our scorekeeper for the last game was (he, him).
  18. That is (he, him) in the blue shirt.
  19. The highest scorers will be (she, her) and (I, me).
  20. It was (them, they) who won last year's bowling trophy.

- **Compound Subjects and Objects** *(pp. 130-131)* Write the correct compound subject or compound object from the parentheses in each sentence. Then label the compound subjects you wrote *CS* and the compound objects *CO*.

  21. (Juan and I, Juan and me) train animals for television.
  22. Animal shelters and breeders call (Juan and I, Juan and me).
  23. (He and I, Him and me) take a van to the donor.
  24. The (donor and us, donor and we) choose the most agreeable animals to train.

- **Using Words Correctly** *(pp. 132-133)* Write the pronoun that best fits in each sentence. Rearrange the sentence to check your answer.

  25. (Who, Whom) invited all these people?
  26. (Who, Whom) do I ask for a glass of juice?
  27. (Who, Whom) found these old photographs of me?
  28. (Who, Whom) should I thank for this surprise party?
  29. (Who, Whom) did you see at the store?
  30. (Who, Whom) gave you that bracelet?

- **Building Vocabulary** *(pp. 134-135)* Copy the idiom from each of the following sentences.

  31. His explanation was too cut and dried.
  32. I wish she would give me a break sometime.
  33. They were talking up a storm in the kitchen.
  34. She saved her money for a rainy day.

Maintain

- **Verbs and Direct Objects** *(pp. 87–90)* Write the verb in each sentence below. Beside it, write *action verb* or *being verb*. Then write the direct object that follows each action verb.

  1. Mammoth Cave is special.

  2. Rock forms fill the cave.

  3. The shapes seem treelike.

  4. We visit the cave's lakes.

- **Linking Verbs** *(pp. 91–92)* Copy each sentence. Draw a line under the linking verbs. Label each predicate noun *PN* and each predicate adjective *PA*.

  5. Alaska is beautiful.

  6. The air smells fresh.

  7. The mosquitoes are huge.

  8. The roads are swamps.

- **Main Verbs and Auxiliaries** *(pp. 93–95)* Write the verb phrase in each sentence. Draw a line under the main verb.

  9. Sandy has written a report on Canada.

  10. She didn't use any magazine articles.

  11. The report will be due next week.

  12. She has completed her assignment successfully.

- **Verb Tenses** *(pp. 96–99)* Write the verb for each sentence correctly. Then write the past participle of the verb.

  13. She ____ the newborn kitten very gently. (hold)

  14. Yesterday the tiny kitten ____ on an old coat. (stay)

  15. In a few days it will ____ its eyes. (open)

- **Subject-Verb Agreement** *(pp. 102–103)* Write the verb form that agrees with the subject of each sentence.

  16. The lecture and exhibit (is, are) free.

  17. Either Sally or her grandfather (take, takes) pictures.

  18. Neither parents nor teachers (has, have) photos here.

- **Pronouns** *(pp. 121–125)* Copy each sentence. Underline the pronouns. Draw an arrow from each pronoun to its antecedent(s).

  19. Al saw Harry and Elaine and recognized them immediately.
  20. Many people like skiing. It is exciting.
  21. Rufus ran out the back door, but he didn't escape.

  Label subject pronouns *S* and object pronouns *O* in exercises 19–21.

- **Possessive Pronouns** *(pp. 126–127)* Write the pronouns.

  22. (Your, You're) jar has more plants than (my, mine).
  23. (It's, Its) soil looks rich and moist.
  24. Is this glass jar (your, yours)?
  25. (Who's, Whose) jar will you choose?

- **Pronouns After Linking Verbs** *(pp. 128–129)* Write the correct pronoun in parentheses.

  26. It is (I, me).   **28.** Ed and I are (they, them).
  27. That was (him, he).   **29.** One guest was (her, she).

- **Compound Subjects and Objects** *(pp. 130–131)* Write the correct compound subject or object in parentheses.

  30. (Tammy and I, I and Tammy) ride horses on weekends.
  31. Joel asked (Hal and I, Hal and me) to go skating.
  32. (My parents and me, My parents and I) are having a sale.

- **Using Words Correctly** *(pp. 104, 132–133)* Write the correct word in parentheses.

  33. (Who, Whom) should I ask?
  34. (Who, Whom) will discover our next Olympic champion?
  35. We can (sit, set) this chair in a quiet corner.
  36. I'll (lie, lay) this book here and review it with you.

- **Building Vocabulary** *(p. 105)* Write the roots of these words: *react, peaceful, governor.*

8 Writing About Yourself

1 | Writing a Good Beginning

A good beginning is an invitation to read. It gets your attention. Then it takes you into the story. Is this a good beginning?

> I was sleeping overnight at my friend's house. We were in her bedroom in the attic. I heard something on the stairs. It was just her pesty little brother coming to bother us.

Does this beginning catch your attention and leave you wondering about who? when? where? or why?

Read the next beginning, and compare it with the first one.

> "Psst!" I whispered as I poked Wendy. I hated to wake her up, but the creaking noise was scary. I had a shivery feeling that we were not alone in her attic bedroom. What could be creeping around up here in the darkness?

How does the writer catch your attention? What words or sentences stir your curiosity? What is left to your imagination?

In your own story, you will want a strong opening. Your first sentence should capture a reader's attention. The next three or four sentences should make your reader curious about what will happen next.

Practice

The following paragraph is the second paragraph in a story. Write a good beginning of four or five sentences to come before it. Remember, an opening paragraph should invite the reader into the story and leave him or her curious about what will happen.

> We realized then that we were lost. I looked up at the gray sky. Without the sun, would we be able to figure out our direction? Suddenly, Thad pointed and yelled, "Look, Joey! We're going to be OK!"

2 | Telling Enough

Have you ever read something so interesting you could not put it down? Most writers want their readers to feel this way.

One way to make your own story lively and interesting is to include the right details. Let the characters and events come alive in your readers' minds. Help them picture the story that is unfolding and feel as the character feels. This means including details that allow your readers to picture the events as they really happened. It also means describing the feeling of the characters so that the reader can imagine those feelings.

Read these two paragraphs, and compare them. Decide which one does a better job of making the situation and the characters seem real.

1.   My best friend was moving away. We had been classmates and friends for many years. I would miss her. When it was moving day, I went to her house. I had a farewell present to give her. I thought it would remind her of some of the fun times we had spent together.

2.   Talia's moving day had arrived. Unfortunately, so had the movers! As I raced to her house, I thought back on all the years since kindergarten. How would school seem without my best friend? I tightened my fingers around the "good-by and good luck" token—the sand dollar we'd found two summers ago at Sea Gull Cove—and I blinked hard.

- How do the two paragraphs differ?
- Which one is better? Why?
- Which one lets you know the writer's feelings? How?
- Which one gives a clearer picture of what happened? How?

When you write your story, be sure to include enough details to hold a reader's interest. Tell enough so that anyone who reads your story can see the events as they really happened and imagine the feelings you had at the time. Describe feelings such as excitement, surprise, sadness, disappointment, or happiness.

Practice

Rewrite the following paragraph as if it were your own. Make up details so that the reader can feel what it was like to be in the situation. Do not try to tell everything, but tell enough to hold a reader's interest.

This was the day my friends and I were going horseback riding. We had planned it for a long time. This would be my first time on horseback. My horse looked so big. He was friskier than the others and probably faster, too. I just held on and hoped he would go along the trail slowly.

3 | Writing Dialogue

Conversation in a story is called **dialogue.** Dialogue helps to make your story lively and interesting. When writing dialogue, you quote a person's exact words.

Read this example, showing how a writer used dialogue in her story.

It was last Sunday, and we were all getting ready to go to the beach. Chip, my little brother, was getting yogurt all over his face, and my mother was starting to get upset. My father was out in the car, leaning on the horn and yelling, "What's holding up the show?"

The thing that was holding up the show was my yellow bathing suit. I couldn't find it anywhere.

"It's got to be *someplace,*" my mother said.

"Let's look for it," my father said.

We looked in the back hall closet. We found half a box of cereal, my mother's favorite furry boots, and Hickory and Dickory, my brother's pet mice, which we thought had escaped.

My mother said, "My mukluks!"

My brother said, "My mice!"

My father said, "My, my . . ."

And I said, "That still doesn't find my yellow bathing suit."

Then my little brother started to laugh. He pointed to Little Baby One Arm, my old doll left over from my childhood. There, on her head . . . was the top of my yellow bathing suit. And right at that second, I remembered where the bottom was. It was in my school bag—the one with the missing strap.

The whole day wasn't spoiled. By two o'clock, we found a good parking space at the beach. The beach was really great. Chip only got lost once. I found my old green knee socks rolled up in my bathing cap, and I found a million fantastic shells to take home.   *-Robyn Supraner*

- How did the writer's father feel when he yelled, *"What's holding up the show?"*? How is this quotation different from this sentence? *My father wanted to know what was holding everyone up.*
- How is *My mother said, "My mukluks!"* different from this sentence? *My mother said that the mukluks were hers.*
- Which sentence might have been written this way? *"What a great beach this is!" I said.*

Practice

Change these sentences to dialogue. Try to make the speaker's feelings show. (Page 357 in the Handbook will help you with punctuation.) The first one has been done for you.

1. Gramp complained that his feet hurt from hiking.
   "My feet are killing me from all this hiking," grumbled Gramp.
2. Darren said that his feet were sore, too, and suggested that he and Gramp rest for a while.
3. Gramp thought that that was a really good idea.
4. Darren wanted to know where they should set up camp.
5. Gramp told Darren about a campsite with a stream nearby.
6. Darren said they could soak their feet in the cool water.

4 | Improving Your Sentences

You know how important a catchy beginning is, and you know how important specific details are. Do you realize how important the style of your writing is? Imagine what it would be like to read a whole story written in sentences like these.

I enjoyed sightseeing. I liked the marketplace the best. Everything looked so colorful! The watermelon vendor was busy. He was also generous. He gave me a huge slice of watermelon. What a tasty lunch it made! The watermelon was juicy. It gave me a wide pink smile. I looked like a clown.

How would you describe the sentences above? Short, choppy sentences can make a story dull and difficult to read. How can sentences like these be improved?

The same paragraph might be written a different way. What is the problem now?

I enjoyed sightseeing and I liked the marketplace the best and everything looked so colorful! The watermelon vendor was busy but he was also generous and he gave me a huge slice of watermelon. What a tasty lunch it made! The watermelon was juicy and so it gave me a wide pink smile, I looked like a clown.

Is the style of these sentences better than the style in the first paragraph? Long, stringy sentences that run together are also boring and difficult to read. How could you improve sentences like these?

One way to make your sentences interesting and appealing is to vary their lengths. Write some short sentences and some long ones. The following paragraph gives you an example.

I enjoyed sightseeing, and I liked the marketplace the best. Everything looked so colorful! The watermelon vendor was busy, but he was also generous. He gave me a huge slice of watermelon. What a tasty lunch it made! The watermelon was juicy, and it gave me a wide pink smile. I looked like a clown!

Practice

Rewrite each paragraph so that some of the sentences are short and some are long.

1.   Once my little brother Stan set up a store. I'll never forget it! He found an old table. He carried it to the front yard. He went back to the kitchen. He got himself a chair. He climbed up on the counter. He raided the cabinets. All the cans and boxes came out. He carried them outside. Lots of cars stopped. People bought soup. They stocked up on cereal. Someone bought two jars of peanut butter. Then my mother arrived home. Stan's store went bankrupt.

2.   My dog Napoleon is so big and clumsy and I knew we would have to train him but I wasn't having any luck by myself and then my dad told me I could enroll him in obedience school. Napoleon would have to behave better at home and I thought the neighbors in the other apartments would be pleased and they were. Now they could walk down the sidewalk and Napoleon wouldn't bound up to them and he wouldn't give them clumsy hellos and he wouldn't scare their children. Napoleon didn't mean to be scary and he was only trying to be friendly but now he would be polite.

5 | Getting Started

Your own story is mainly about *you*. Because you are the designer of your own story, you will want to choose a single event that lets you, the main character, speak, act, react, and come alive. Ask yourself these questions to warm up your brain cells.

1. What happened that made you laugh until you cried?
2. When did you think you might burst with excitement?
3. What situation made you feel as if you wanted to melt away?
4. What happened to you today, last week, or last summer that could be material for a story about you?

We all enjoy *telling* stories about ourselves. *Writing* about an experience gives you a chance to include the best details.

Practice

A. Your memory is like a diary. Think of those moments that touched you. What happened? How did you feel? How did you act or react? Choose one experience.

B. Now tell a classmate about your experience. Include enough details so that your listener will feel the pleasure, surprise, excitement, or sadness that you felt at the time. Have your listener ask questions about anything that was not clear or anything you could tell more about.

Steps for Writing About Yourself Here are the steps for writing a story about yourself. You will follow these steps to write your own story.

Step One	Choose a topic.
Step Two	Write your story.
Step Three	Revise your story.
Step Four	Proofread your story.
Step Five	Make a final copy to share.

6 | Step One
Choose a Topic

The event you choose to write about does not have to be exciting. It can be as ordinary as a gray day, as long as it has some meaning for you. Your topic should be one that you can develop in a way that is interesting to read. You should highlight a single experience, not try to write about a whole summer, a whole week, or even a whole day.

Felicia had gathered ideas about small but important events in her life. She jotted down a list of several topics.

caring for my turtle   *going to Aunt May's*
my first day at Jefferson   *my birthday*

Felicia turned her topics over in her mind. She decided that she preferred two—the visit with Aunt May and her first day at Jefferson. As she dug into her memory, she quickly wrote down details about each one. Then she looked over her notes. Although the visit had been especially fun, she did not have strong feelings about it; it had been one of many. Her first day at Jefferson was still vivid in her mind. It had been a completely new and different experience. Felicia circled that topic.

Assignment
- **Make a List**
- **Make Notes**
- **Choose a Topic**

A. List several of your personal experiences. Use the ones you thought of for the Practice exercise on page 148. Remember, each topic should center on a single event.

B. Decide which two topics you like best, and make notes about each one. Jot down some details that make the event seem real. Also note your feelings at the time.

C. Look at your notes, and choose the best topic. Circle it.

7 | Step Two
Write Your Story

Once you have chosen your topic, you should let your thoughts flow onto the paper. Your first draft is rough, so you can just write, write, write, and correct any mistakes later on.

Felicia thought back to that first day. She wrote whatever important details came into her mind without worrying about mistakes in spelling, punctuation, or handwriting.

Felicia's first draft

A Day to Remember

Mama called to me. It was time to get up. It was my first day at school Jefferson and she had my breakfast on the table. Mama wanted me to eat it before it got cold.

I put on dressed quickly and went downstairs. I sat down to eat, but I couldn't eat. Then Mama asked me what was the matter because she knew I was worryed and nervous and Mama seems to be able to read our minds.

I drank some milk. I picked up my bag. I said good-by to Mama and the boys. Then I walked to school.

When I got there, the bell rang and I was swept along with the crowd. I looked for room number 7. Then, just as we I saw it, someone touched my arm and said, "Hi! I'm Carrie. I'm new here and I'm looking for Room 7. Can you help me?"

Suddenly my first day at Jefferson seemed fine.

- Does Felicia's beginning catch your attention and draw you into her story? How could she improve it?
- Has Felicia let you know exactly how she felt on her first day at Jefferson? What details could she add to give a clearer picture of how she felt?
- Which sentences in this story would make good dialogue?
- Do any of Felicia's paragraphs contain short, choppy sentences? long, stringy sentences? If so, which ones?

Assignment • Write Your First Draft

Write the first draft of your story. Get your thoughts down on paper without worrying about mistakes. You may want to write on every other line so that you have plenty of space for making changes later on. As you write, keep these things in mind.

1. Write about one particular experience.
2. Write a lively beginning that will capture the interest of your readers.
3. Tell enough to make your story interesting, but do not try to tell everything that happened.

8 | Step Three
Revise Your Story

Felicia reread her story thoughtfully. She spent several minutes thinking about how she could make her beginning catchier and more inviting. It seemed too dull. Felicia tried out two new beginnings. She also decided to change some sentences into dialogue to make the characters come alive.

Then Felicia read her story to Carrie. She also read her new beginnings to her and asked which one she thought was better. Carrie agreed that the first beginning was dull, and helped her choose a new one.

Then Carrie said, "I like your ending, but I think you should tell more about how you felt. I have never changed schools, and it would give me the jitters!"

Carrie also thought that the title could be about any day and suggested that a different title could give a hint about the story.

After the discussion, Felicia added stronger words to express her nervousness. She changed other weak words, too. Finally, she worked on a better title.

Here are the changes Felicia made.

Felicia's new beginning paragraph

> I felt the warm morning sun in my bedroom, but I refused to open my eyes. I pulled the covers over my head. Why wasn't it tomorrow, or next weak, or any day but today

- Do you agree that this beginning is better than the old one? Why or why not?
- What words in the new beginning express her nervousness?

Felicia's revision

~~First-Day Jitters at Jefferson~~
A Day to Remember

New beginning goes here Mama called, ~~to~~ me. "Fee! It's time to get up." It was my first day at ~~school~~ Jefferson and she had ~~my~~ You're breakfast is on the table." Mama wanted me to eat it before it got cold. Mama didn't want me to be late.

I ~~put on~~ dressed quickly and ~~went~~ flew downstairs. I sat down to eat, but I couldn't eat. Then Mama asked me "What's the matter, Fee? Do you have butterflies in your stomach. ~~what was the matter because she knew I~~ Try not to worry. It'll be fine." ~~was worried and nervous and Mama seems to be able to read our minds.~~

I ~~drank~~ gulped down some milk. I picked up my book ~~bag,~~ and waved I said good-by to Mama and the boys. Then I walked to school. My legs felt like rubber.

When I got there, the bell rang and I was swept along with the noisy crowd. I looked for room number 7. Then, just as ~~we~~ I saw it, a girl someone touched my arm and said, "Hi! I'm Carrie. I'm

new here and I'm looking for Room 7.
Can you help me?"
 jitters
Suddenly my first-day at Jefferson
just melted away.
~~*seemed fine.*~~

Check Felicia's revised story.

- Do you think Felicia's new title suits her story? Why or why not? Did she capitalize it correctly?
- Where did Felicia add dialogue? Do you think the dialogue improves the story? Why or why not?
- What details did Felicia add to her story? How do these details improve the story?
- What short, choppy sentences did she change? How did she change them?

Assignment
- **Revise Your Story**
- **Discuss Your Story**

A. Reread your story carefully, and think about changes that would improve it. Ask yourself these questions.

1. How could I improve my beginning?
2. Have I made the characters and events seem real?
3. Have I varied the lengths of my sentences?
4. Did I write a good title that gives a hint about my story?

B. Write two new beginnings. Then decide which one is better. (You may still like your first beginning best.)

C. Make changes in your story. Cross out words that are weak, and add new words that give a clearer picture.

D. Read your story to a classmate. Decide together which is the best beginning. Discuss ways your story might be improved. If you like your listener's suggestions or if any new ideas have occurred to you, make the changes on your paper.

9 | Step Four
Proofread Your Story

You have learned that proofreading gives you a chance to correct errors in spelling, capitalization, and punctuation. You also can check sentences for run-ons and fragments.

Before Felicia proofread her story, she copied part of it over so that it would be easier to read. Her changes had made her paper messy. Since she had not made many changes in the ending, she did not copy it. Felicia used the dictionary to check the spellings of words she was unsure of.

Felicia's first two paragraphs after proofreading

> First-Day Jitters *a*t Jefferson
>
> I felt the warm morning sun in my bedroom, but I refused to open my eyes. *I* pulled the covers over my head. Why wasn't it tomorrow, or next ~~weak~~ *week*, or any day but today ?
>
> Mama called, "Fee! It's time to get up! ~~You're~~ *Your* breakfast is on the table." It was my first day at Jefferson, and Mama didn't want me to be late.

- What correction did Felicia make in her title?
- What punctuation and capitalization changes did she make?
- In two places Felicia chose an incorrect homophone. How did she correct both mistakes? What does each of those four homophones mean?

Practice

Felicia found six other proofreading errors. They were all in the following section of her story. Copy these paragraphs, and correct the errors. Use a dictionary to check spellings.

I dressed quickly and flew downstairs. I sat down but I couldn't eat. Then Mama asked, "Whats the matter, Fee? Do you have butterflies in your stomach. Try not to wory. It'll be fine."

I gulped down some milk, picked up my book bag, and waved good-by to Mama and the boys. Then I walked to school My legs felt like rubber

Assignment   • Proofread Your Story

Proofread your own story. Ask yourself these questions.

1. Have I written my title correctly?
2. Are my paragraphs indented?
3. Did I spell all the words correctly?

Grammar skills checklist

4. Have I capitalized and punctuated sentences correctly?
5. Have I corrected run-on sentences and sentence fragments?
6. Have I used apostrophes correctly?
7. Have I used the correct form of subject pronouns, object pronouns, and possessive pronouns?

10 | Step Five
Make a Final Copy

Felicia was ready to share her story, but first she wanted to make it look special. She copied it onto a clean sheet of paper in her best handwriting. Then she thought of a way to share it—she made a story folder.

First, Felicia folded a large sheet of drawing paper in thirds. She printed the title of her story and her name, as the author, on the outside of the top fold. She opened the folder and drew lines on the vertical folds.

Next, Felicia drew three illustrations to go with her story—one for the beginning in the left-hand section, one for the middle in the center section, and one for the ending in the right-hand section. She left room below each picture for a part of her story. After she had colored in each illustration, Felicia cut her story into three parts and pasted each part below its illustration. Her finished story folder looked like this.

Assignment
- **Make a Final Copy**
- **Share Your Story**

A. Write your story in your best handwriting on clean paper.

B. Check to be sure you have copied your story correctly.

C. Think of a special way to share your story.

- Make an illustrated folder, as Felicia did, or a booklet.
- Plan a skit from your story, and dramatize it.

1 | Getting Meaning from Context

The following sentence contains a word that may be unfamiliar to you. If you read the sentence carefully, you will find clues about the meaning of the word.

> We had to turn back because a fallen tree *obstructed* the hiking trail.

Did you figure out the meaning of *obstructed*? If you used the **context**—the other words in the sentence—you probably concluded that *obstructed* means "blocked" in the sentence above.

Context clues may be a word, a group of words, a sentence, or even a group of sentences. The clues may appear before, after, or before *and* after a word with an unfamiliar meaning. Always look for clues to meaning.

What does *parrot* mean to you? Notice that this familiar word has a meaning that may be unfamiliar in the following sentence: *John simply parrots the words of the song—he doesn't understand what he's repeating.* Sometimes words in a sentence, such as *he doesn't understand what he's repeating,* will define an unfamiliar word.

What word in this sentence tells you the meaning of *refuge*? *We searched for hours for shelter and finally found refuge in a cave.* Did you figure out that *shelter* is a synonym for *refuge*? The two words have the same meaning in this sentence.

What does *morsel* mean in this sentence? *I offered the kitten a chunk of cheese, but it would eat only a morsel.* In this sentence, *chunk* is an antonym of *morsel*; a *chunk* is a big piece while a *morsel* is a small piece. Sometimes a familiar word will be an antonym for an unfamiliar word.

To figure out the meaning of *decrepit* in the following passage, you will have to use several clues that appear in the sentences.

> The old Barnard place is decrepit. The worn-out roof is leaking badly. The creaky porch is falling apart.

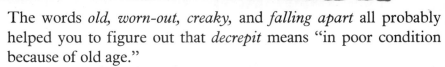

The words *old, worn-out, creaky,* and *falling apart* all probably helped you to figure out that *decrepit* means "in poor condition because of old age."

Sometimes, the context will not help you to understand the meaning of a word. In those cases, turn to a dictionary for help.

Practice

Use the context to figure out the meaning of each underlined word. Write the meaning on your paper.

1. Outwardly, Rona seems <u>placid</u>, but she's probably very nervous.
2. A little tree has grown out of the <u>rupture</u> in the rock.
3. At the beginning of a project, Jim is filled with <u>zeal</u>, but he often runs out of enthusiasm.
4. You have the <u>option</u> to either make dinner or wash the dishes.
5. Ms. Schultz was <u>agitated</u> with the clerk, but she calmed down when she heard the explanation for the mistake.
6. The bus <u>jounced</u> along the rocky dirt road.
7. I <u>relish</u> my afternoons at the movies. I particularly enjoy science-fiction films.
8. Please <u>file</u> quietly into the room. Don't all of you try to squeeze through the door at once.
9. Try not to <u>slur</u> your words. Pronounce them carefully.
10. I like newspaper articles that are <u>succinct</u>. Facts should be presented briefly and clearly.
11. Florida winter weather is more <u>moderate</u> than Ohio's. It rarely freezes.
12. The police and safety inspectors studied the <u>derailment</u> for days, but they could not discover the reason the train went off the track.

2 | Finding Words in a Dictionary

When looking for an entry word in the dictionary, you can save time by trying to open the dictionary near the page where the word is listed. Think of the words as being grouped in three parts of the dictionary—the front, middle, and back. In which part of a dictionary would you find the word *neon*?

After you turn to the correct part of the dictionary, use guide words to locate the word. **Guide words** are listed at the top of each page. They tell you the first and last words listed on that page. If you were looking for the word *nourish*, would you find it on a page with the guide words *notebook/novel*?

Quite often, all the words on a dictionary page begin with the same two or three letters. You use the first different letter to determine alphabetical order. Would you find *fringe* before or after *frighten*? Would *reclaim* come before or after *recognize*?

Suppose you want to know the meaning of the word *refining* but cannot find it listed in the dictionary. Look for the word *refine*. Entry words usually are listed in simple forms, without endings such as *-ing, -ed, -s, -er,* and *-est*. Under what entry word will you find the meaning of the word *boldest*?

Practice

A. Write these words in alphabetical order.

balance	ginger	adequate	drop	excavate	equip
aqua	coax	gentle	dual	feud	bolt
prey	excuse	python	mile	verify	stance

B. Write each word below. Tell if you would find it *before, after,* or *on* the page with the guide words *regiment/rehearsal.*

| register | relative | regret | refrigerator | reject |
| region | regular | reform | release | regard |

3 | Using Dictionary Definitions

If you cannot figure out the meaning of a word by using the context in which it appears, you turn to a dictionary for help. Many words have more than one meaning. Suppose you want to know what *glimmer* means in this sentence: *Patty saw a glimmer of anger in Ryan's eyes.* Carefully read the definitions and examples in italics below to determine which meaning fits the sentence.

> **glim•mer** |glĭm′ər| *n.* **1.** A dim or unsteady light; a flicker: *the glimmer of fireflies.* **2.** A faint trace or indication; a glimpse: *a glimmer of her old sense of humor.* —*v.* **1.** To give off a dim or flickering light: *a single lamp seen glimmering through the window.* **2.** To appear or be indicated faintly: *The Colorado River from the plane seemed a greenish snake glimmering far below.*

Two meanings are given for the noun (*n.*) *glimmer,* and two meanings are listed for the verb (*v.*) *glimmer.* How is *glimmer* used in this sentence: *A distant lantern glimmered in the dark.* Which verb definition fits the context of the sentence?

Some words are **homographs,** words that are spelled like other words. Homographs have different meanings because they come from different roots or languages. Look below at the entries for *steep.* Each homograph is marked with a small raised number.

> **steep¹** |stēp| *adj.* **steep•er, steep•est. 1.** Rising or falling abruptly; sharply sloped: *a steep hill; a steep stairway.* **2.** Very high: *a steep price to pay.*
> **steep²** |stēp| *v.* **1.** To soak or be soaked in a liquid: *The meat was steeped in its own juices.* **2.** To involve or preoccupy thoroughly; immerse: *As a child, she steeped herself in adventure stories.*

Notice that *steep¹* is an adjective (*adj.*) and *steep²* is a verb (*v.*). Which entry word is used in this sentence: *When Barbara goes to Spain, she wants to steep herself in the daily life of the people.* First, you must decide whether *steep* is used as an adjective or a verb in this sentence. *Steep* is used here as a verb. Which meaning of *steep²* fits the sentence?

Practice

A. Use the dictionary entries below to figure out the meaning of *reel* in each of the following sentences. Indicate which entry word and meaning is used in each sentence.

> **reel¹** |rēl| *n.* **1.** A spoollike device that turns on a central bar, used for winding a hose, rope, film, tape, fishing line, etc. **2.** The amount held by a reel. —*v.* **1.** To wind onto a reel. **2.** To pull in (a fish) by winding on a reel: *reel in a marlin.*
> **reel²** |rēl| *v.* **1.** To stagger: *reeling out of the smoky room, half-suffocated.* **2.** To go round and round in a whirling motion: *The events of the day reeled in his mind.*
> **reel³** |rēl| *n.* **1.** Any of several fast, lively folk dances. **2.** Music written to accompany or as if to accompany any of these dances.

Example: Joe *reeled* his fishing line. reel ¹—v.l.

1. My album of folk music includes a Virginia *reel.*

2. Wayne needs a new *reel* for his movie projector.

3. After a dizzying ride on the roller coaster, we *reeled* slowly through the crowd.

4. Hazel is trying to *reel* in a hundred-pound swordfish.

B. Write sentences using each of the following meanings of the word *season.*

5. noun, meaning 1.a. **6.** noun, meaning 2 **7.** verb, meaning 1

> **sea•son** |sē′zən| *n.* **1. a.** One of the four equal natural divisions of the year, spring, summer, autumn, and winter, each beginning as the sun passes through the corresponding solstice or equinox. **b.** Either of the two parts, rainy and dry, into which the year is divided in tropical climates. **2.** A period of the year devoted to or marked by a certain activity or by the appearance of something: *the hunting season; the hurricane season.* —*v.* **1.** To give (food) extra flavor by adding salt, pepper, spices, etc. **2.** To add enjoyment or interest to: *seasoned his writing with a dry Yankee wit.* **3.** To dry (lumber) until it is usable; cure. **4.** To make (a person or persons) capable or fit through trial and experience: *hard training to season recruits.*

C. Locate these words in a dictionary. Use each in a sentence.

8. lope **9.** jovial **10.** crest **11.** trickle **12.** nerve

4 | Using a Dictionary for Pronunciation

This drawing shows a type of fish that has lived for millions of years. Can you pronounce the name?

If you look up *coelacanth* in a dictionary, you will find this listing: **coe•la•canth** |sē′lə kănth′|. Notice that the entry word is broken into three syllables. In the special spelling that tells you how to say the word, the consonant letters stand for the common sounds of those letters. However, you may need to refer to a **pronunciation key** to understand the vowel sounds in a special spelling. A key such as this one appears on every page or every other page of a dictionary.

ă pat/ā pay/â care/ä father/ĕ pet/
ē be/ĭ pit/ī ice/î neat/ŏ pot/
ō go/ô paw, for/oi oil/o͝o book/
o͞o boot/ou out/ŭ cut/û fur/
th the/th thin/hw which/zh usual/
ə ago, item, pencil, atom, circus

Look at the first syllable of the special spelling of *coelacanth*: sē. Use the pronunciation key to figure out how to pronounce ē. The word *be* is given as an example of the *ē* sound.

In the second syllable of the special spelling, you see this mark: ə. Find this symbol in the key. After ə are five words: ***ago, item, pencil, atom, circus***. The dark letters in these words stand for the ə sound, which is called the **schwa sound.**

When a word has more than one syllable, you say one of the syllables with more stress, or force, than the others. The heavy dark mark after the first syllable of *coelacanth* is called an **accent mark.** It tells you that this syllable is spoken with the most stress. Notice that there is a lighter mark after the last syllable. That syllable is spoken with more stress than the second syllable but is not pronounced as forcefully as the first syllable.

You will come across some homographs that have different pronunciations. Look below at the special spellings for *refuse*[1] and *refuse*[2]. Which pronunciation fits this sentence? *The truck carried the refuse to the dump.*

> **re·fuse**[1] [ri fyo͞oz′] *v.* **re·fused, re·fusing. 1.** To decline to do (something). **2.** To decline to accept; turn down; *refuse an offer.* **3.** To decline to give; *refused permission.*
> **re·fuse**[2] [rĕf yo͞os] *n.* Worthless matter; waste.

Within a single entry, there is also sometimes more than one pronunciation. Notice below that there are two special spellings for the noun *progress:* The second syllable may be pronounced either as *-rĕs* or *-rĭs.* Either of those pronunciations is acceptable, although the first one probably is more common.

Now look at the special spelling that appears before the definitions for *progress* used as a verb. Notice that when used as a noun, the first syllable of *progress* is stressed. When used as a verb, the second syllable is stressed. A word may have different pronunciations when it is used as more than one part of speech.

> **prog·ress** [prŏg′ rĕs′] or [-rĭs] *n.* **1.** Onward movement; advance. **2.** Steady improvement, as in a civilization or individual. —*v.* **pro·gress** [prə grĕs′]. **1.** To move along; advance; proceed. **2.** To make steady or regular improvement.

Practice

A. Use these special spellings to answer the following questions.

gyrate |jī′rāt′| lineage |lĭn′ē ĭj| ensemble |än säm′bəl|

1. Which syllable of *gyrate* is spoken with more stress?
2. How many syllables does *lineage* have?
3. Does the first syllable of *lineage* rhyme with *pin* or *pine*?
4. Does the first syllable of *ensemble* rhyme with *fan* or *farm*?

B. Use the entry for *progress* above to choose the pronunciation for the underlined word below. Write the special spelling.

5. You can <u>progress</u> if you work harder.
6. Slow progress is better than no <u>progress</u>.

5 | Using the Library

Do you know how to find materials in a library? How do you locate fiction books? How do you find nonfiction books? How do you learn what books the library has?

You know that **fiction** is created from an author's imagination. Sometimes fiction may be about real people and events, but the other parts of the story are made up by the author. Fiction books are grouped together in a library, arranged alphabetically by the authors' last names. To make it easy for you to find a fiction book, the first letters of the author's last name are printed on the spine, or narrow back edge, of the book. To find the book *Johnny Tremain,* by Esther Forbes, you would look for shelves with books by fiction writers whose last names begin with *F.* Then you would look for the letters *Fo.*

You know that **nonfiction** books contain factual information. They are about real people and events from the past or present. They also give information about subjects such as painting and medicine. Nonfiction books are arranged according to subject, and each subject area has a number. This number appears under the author's name on the spine of the book. To find a nonfiction book, think of the general category in which the book probably belongs. For example, if you want a book about undersea exploration, you would find it with books about the ocean.

In another part of the library, you will find **reference books.** These special nonfiction books include dictionaries, encyclopedias, atlases, and almanacs. Usually you must use reference books in the library. They cannot be borrowed from the library to use at home.

How do you find a fiction book if you do not know the author's name? How do you locate a nonfiction book if you do not know the number by which it is shelved? You check the **card catalog,** which contains cards that list all the books in the library. Each drawer of the catalog is labeled with one or more letters. The cards inside are arranged alphabetically.

For every book in the library, the card catalog contains an author card and a title card. A third card—a subject card—is included for each nonfiction book and some fiction books.

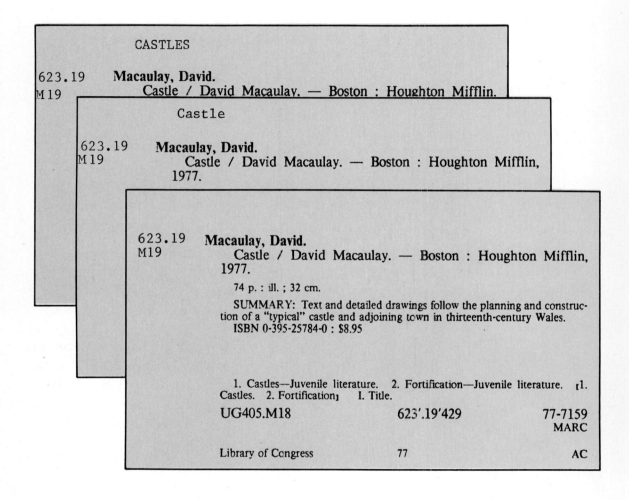

CASTLES

623.19 **Macaulay, David.**
M19 Castle / David Macaulay. — Boston : Houghton Mifflin,

Castle

623.19 **Macaulay, David.**
M19 Castle / David Macaulay. — Boston : Houghton Mifflin,
1977.

623.19 **Macaulay, David.**
M19 Castle / David Macaulay. — Boston : Houghton Mifflin,
1977.
74 p. : ill. ; 32 cm.
SUMMARY: Text and detailed drawings follow the planning and construction of a "typical" castle and adjoining town in thirteenth-century Wales.
ISBN 0-395-25784-0 : $8.95

1. Castles—Juvenile literature. 2. Fortification—Juvenile literature. ⌊1. Castles. 2. Fortification⌋ I. Title.
UG405.M18 623'.19'429 77-7159
MARC

Library of Congress 77 AC

If you know a writer's name and want to find out the titles of books the person has written, you check an **author card.** A separate card is filed for each of an author's books. Below the author's name and the book title, there is other information: the name of the publisher, the year of publication, and the number of pages. There also may be mention of illustrations.

What if you know only the title of a book? Then you look for a **title card,** on which the book title appears on the top line. All the information on the title card is the same as that on the author card. A title card is filed alphabetically by the first word in the title. However, if the first word is *A, An,* or *The,* the card is filed by the second word. The card for *A Day at the Races* would be in the drawer labeled *D.*

What if you want to find a book on a particular topic but have no titles or authors in mind? Then you look for a **subject card,** on which a subject area is listed at the top. One book title is listed below. The other information is the same as that on the author and title cards.

You will sometimes find subject cards that list **cross-references.** They refer you to other subject cards. For example, if you want to find books about veterinarians, or animal doctors, you might discover that the subject card labeled VETERINARIANS has the following information: *See* ANIMALS. This card tells you that no books are listed under VETERINARIANS. Occasionally, you will come across a subject card that refers you to an *additional* subject area. For example, if you looked under the subject SKIN DIVING, you might find a few cards that list specific book titles and one card with this information: *See also* OCEAN; WATER SPORTS.

On the sample cards on page 167, notice the **call number** to the left of the author's name. Every nonfiction book has a call number, which tells how the book is classified. Many libraries use the Dewey Decimal System. To each category of books, a range of numbers is assigned. For example, books about science have the numbers 500–599.

One group of nonfiction books—biographies and autobiographies, the life stories of real people—are arranged in a special way. They are usually alphabetized by the last name of the person the book is about. A book about Amelia Earhart, the aviator, would be shelved by the letter *E.*

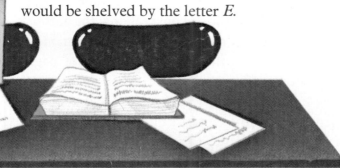

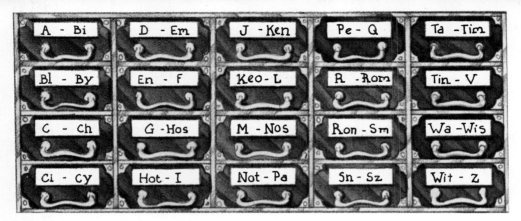

Practice

A. Use the card catalog above to answer the following questions. Decide which drawer probably contains the card you need, and write the letter or letters that appear on that drawer.

1. Does the library have any books by Robert Lawson?
2. Does the library have any books about Chinese cooking?
3. Is *April Morning* in the library?
4. Does the library have a biography of Harriet Tubman?
5. Is *The Wind in the Willows* in the library?
6. Besides *Summer of the Swans,* does the library have other books by Betsy Byars?
7. What books about soccer does the library have?
8. What poetry books by Eve Merriam does the library have?
9. Does the library have a biography of the inventor Thomas A. Edison?

B. Use the card catalog in a library to find answers to these questions. Write either the title of a book or an author's name.

10. What is the title of a nonfiction book about reptiles?
11. Who is the author of *Call It Courage?*
12. Who is the author of *A Wrinkle in Time?*
13. What is the title of a nonfiction book about sports?
14. Who is the author of *Mrs. Frisby and the Rats of NIMH?*
15. What is the title of a book written by Mary Stolz?

6 | Using an Encyclopedia

An encyclopedia is one of the most useful references in a classroom or library. This set of books contains articles that give information about people, places, things, events, and ideas. You can find answers to many questions in an encyclopedia.

Encyclopedia articles are arranged in alphabetical order in a set of books, or **volumes.** Each volume is labeled to tell you the beginning letter or letters of all the main topics in that book.

To find information in an encyclopedia, you must have a **key word** in mind. Suppose you want to answer this question: *What equipment is used for cross-country skiing?* SKIING is the topic you would look for. Sometimes you will have to look up two or more topics to get information. What are the key words in this question? *What is the major language of both Austria and Switzerland?*

Guide words, like those in a dictionary, will help you to locate your topic quickly. Guide words are printed in dark type at the tops of most pages. The word listed at the top of a left-hand page is the topic of the *first* article on that page; the word or words at the top of a right-hand page name the topic of the *last* article on that page. Would you find the topic ARMADILLO between the guide words ARCTIC OCEAN and ARROW? Would you find ARTIFACTS there?

Sometimes instead of an article after a main topic there is a **cross-reference.** This tells you to look under another topic. For example, listed after the topic PING-PONG, you may see this cross-reference: *See TABLE TENNIS.*

Some cross-references tell you where to find additional information. For instance, at the end of an article about Grand Canyon National Park, this cross-reference might be listed: *See also ARIZONA; COLORADO RIVER; NATIONAL PARK SYSTEM; POWELL, JOHN WESLEY.*

You may find very long articles about some topics. For example, if you look up HORSE in an encyclopedia, you may find twenty to thirty pages of information. Such lengthy articles usually are divided into sections. Each has a heading in heavy type that tells what the section is about. These are some of the headings you may find in an article about horses: *Kinds of Horses, The Body of a Horse, How to Ride, Care of Horses,* and *The History of the Horse.* There also may be several subsections within a section. Under *Care of Horses,* you may find subsections with these headings: *Food, Grooming, Medical Care.* By quickly reading the section and subsection headings in a long article, you can easily locate the information you need.

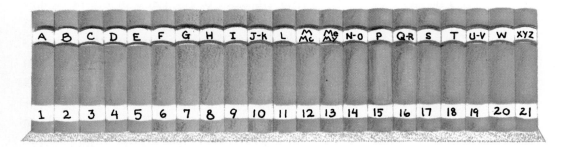

Practice

A. Which volume of the pictured encyclopedia would contain the answer to each question below? Write the letters of the volume you would choose. You may find some answers in *two* volumes.

1. Why is Oklahoma called the Sooner State?
2. What are the four blood types?
3. In track and field events, what is the decathlon?
4. What is a famous geyser in the United States?
5. What percentage of the earth's surface is water?
6. Why is Charles A. Lindbergh famous?
7. What are five types of grain?
8. When did Marconi send the first radio signals?
9. What are the three primary colors?
10. What is the official language of Kenya in Africa?

B. Use an encyclopedia to answer five of the questions above.

7 | The Parts of a Book

When you open a nonfiction book, you may not sit down and read the whole book as you would a book of fiction. Often you are looking for specific information. Nonfiction books usually have two parts that can be particularly useful to you.

In the front of most nonfiction books is a **table of contents.** The table of contents lists the titles of the parts of the book and the page numbers on which the parts begin. The largest parts may be called *units.* How many units are shown on the contents pages below? Often, additional topics are listed under the main parts, and page numbers are given for these topics. The parts within a unit may be called *chapters* or *sections.* How many chapters are there in Unit 1 of the book shown below? By looking quickly at the table of contents, you can tell how a book is organized, what topics are covered, and how many pages are devoted to each topic.

Contents

In the back of many nonfiction books is an **index,** an alphabetical list of topics and names that appear in the book. Because it is organized alphabetically, an index is very helpful when you are searching for specific information. Page numbers tell you where to look.

The index below is from the book *Around Our World.* The words printed farthest to the left in each column are called **main topics.** If the main topic is a person, the last name is listed first. You will sometimes find **subtopics** listed after a main topic. They tell what types of information are given about the main topic. Find the main topic *Africa.* How many subtopics are listed? Notice that these subtopics are listed in alphabetical order.

Find the main topic *Agriculture*. A **cross-reference** directs you to the main topic *Farming,* where you will find page numbers. Another type of cross-reference appears after the listing for *Astronomers.* The words *See also Stars* tell you that more information about astronomers (who study the universe beyond the earth) appears on the pages on which stars are discussed.

Now look at the listing *Andes Mountains.* Do you know what is meant by the letters *p* and *m* that appear before some of the page numbers? Read the paragraph at the beginning of the index. It tells you what *m, c, g,* and *p* stand for in this index. Different indexes may use different abbreviations. If you come across an unfamiliar symbol in an index, always check the first page of the index for an explanation.

Practice

A. Use the table of contents on page 172 to answer each of these questions.

1. Which unit contains information about language?
2. On which page would you begin reading about rapid changes in language?
3. In Unit 1, which chapter probably tells about where people live on the earth?
4. On which page would you begin reading about city life?
5. In which chapter in Unit 2 is there probably an explanation of human behavior?
6. Which chapter in which unit tells about names?

B. Use the index on page 173 to answer these questions. On which pages in the book could you probably find the answers?

7. How does television advertising affect viewers?
8. On which page is there a map of Alaska?
9. Who are the Bushmen of Africa?
10. Which pages show pictures of Mexican art?
11. Why is Athens called the birthplace of democracy?
12. Which English words are borrowed from Arabic?

8 | The Newspaper

You know that newspapers contain articles about recent events in your town, state, nation, and the world. What other information may be found in newspapers? If you take a look at a daily paper, you will find answers to questions such as these.

- What weather is predicted for today?
- Are there any after-school jobs available?
- What do readers have to say about recent articles in the paper?
- Are any of the nearby stores having sales?
- Did your favorite sports team win yesterday's game?

News stories are the most important part of a newspaper. They help you learn about what is happening in the world. The most important articles usually appear on the front page. Check the headlines, or titles, to find the news stories that you want to read. When you read the first paragraph of a news story, look for answers to these questions: Who is it about? Where did it happen? When did it happen? What happened? The answers will help you decide if you want to read the entire article.

In addition to the pages of news reports, most newspapers contain sections with articles about business, sports, entertainment, home, family, and health. The entertainment section includes articles about movies, plays, concerts, and other presentations.

There are reviews of movies and television programs that can help you decide what you want to see. Also listed are schedules for local movie theaters. A section with a title such as LIFESTYLES or AT HOME may include advice on home care and activities, health facts, and community announcements. The SPORTS section should include scores and details for a variety of sports events. If you want to find a job or buy or sell something, you would turn to the section entitled WANT ADS or CLASSIFIED. A section labeled EDITORIALS contains the opinions of writers, including letters from readers. Editorials are usually about current events.

In addition to the major sections, most newspapers also have other regular features. A brief weather prediction may appear on the front page, and there may be additional information and forecasts elsewhere in the paper. There may be comic strips and a crossword puzzle. Most newspapers have special columns. Some columns have answers to readers' questions. Some are meant to amuse you, and others contain opinions about subjects not usually covered in the editorial section. Just about every newspaper has advertisements for products to buy and places to shop or to visit.

When you are looking for a section or feature, you can find it by using the index, which appears on the first or second page of most newspapers. See the sample index below. It lists the sections and features in alphabetical order. If a newspaper is arranged in several separate parts, each part may be labeled with a letter, such as *A, B, C,* and so on. For example, you may find the sports stories on pages B9–14, in the second part of the paper. When you are looking for something *not* listed in the index, decide which section probably contains the information. For example, if you want advice on home repair, you would look in the section entitled LIFESTYLE.

Business	C1–8	Entertainment	C9–12
Classified	D6–15	Lifestyle	D1–10
Comics	C12	Sports	B9–14
Crossword	C13	TV/Radio	C13
Editorials	A12–13	Weather	D11

Practice

Use the index on page 176 to answer these questions. Write the correct letters and page numbers for the sections or features you would turn to.

1. What personal advice is given in the "Ask Maggie" column?
2. For how many weeks will the circus be in town?
3. Are there any used tape recorders for sale?
4. Does the paper contain any recipes today?
5. Did the new science-fiction movie get a good review?
6. When will the gymnastics program begin?
7. Will temperatures be lower tomorrow?
8. Does the newspaper express an opinion about the increased bus fares?
9. How did the high-school team perform in its recent game?
10. What do readers have to say about the new highway?

9 | Choosing Reference Aids

If you want to write a report or to find the answer to a question, where do you look for facts? Different types of questions require different types of reference aids. If you know what kind of information can be found in various sources, then you can quickly choose the reference aid you need.

You know that an **encyclopedia** is a set of books containing articles about hundreds of subjects, arranged alphabetically. You use an encyclopedia when you need general information.

Another reference aid is an **almanac,** a book published yearly. The almanac contains facts relating to the previous year or years. For example, most information in a 1982 almanac is about 1981 or before. An almanac gives brief descriptions, statistics (numerical information), and dates, often in the form of lists, tables, and charts. Almanacs contain facts about subjects such as historical events; government and government leaders; cities, states, and other areas of the U.S.; nations of the world; agriculture; achievements and awards; science, including inventions and discoveries; weather; entertainment; sports; and geography. If you want up-to-date information, use the most recently published almanac.

If you need a map, use an **atlas**—a book of maps. There are many different atlases. An atlas of the world contains maps of all the nations. A United States atlas includes maps of all the states. A regional atlas shows various sections of a nation or state. Although you can find maps in an encyclopedia, atlas maps are usually more detailed. They show towns and highways and points of interest, such as museums and historical sites, that may not be noted on an encyclopedia map.

What reference aid do you use if you want information about a very recent event? You should check a daily **newspaper,** which contains news about local towns, the state, the nation, and the world. If you want to know about yesterday's city council meeting, look for the answer in a newspaper.

More than one reference aid may have information on the subject you are investigating. However, usually you will find that one of the aids has more detailed information or can be used more quickly. If you select the best reference aid for your research, you will save time and effort.

Here is the first verse of an American folk song. Suppose you want to learn about the history the song is about. What reference aids would you use?

> We've formed our band and are well manned,
> To journey afar to the promised land,
> Where the golden ore is rich in store
> On the banks of the Sacramento shore.

If you look up GOLD in an encyclopedia, you will find information about the California gold rush. To find out where Sacramento is located in California, you can use an atlas. If you want current facts about gold mining, check an atlas to find out how much gold is now produced in the U.S. and where such mining is done. Then go to today's newspaper to find out the current price per ounce of gold. Reference aids provide a mine of information!

Practice

A. For each question, tell whether you would find the answer in an encyclopedia, an almanac, an atlas, or a newspaper.

1. What are two endangered species of mammals?
2. What road in Vermont would you take from Chester to Ludlow?
3. What is letterpress printing?
4. What is the latest report on the satellite orbiting Saturn?
5. Who holds the record number of Olympic gold medals?
6. How far is it from Lima, Ohio, to Akron, Ohio?
7. How did the U.S. Senate vote yesterday on the tax bill?
8. What TV program won the most recent Emmy Award for best comedy series?
9. How did Iowa get its nickname, the Hawkeye State?
10. What U.S. city had the coldest temperature yesterday?

B. Find the answers to five of the questions above.

Mid-Book Test

- **Sentences** Write each sentence, adding end punctuation. Then write *declarative, interrogative, imperative,* or *exclamatory* to identify each type of sentence.

   1. Have you ever flown a kite
   2. How beautiful they are
   3. My kite has a long tail
   4. Unwind some more string

- **Subjects and Predicates** Write each sentence. Draw a line between the complete subject and complete predicate. Underline the simple subject once and the simple predicate twice.

   5. My best friend joined a hiking club.
   6. Members of the club went to a wildlife preserve.
   7. Some people brought their cameras with them.
   8. Everyone in the group carried a pack.

- **Finding the Subject** Write the subject of each sentence.

   9. Have you seen the daffodils?
   10. Please pick some for me.
   11. There are the apple trees.
   12. Here are some flower buds.

- **Compound Subjects and Predicates** Write the compound subject or compound predicate of each sentence.

   13. The car keys and theater tickets were lost.
   14. Marian and her mother searched for them.
   15. Marian's mother knelt and looked under the sofa.
   16. Marian opened and closed all the dresser drawers.

- **Compound Sentences** Combine each pair of sentences into a compound sentence.

   17. The cars are moving. Jane cannot cross the street.
   18. The deer spotted us. They bounded into the deep woods.
   19. Jack bought groceries. First he made a shopping list.

- **Fragments and Run-ons**   Correct each fragment or run-on.

  20. Roaming the wilderness.
  21. He worried about the test how should he study?
  22. The skirt was long she shortened the hem.
  23. For at least two hours.

- **Nouns**   Write each noun. Label it *common* or *proper*.

  24. Dr. Angelo, the dentist, is on Chauncey Street.
  25. Edward wears a watch that loses ten minutes a day.
  26. Edward was late for his dental appointment last Tuesday.
  27. He looked at some watches in a window at Ivy Mall.

- **Plural Nouns**   Write the plural form of each noun below.

  28. desk
  29. watch
  30. country
  31. brush
  32. tax
  33. rose
  34. solo
  35. life

- **Possessive Nouns**   Write the possessive for each sentence.

  36. The _____ long day was over. (sailors)
  37. _____ boat approached the dock first. (Fred)
  38. The _____ sails fluttered aimlessly in the breeze. (boats)
  39. The _____ boat is still out in the harbor. (Perkinses)

- **Appositives**   Rewrite each pair of sentences into a single sentence containing an appositive. Punctuate it correctly.

  40. The hurricane was the worst storm of the season. The hurricane destroyed many beautiful trees.
  41. The 1852 House was hit. It is the oldest house in town.
  42. The Historical Preservation Fund is a fund to repair the house. The fund was started last month.

- **Verbs**   Write *action* or *being* for each verb below.

  43. Leopards hunt their prey at night.
  44. Leopards are smaller than lions or tigers.
  45. Leopards drink water every two or three days.

- **Direct Objects**   Write each direct object in exercises 43–45.

- **Linking Verbs** Copy these sentences. Underline the linking verbs. Label predicate nouns *PN* and predicate adjectives *PA*.

  46. The leopard is a cat.
  47. Leopards are climbers.
  48. Newborn cubs are blind.
  49. Their fur is spotted.

- **Main Verbs and Auxiliaries** Write each verb phrase below. Underline the auxiliary once and main verb twice.

  50. Ali has studied color photography.
  51. She'll print her own photographs in a darkroom.
  52. Should she exhibit them?
  53. She must have learned about light meters and lens filters.

- **Principal Parts of Verbs** Write the correct form of the verb for each sentence. Then write its past participle.

  54. Last month Tom ＿＿ in a marathon. (run)
  55. He ＿＿ the race ahead of forty runners. (finish)
  56. Tom ＿＿ the race again next year. (enter)
  57. He still ＿＿ running every day. (practice)

- **Regular and Irregular Verbs** Label each verb you wrote for exercises 54–57 *R* for regular or *IR* for irregular.

- **Subject-Verb Agreement** Write the verb that agrees with each subject.

  58. Vi (has, have) bought a new car.
  59. Mo and Al (like, likes) it.
  60. Neither her sister nor her brothers (has, have) driven it.

- **Pronouns** Copy each pronoun, and write its antecedent.

  61. Pierre saw the other skiers ahead. They spotted him, too.
  62. Pierre skied fast, but they moved even faster.
  63. He dropped one ski pole. It slid down the icy slope.

- **Subject and Object Pronouns** Write *S* above each subject pronoun you wrote for exercises 61–63. Write *O* above each object pronoun.

- **Possessive Pronouns** Write the correct pronoun.

64. May I use (your, you're) stereo equipment?
65. (Its, It's) sound is excellent.
66. I would like to tape some of (my, mine) records.
67. The singers blend (they're, their, theirs) voices well.
68. (Who's, Whose) records shall I borrow?

- **Pronouns in Compounds and After Linking Verbs** Write the correct word or words to complete each sentence.

69. The taxi driver noticed (Debbie and I, Debbie and me).
70. (Debbie and I, Me and Debbie) rode to the airport together.
71. The last person to board the plane will be (she, her).

- **Using Words Correctly** Write the word in parentheses that correctly completes each sentence.

72. We can (teach, learn) the class some facts about rocks.
73. First, ask them to (sit, set) down and listen to directions.
74. (Who, Whom) will (lend, borrow) your map from you?
75. (Who, Whom) did you bring on the mountain-climbing trip?
76. (Sit, Set) the tripod on that rock.
77. (Let, Leave) me take a photograph of the entire group.
78. Anthony might (lend, borrow) his gear to you.
79. The mountain (rises, raises) high above the valley.
80. (Who, Whom) will reach the mountaintop first?
81. The village (lies, lays) miles below the exhausted climbers.
82. The climbers will (lie, lay) their packs down.
83. They will (rise, raise) a flag when they reach the summit.

- **Building Vocabulary** Write a synonym and an antonym for each word.

84. ancient   85. joyful   86. cold   87. frightened

Write the root of each of these words.

88. believable   90. repay   92. exchange   94. stressful
89. governor   91. preview   93. discount   95. actor

Writing a Report

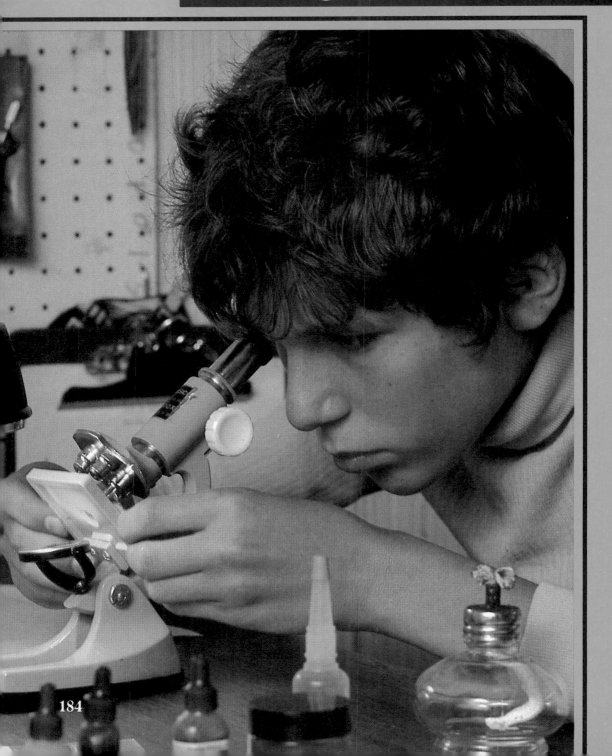

1 | Taking Notes

Taking notes is a shortcut for writing down information you want to remember. When you take notes, you write only key words that will help you recall particular ideas or facts.

You can take notes to help you study a subject like science. You can also take notes to help you write about a topic. Suppose you are writing a report about how trees became petrified, or changed to rock. When you read, you would take notes to tell you that information. Read the paragraph and notes below.

In the Petrified Forest National Park, you can see solid rocks that were tree trunks 150 million years ago. The trees died and were buried in mud, sand, or ash. Water seeped into the logs, leaving behind mineral deposits. As the trees rotted, the minerals filled the spaces in the logs. Over time, the minerals replaced the wood and became solid rock.

How were trees changed into rock?
—trees buried in mud, sand, or ash
—water in logs left behind mineral deposits
—minerals filled the spaces in the log when wood rotted
—wood completely replaced by rock

• What facts were left out of the notes? Why?

Practice

Read the paragraph below. Take notes to answer the question *How did the pony express service work?*

In the early 1860's, daring pony express riders carried mail between Missouri and California in only ten days. The pony express had a relay system. A rider rode from one home station to the next, about 75 miles away. A second rider carried the mail from the second station to the third. The mail was passed from rider to rider for 2000 miles.

2 | Making an Outline

An outline is a plan for organizing information. It can have several parts. The **main topics** tell what each section of the outline is about. The **subtopics** are facts and ideas that support the main topics. **Details** give more information about subtopics. An outline also has a title.

Roman numerals are used for main topics. Capital letters are used for subtopics. Numbers are used for details.

Study how one section of an outline is formed from these notes.

What kinds of contests are in a rodeo?
—grand parade at beginning
—rough stock events and timed events
—rough stock events done for certain length of time
—timed events done as quickly as possible
—rough stock events include bareback riding, saddle bronco riding, bull riding
—timed events are calf roping, steer wrestling, steer roping

Rodeos
I. Kinds of contests   **main topic**
   A. Rough stock events   **subtopic**
      1. Done for certain length of time   **detail**
      2. Bareback riding
      3. Saddle bronco riding
      4. Bull riding
   B. Timed events
      1. Done as quickly as possible
      2. Calf roping
      3. Steer wrestling
      4. Steer roping

- What parts of the notes became a main topic?
- What information in the notes became subtopics? details?
- What fact in the notes was left out of the outline? Why?
- Are the details in a logical order? Why or why not?

Practice

Use the notes below to complete the outline. Turn each question in the notes into a main topic. Write the facts in the notes that support the main topics as subtopics. Write the facts that tell about a subtopic as details under that subtopic. Write the details in a logical order. Write a title.

What was early armor made of?
—cave dwellers wore thick animal skins
—Greeks wore bronze helmets and body plates
—Romans wore leather and iron armor

What kinds of armor did knights wear in the Middle Ages?
—mail and plate armor
—mail made of thousands of interlocking metal rings
—mail was lightweight and easy to move in
—mail was worn over padded clothing
—plate armor made by joining together metal plates
—plate weighed fifty to sixty pounds
—plate covered knight from head to toe

   I. Early armor
      A. Cave dwellers—animal hides
      B.
      C.
  II.
      A. Mail
         1. Made of thousands of interlocking metal rings
         2.
         3.
      B.
         1.
         2.
         3. Covered knight from head to toe

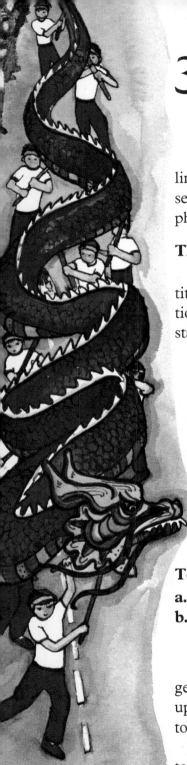

3 | Writing a Paragraph from an Outline

Just as a skeleton provides the structure for your body, an outline provides the structure for your paragraphs. You expand each section of an outline into a full paragraph by adding words and phrases that explain, describe, and give interest to the facts.

The Topic Sentence

How do you write a paragraph from an outline? First, read the title and the main topic, subtopics, and details of the outline section. Think about the main idea. Then write a topic sentence that states the main idea.

Read the outline section and the topic sentences below.

Chinese New Year

I. Dragon parade
    A. Acrobats in colorful costumes
    B. Musicians playing gongs, cymbals, other instruments
    C. Lighted floats
    D. Dragon
        1. Made of cloth, often red silk or velvet
        2. Held up by people with poles
        3. Weaves back and forth in the street

Topic sentences:

a. The dragon parade is one of the Chinese New Year's events.

b. The dragon parade is a colorful and lively event of the Chinese New Year.

Both topic sentences state the main idea. Sentence **a** is very general. Sentence **b** uses the adjectives *colorful* and *lively* to sum up facts given in the subtopics. Sentence **b** is a more interesting topic sentence because it gives more information.

Sometimes facts taken from the subtopics can be used in an interesting way in the topic sentence. Read the section of an outline and the topic sentences on the next page.

Extinct Animals

I. Woolly mammoth
  A. Appearance
    1. Looked somewhat like a very big elephant
    2. Hairy body
    3. Back legs shorter than front legs
    4. Short tail with hair at end
  B. Lived about ten thousand years ago
  C. Some found frozen in ice in Alaska and other cold areas

Topic sentences:

a. Elephant-like animals called woolly mammoths lived long ago.

b. If you had lived in Alaska ten thousand years ago, you might have met a woolly mammoth.

Both sentences state the main idea. Sentence **b,** though, uses the information in the outline to state the main idea in an unusual way.

The Paragraph

The rest of the sentences in the paragraph give the supporting details. The supporting details are the other facts in the outline not included in the topic sentence. Add words and phrases to expand these facts into clear, interesting sentences.

Read the following paragraph. It was written from the outline about the woolly mammoth.

If you had lived in Alaska ten thousand years ago, you might have met a woolly mammoth. The woolly mammoth looked somewhat like a very large elephant, but it was different in some ways. As its name tells you, long hair covered its huge body. Its back legs were shorter than its front legs, and its short tail had a hairy fringe at the end. We know about woolly mammoths because some have been found frozen in ice in Alaska and other cold places.

- Which sentences combined facts from two subtopics or details in the outline?
- What words or phrases were added that help you understand or picture the woolly mammoth more clearly?

Practice

Read the two outline sections below. Write two topic sentences for each one. Each topic sentence should state the main idea. Perhaps you can state it in an unusual way. Use the titles, main topics, and subtopics of the outlines to help you.

For each outline, choose the topic sentence you think is better. Write a paragraph for each outline section. Use words and phrases that will make your paragraph interesting to read.

Major Storms

I. Tornado
   A. Twisting wind storm
   B. Cone-shaped cloud
   C. Strongest winds of any storm on earth
      1. Whirls around at more than 300 miles per hour
      2. Can pull up large trees, carry cars hundreds of feet

Native Americans

I. Some early kinds of homes
   A. Long houses
      1. Iroquois tribes
      2. Rectangular long houses
      3. Made of poles covered with bark or leaves
   B. Tepees
      1. Plains Indians
      2. Cones made of buffalo skins
      3. Easy to move
   C. Adobe homes
      1. Pueblo Indians
      2. Made of sun-dried brick
      3. Built in levels like apartments

4 | Getting Started

What topics tickle your imagination—penguins? pioneer life? careers in radio broadcasting? how money is manufactured?

Doing research for a report can be a great way to learn about a topic. It is like going on a treasure hunt. You search for clues, then put the clues together to find the treasure—in this case, information that interests and informs you. Along the way, you develop thinking and writing skills you can use all your life.

A report tells only facts. A **fact** is information that can be proven true. In a report, you do not tell about yourself or your **opinions,** your thoughts and feelings.

The sentence *The average daily temperature in Florida is higher than in Montana* could be in a report, for example. It states a fact that can be proven. The sentence *Everyone loves warm weather* states an opinion.

Practice

A. Write three sentences that state facts and three sentences that state opinions.

B. List five possible report topics. Be specific. For example, name a particular person instead of just listing "a famous person," or list "pilot" instead of just "careers."

Steps for Writing a Report   Here are the steps for writing a report. You will follow these steps to write your own report.

Step One   Choose a topic.
Step Two   Plan your report.
Step Three   Write your first draft.
Step Four   Revise your report.
Step Five   Proofread your report.
Step Six   Make a final copy to share.

5 | Step One
Choose a Topic

Choosing a topic for your report is an important first step. When thinking about topics, ask yourself these questions.

1. How much does this topic interest me?
2. Can I find information about this topic easily?
3. Can I tell about this topic in a short report?

Leon thought of several subjects for a report.

London Bridge
the author Lloyd Alexander

microscopic life
laser beams

He asked himself the three questions for choosing a report topic for each idea. He thought it might be difficult to find much information about Lloyd Alexander. He was not as interested in London Bridge as in some of the other topics.

Microscopic life was too big a topic, but Leon was really curious about it. How could he narrow, or shorten, it? He remembered looking through a microscope in science class one day. He had seen several kinds of tiny animals. Then he knew! He could narrow his topic to *one* microscopic animal. He remembered one animal was called the amoeba. Leon decided to write about the amoeba for his report.

Assignment • Choose a Topic

A. Make a list of at least five report topics that interest you.
B. Ask yourself the three questions for choosing a report topic. Narrow any topics that are too big. Cross out any topics that would be difficult to find information about.
C. Look at your topics again. Which topics are you most excited about? Choose one of those topics for your report, and circle it on your paper.

6 | Step Two
Plan Your Report

Planning your report involves several steps: (1) deciding what kind of facts to include, (2) finding the facts and taking notes, and (3) organizing the notes into an outline.

Leon wrote the questions he wanted his report to answer.

1. *How does an amoeba move?*

2. *What is an amoeba?*

3. *What and how does an amoeba eat?*

Leon checked library books and encyclopedias for answers to his questions. From his reading, he learned that amoebas increase their population in an unusual way. He wanted to put that information in his report. He added this question to his list.

4. *How does the number of amoebas increase?*

When Leon found facts that answered his questions, he took notes. He wrote his notes on note cards, putting one note on each card. Leon wrote the question the fact answered. Below it, he wrote the fact. At the bottom of the card, he wrote where he found the fact.

Here is one of Leon's note cards.

What is an amoeba?

—made of cytoplasm, a kind of clear jelly

The Amoeba, Sean Morrison, page 19.

After Leon had gathered the facts to answer his questions, he needed to organize them into an outline.

1. Leon put together all the note cards that answered each of his four questions. He made four piles of cards.
2. He reread his notes for one question. He put the cards in an order that made sense. He did this for all four questions.
3. He turned each question into a main topic heading.
4. He wrote the facts that answered each question as subtopics.
5. He wrote any facts that told about a subtopic as details.

Look at part of Leon's outline below.

part of Leon's outline

The Amoeba

~~II.~~ I. How an amoeba moves
  A. Changes shape
  B. Pulled along by pseudopods
  C. Travels only a few inches a day

~~I.~~ II. What an amoeba is
  A. Pond animal
  B. Very tiny
    1. Only one cell
    2. Can be seen with microscope
    3. ~~C.~~ About one one-hundredth inch
  C. What an amoeba is like
    1. ~~D.~~ Made of clear jelly called cytoplasm
    2. ~~E.~~ Outer covering = cell membrane
    3. ~~F.~~ Has nucleus that controls what the amoeba does

- What are the main topics? the subtopics? the details?
- Why did Leon change the order of the two sections in this part of the outline?
- What other changes did he make? Why?

After Leon wrote his outline, he checked that the main topics, subtopics, and details were in the best order. He decided that the second section should be first. After all, why would readers care how an amoeba moves if they do not know what one is! He circled that section and then drew an arrow to show where it would go.

Leon looked again at the subtopics and details in the section that told what an amoeba is. He noticed that subtopic C told about the amoeba's size. He made it a detail under subtopic B. He also saw that subtopics D, E, and F all told what an amoeba was made of. He wrote a new subtopic and listed them as details.

Assignment
- **Write Questions**
- **Take Notes**
- **Make an Outline**

A. What information would you like to learn about your topic? Write three or four questions to answer in your report.
B. Find books or encyclopedia articles about your topic.
C. Take notes that answer the questions you wrote. Write your notes on note cards. Write one fact on each card.

1. At the top, write the question the fact answers.
2. Write the fact or information below the question.
3. At the bottom, write the title, author, and page numbers of the book you used or the title, volume number, and page numbers of the encyclopedia.

D. Write an outline, using your notes. Turn your questions into main topics. Write facts that support the main topics as subtopics. Write facts that tell about a subtopic as details. Write a title for your outline.
E. Check your outline. Are the main topics, subtopics, and details in the best order?

7 | Step Three
Write Your Report

Leon began his report with an introduction to give a general idea of what the report was about. Then he followed his outline to write the body of his report. He wrote one paragraph for each section of his outline. At the end, Leon wrote a conclusion to sum up his report. He also listed the sources of his information.

Leon did not worry about making mistakes as he wrote. He knew he would be able to revise and proofread his paper later.

Leon's first draft

My report is about the amoeba. ~~You cannot.~~ It is so tiny you need a ~~tele~~ microscope to see it. You will find this report very interesting.

The amoeba is a very tiny animal that lives in pond water. It is about one one-hundredth of an inch across. It has just one cell. It looks like a blob. It is made of a clear jelly stuff called cytoplasm. The ~~cytopl~~ outer covering of the cell is the cell membrane. It keeps the cell together. Inside is a nucleus. It controls what the amoeba does. It just helps the amoeba react.

An amoeba chang moves by changing shape. The pseudopods reach out and pull it along. The amoeba can push out pseudopods in any direction. An amoeba moves only a few inches a day.

The amoeba eats other tiny animals and plants. It traps food with it's pseudopods. They suround the food and make a food vacuole. The amoeba dijests the food in the food vacuole just like are stomachs dijests food.

The amoeba pulls itself apart in the middle. It divides in two. Both new amoebas are just like the old one.

The amoeba is an amazing animal.

The Amoeba, Sean Morrison, pages 11–40.
World Book Encyclopedia, Volume 1, page 387.

- Which paragraph needs a topic sentence?
- Is the first paragraph a good introduction? Why or why not?
- Is the last paragraph a good conclusion? Why or why not?
- Which scientific words are not clearly explained?
- Which short, choppy sentences should Leon rewrite?

An Amoeba (ə mē′bə)

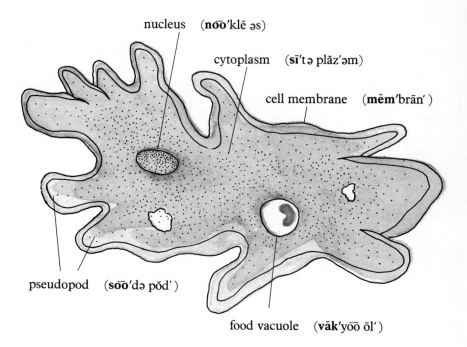

nucleus   (noo′klē əs)

cytoplasm   (sī′tə plăz′əm)

cell membrane   (mĕm′brān′)

pseudopod   (soo′də pŏd′)

food vacuole   (văk′yoo ōl′)

Assignment • Write Your First Draft

Use your outline to write your first draft. Write one paragraph for each section of your outline. You may want to skip a line as you write. Follow these steps.

1. Write an introduction that leads into your report topic. Keep your introduction short. Include information to make a reader interested in learning about your topic.
2. For each paragraph in the body of the report, first write a topic sentence. Use the title, main topic, and subtopics to help you. Then write the subtopics and details as complete sentences. Add words and phrases to the facts in your outline to make your sentences more descriptive and interesting.
3. Write a conclusion, or ending, to let the reader know the report is finished. In your conclusion, sum up the topic or the most important ideas. Keep the conclusion brief.
4. At the end of the report, write the information about the books and encyclopedias where you found your facts.

8 | Step Four
Revise Your Report

When Leon reread his report, he tried to imagine what he would think of it if someone else had written it. As he read, he saw several parts that needed revising.

Leon realized that the report needed a better introduction and conclusion. The first sentence of his introduction was very weak, and the last sentence stated an opinion. Leon thought carefully about a new first sentence. He needed to tell that the report was about the amoeba in a way that would interest the reader.

Leon thought his conclusion cut off the report too quickly. The conclusion needed to give a better summary.

Leon wrote a new introduction and conclusion. He pasted the new paragraphs over the ones on his first draft.

Leon noticed that there was a big jump between the paragraphs about how an amoeba moves and what it eats. He wrote another topic sentence for the paragraph about what an amoeba eats. He liked the way the new topic sentence tied the two paragraphs together. Leon also added a topic sentence for the paragraph about how an amoeba divides itself in two.

Then he asked Megan to listen to his report.

"I never knew pond water had those tiny animals in it!" exclaimed Megan. "Your report is really interesting. I thought everything seemed in the right order, too."

"Were all the facts explained clearly?" asked Leon.

"Well," Megan said thoughtfully, "you didn't really explain pseudopods, and I wasn't sure how a food vacuole looks. Is the nucleus the amoeba's brain? That wasn't clear."

Leon took a few notes to remind him of Megan's comments.

"Are there other things I should change?" he asked.

"Well," she said, "I wouldn't use the word *stuff*."

Leon thanked Megan for her suggestions. He made more changes to clear up the facts Megan did not understand. He also combined several short sentences that had sounded choppy when he read the report aloud. Finally, he added a title.

The Amoeba

A drop of pond water holds a whole world of animal life that can be seen only with a microscope. One of these microscopic creatures is the amoeba.

The amoeba is a very tiny ~~animal~~ *and simpel* that lives in pond water. It is about one one-hundredth of an inch across. ~~It~~ *and* has just one cell. It looks like a blob, *because* It is made of a clear jelly stuff called cytoplasm. The ~~cytopl~~ outer covering of the cell, is the cell membrane. It keeps the cell together. Inside *the cell,* is a nucleus. ~~It~~ *The nucleus is like a Brain but it can not think.* controls what the amoeba does. It just helps the amoeba react.

An amoeba ~~chang~~ moves by changing shape. *the amoeba* The pseudopods reach out and pull it along. The amoeba can push out pseudo-pods in any direction. An amoeba moves only a few inches a day. *The amoeba extends part of the cytoplasm to form false feet called pseudopods.*

The pseudopods helps   *catch*

∧ The amoeba ~~eats~~ other tiny animals
for food.
and plants, ~~It traps food with it's pseudo-~~
                         a pocket called
~~pods.~~ They suround the food, ~~and make~~ ∧
   and trap the food.
a food vacuole. The amoeba dijests the
food in the food vacuole just like are
stomachs dijests food.
number of amoebas increases in an unusual way. When full size, an
     The ∧ amoeba pulls itself apart in
       and
the middle. ~~It divides in two.~~ Both new
amoebas are just like the old one.

     Even though it has only one cell, the
amoeba can move, gather food, and
divide itself in two. The amoeba is
a microscopic marvel.

The Amoeba, Sean Morrison, pages 11–40.
World Book Encyclopedia, Volume 1,
page 387.

- Why are Leon's new introduction and conclusion better?
- He changed the beginning of the second paragraph. Why?
- What information did Leon add to explain pseudopods, a food vacuole, and the nucleus?
- Look at Leon's new topic sentence for his fourth paragraph. How does it tie together the third and fourth paragraphs?
- What other topic sentence did Leon add?
- What other changes did Leon make in his report?

Revise Your Report   **201**

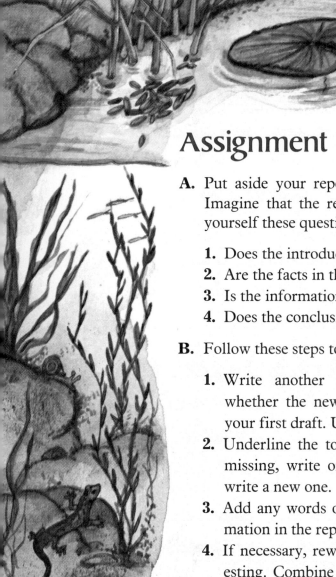

Assignment

- **Revise Your Report**
- **Discuss Your Report**

A. Put aside your report for a few days. Then read it again. Imagine that the report was written by someone else. Ask yourself these questions.

1. Does the introduction interest you in the topic?
2. Are the facts in the report clearly explained?
3. Is the information presented in an order that makes sense?
4. Does the conclusion summarize the report?

B. Follow these steps to revise your report.

1. Write another introduction for your report. Decide whether the new introduction is better than the one in your first draft. Use the introduction you think is better.
2. Underline the topic sentence in each paragraph. If it is missing, write one. If a topic sentence is dull or weak, write a new one.
3. Add any words or sentences needed to explain the information in the report more clearly.
4. If necessary, rewrite sentences to make them more interesting. Combine choppy sentences into longer sentences. Shorten any stringy sentences.
5. Write another conclusion. Choose the conclusion you like better.
6. Write a title for your report.

C. Read your report to a classmate or your teacher. Make notes of any suggestions or comments your listener has. If you think your listener's suggestions will improve your report or if you think of any ideas on your own during the discussion, make those changes on your paper.

9 | Step Five
Proofread Your Report

Leon had made so many revisions on his first draft that he could not follow it well. He copied over his report so that he could proofread it.

Leon checked his capitalization and punctuation. He looked up in the dictionary the spelling of several words he was unsure of. He also checked that he had used correct verb tenses and the correct forms of pronouns.

Look at one of Leon's paragraphs after he proofread it.

Leon's second paragraph after proofreading

> The amoeba is very tiny and simpel *simple.*
> It is about one one-hundredth of an inch across and has just one cell. It looks like a blob because it is made of a clear jelly called cytoplasm. The outer covering of the cell, the cell membrane, keeps the cell together. Inside the cell, a nucleus controls what the amoeba does. The nucleus is like a *b* Brain, but it can not *cannot* think. It just helps the amoeba react.

- What spelling mistakes did Leon correct?
- What capitalization and punctuation changes did he make? Why?

Practice

Proofread the paragraph below from Leon's report. If you are unsure how to spell a word, check a dictionary. There are nine mistakes.

The pseudopods helps The amoeba catch other tiny animals and plants for food. They suround the food, make a pocket called a food vacuole and trap the food. The amoeba dijests the food in the food vacuole just like are stomachs dijests food.

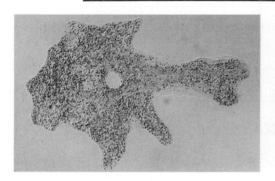 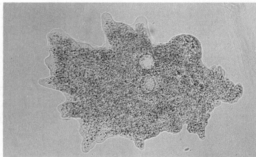

Assignment • **Proofread Your Report**

Proofread your own report. Use the questions below to help you.

1. Have I indented each paragraph?
2. Is every word spelled correctly?

Grammar skills checklist

3. Does every sentence express one complete thought?
4. Have I used commas correctly to join the parts of compound sentences and to set off appositives and items in a series?
5. Have I used capital letters correctly with proper nouns and titles?
6. Does the subject of each sentence agree with the verb?
7. Have I used the correct form for each subject pronoun, object pronoun, and possessive pronoun?

10 | Step Six
Make a Final Copy

Now that Leon had revised and proofread his report, he could turn his attention to making it look neat. He recopied the report in his best handwriting. Then he checked his final copy to be sure he had not made any copying mistakes.

The students in Leon's class decided to present their reports aloud to the class. There were many different topics, and they wanted to learn about all of them.

Leon practiced reading his report aloud. He made sure he could read smoothly and clearly and could pronounce all the words. He also prepared a poster for his presentation. He drew a large picture of an amoeba. He labeled the different parts described in his report. He drew other pictures showing how the amoeba moves, catches its food, and divides itself in two. As he read his report to the class, Leon pointed to the different pictures that showed what the report was explaining.

Leon also brought to class several library books that showed photographs of amoebas.

Assignment
- **Make a Final Copy**
- **Share Your Report**

A. Copy your report neatly on a clean piece of paper. Check it for any copying mistakes.

B. If you have not yet written a title for your report, do so now. Use page 358 in the Handbook for help with capitalization.

C. Think of a special way to share your report.

- Make an art project that shows something explained in your report. You might draw a picture, build a model, make a mobile, paint a mural, sew an object, or make a filmstrip.
- Read your report to several students or to the whole class the way Leon did. Practice your oral reading first.
- Make a class booklet of the reports for students to read.

Punctuation

1 | Reviewing End Punctuation

End punctuation gives the same clues in writing as voice changes do in speaking. It tells whether you are asking a question (?), making a statement (.), showing strong feeling(!), or giving a command(.).

Can I take flying lessons?   We'll land at noon.
What a small plane this is!   Check your speed.

Try It Out

Tell which punctuation mark should end each sentence.

1. Our nation's flag has one star for each state
2. What an interesting history it has
3. What was the last state represented by a star
4. The stripes stand for the first thirteen colonies
5. Don't let the flag touch the ground

> There are three end marks. A period (.) ends a statement or a command. A question mark (?) follows a question. An exclamation mark (!) follows an exclamation of strong feeling.

Written Practice

Write these sentences with the correct end punctuation.

1. What is a Southern dinner
2. I am cooking one tonight
3. Did I choose a good ham
4. What a small oven this is
5. We like cooked greens
6. Please mix the biscuits
7. Isn't the dough sticky
8. Let's have some pecans
9. You can shell them first
10. How salty the ham is.

- **Writing Sentences**   Write six sentences. Use each end mark.

2 | Commas in a Series

In a series, the items are separated with a **comma**. A comma tells the reader to pause between the words it separates. Notice how the commas change the meaning of the sentence below.

> I bought fruit salad, tuna sandwiches, and juice.
> I bought fruit, salad, tuna, sandwiches, and juice.

A connecting word such as *or* or *and* usually appears before the last word in a series.

> Do I use one, two, or three teaspoons of parsley?
> Last year my uncle taught me to ski, to scuba dive, and to play chess.

Try It Out

A. Tell where commas belong in these sentences.

1. Red yellow orange green and blue are five of the colors in the rainbow.
2. Red is the color used for stop signs traffic lights and some fire hydrants.
3. Green reminds me of marbles lettuce and Ireland.
4. Colors can make you sleepy wake you up help you think or warn you of danger.
5. Advertisers designers florists and chefs use color to get your attention.

B. For each group, join the four items into a series, and create a sentence. Tell where you would place commas.

6. a pencil   two erasers   a pen   three rulers
7. a half cup of raisins   one cup of milk
   one cup of flour   one teaspoon of water
8. swimming   baseball   tennis   jogging

A comma is used to separate words in a series.
A comma tells the reader to pause between the words that it separates.

Written Practice

Complete each sentence with your own words. Insert commas and connecting words where needed to separate items in a series.

1. The first four months of the year are _____.
2. _____ are three different kinds of flowers.
3. Four former presidents of the United States are _____.
4. The first five notes in the musical scale are _____.
5. The four whole numbers following *one* are _____.
6. The four seasons of the year are _____.
7. The three basic meals we eat are _____.
8. _____ are three countries located in Europe.
9. _____ are four of the world's rivers.
10. Four kinds of wild animals are _____.
11. Three of my favorite foods are _____.
12. Three things I do before leaving on a trip are _____.

- **Writing Sentences**   Make up five series with three or more items in each. Write a sentence, correctly punctuated, for each series you have created.

3 | More Uses for Commas

A comma is used in a compound sentence to separate the simple sentences. Notice the comma in each compound sentence below.

Whales live in the ocean, but they are not fish.
A female whale is called a cow, and a baby whale is a calf.

Commas are used to separate an appositive from the rest of the sentence. You remember that an appositive is a word or a group of words that tells more about the noun it follows.

Mr. Gilmore, a whale expert, works at the aquarium.
Blue whales, the fastest kind, are found in all oceans.

A comma is used after such words as *well*, *yes*, and *no* when they introduce a sentence.

Yes, I have seen a finback whale.
Well, we actually saw its spout first.

Commas are used to set off the name of the person who is being directly spoken to in a sentence.

From this distance, Tim, that looks like a right whale.
Jerry, have you read *Moby Dick*?

Try It Out

Tell where you would insert a comma in each sentence.

1. Class who invented the first workable steamboat?
2. Yes it was Robert Fulton.
3. He was a well-known portrait painter but he became more and more interested in engineering.
4. He ran his first steamboat on the Seine a river in France.
5. No that was not the only boat Fulton built.
6. The *Clermont* another steamboat traveled the Hudson River.
7. Well the steamboat was only one of his projects.

Use a comma to separate simple sentences in a compound sentence.

Use commas to separate an appositive from the rest of the sentence.

A comma is used after words such as *well*, *yes*, and *no* when they begin a sentence.

Commas are used to set off the name of a person being spoken to directly.

Written Practice

Copy these sentences, and add the missing commas.

1. The hornet one of many common insects is much like the yellow jacket.
2. Did you know Jules that all insects have three pairs of legs?
3. Yes I knew that and the body of an adult insect is divided into three parts.
4. What are the three segments of an insect's body Paul?
5. Well the three main sections are called the head the thorax and the abdomen.
6. Some insects help humans and others are very harmful.
7. The honeybee a stinging insect makes honey and pollinates flowers fruits and vegetables.
8. Mosquitoes insects that can carry diseases transmit more than twenty different viruses.
9. Valerie can you name other insects that have wings?
10. Well moths wasps flies and butterflies have wings.
11. An ant a very small insect can lift incredible weights.
12. No ants cannot live in the North Pole.
13. Ants can breathe fresh air but they do not have lungs.
14. Can you describe an ant colony Jeffrey?

- **Writing Sentences** Write two sentences that illustrate each of the statements about commas in the box above. You should have eight sentences in all.

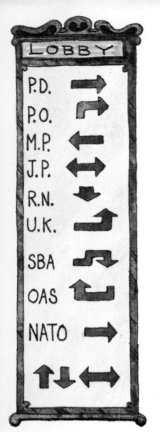

4 | Abbreviations

When you are taking notes or making lists, abbreviations can help you write faster. Using abbreviations can also save you space.

You have seen abbreviations in advertisements and on license plates. An **abbreviation** is a shortened form of a word, usually followed by a period. If you need help writing an abbreviation, check the dictionary.

Study this list of common abbreviations for places.

Apt.	Apartment	Mt.	Mount *or* Mountain
Blvd.	Boulevard	Pkwy.	Parkway
Expy.	Expressway	Rd.	Road

Businesses also use abbreviations as part of their names.

Co.	Company	Inc.	Incorporated

Some abbreviations are written in all capital letters, with each letter standing for a word. You can see from some of the words below that only the important parts are abbreviated.

P.D.	Police Department	P.O.	Post Office
M.P.	Member of Parliament	R.N.	Registered Nurse
J.P.	Justice of the Peace	U.K.	United Kingdom

Abbreviations of government agencies or national organizations do not usually have periods. Read this list.

SBA	Small Business Administration
OAS	Organization of American States
PBS	Public Broadcasting Service
NATO	North Atlantic Treaty Organization

Some abbreviations have neither capital letters nor periods.

mph - miles per hour   hp - horsepower   ft - feet

The United States Postal Service uses two capital letters and no period in each of its state abbreviations.

California	CA	Indiana	IN	South Carolina	SC

Try It Out

How would you abbreviate the following phrases?

1. Pearly Piano Company
2. Fifth Avenue
3. Fun Games, Incorporated
4. Garden State Parkway
5. Apartment 3-A
6. Mount Washington

> ▶ **Abbreviations** are shortened forms of words.
> Most abbreviations begin with capital letters and end with periods.

Written Practice

A. Write abbreviations where you can for the items below.

1. Indiana
2. Doctor Li
3. Mount Snow
4. 55 miles per hour
5. Madison Avenue
6. the Bright Company

B. Copy this registration form for a bicycle. Fill it in, using abbreviations whenever you can.

```
         DEPARTMENT OF PUBLIC SAFETY
    APPLICATION FOR REGISTRATION OF BICYCLE

Name _____
Address _____ City _____ State _____
Zip _____
Telephone Number _____
Make of Bicycle _____ Color(s) _____
Serial Number _____
Other Distinguishing Characteristics _____

                          Signature _____
                          Date _____
```

- **Writing a Paragraph** Write a newspaper advertisement to sell something you own. Use some abbreviations.

5 | Punctuating Dialogue

Dialogue is written conversation. The exact words of a speaker are set apart from the rest of the sentence with **quotation marks**. The first word of a quotation begins with a capital letter. The punctuation at the end of a quotation goes inside the quotation marks.

> Terry said, "Let's go swimming."
> "This beach is closed today," the officer announced.

Notice that a comma sets off the quotation from the rest of the sentence. The comma comes before the quotation marks.

When a quotation ends in a question mark or an exclamation mark, however, you do not need to add a comma to separate it from the rest of the sentence. One end mark is enough.

> "When will it open?" I asked.

A quotation is sometimes interrupted.

> "Oh, no," <u>complained Rob,</u> "we left the raft."
> "It's too late now," <u>I said.</u> "We'll have to come back."

Notice that the second part of the quotation begins with a capital letter only when the first word (*We'll*) begins a new sentence.

Try It Out

Read the sentences below. Tell how you would punctuate and capitalize each one.

1. What time does Mom's train arrive Tim asked.
2. Dad answered it will arrive at noon.
3. Mom will have lots of stories to tell about her trip to the ranch said Tim she'll have presents for us, too.
4. She'll have photos replied Dad and probably movies.
5. I'm sure she missed the city Tim said.
6. Marta sighed it will be good to have her home.

> ▸ **Dialogue** is written conversation.
> ▸ **Quotation marks** are used to set dialogue apart from the rest of the sentence.
> The first word of a quotation begins with a capital letter.
> Punctuation belongs inside the closing quotation marks.
> Commas separate a quotation from the rest of the sentence.

Written Practice

Write these sentences, punctuating and capitalizing the quotations correctly.

1. Benjamin Franklin said little strokes fell great oaks.
2. If our American way of life fails the child, it fails us all said Pearl S. Buck.
3. I am not a Virginian Patrick Henry said but an American.
4. Martin Luther King, Jr. said I have a dream.
5. One has to grow up with good talk in order to form the habit of it Helen Hayes said.
6. Sherlock Holmes said it's elementary, my dear Watson.
7. Success said Emily Dickinson is counted sweetest by those who ne'er succeed.
8. Walt Whitman wrote I hear America singing.
9. Mark Twain said when a teacher calls a boy by his entire name, it means trouble.
10. The mere absence of war is not peace said John F. Kennedy.
11. D.H. Lawrence said the living moment is everything.
12. The road to ignorance said George Bernard Shaw is paved with good intentions.
13. Anything you're good at contributes to happiness said Bertrand Russell.
14. Thomas Mann said thoughts come clearly while one walks.

- **Writing Sentences** Write a dialogue between yourself and a friend, using at least five quotations. Punctuate and capitalize your quotations correctly.

6 | Titles

Titles of books, magazines, newspapers, songs, and other works are treated in special ways. The nouns, verbs, and other important words in a title are always capitalized. Short words such as *a, and, or, an, the, at, to, with, up,* and *for* are capitalized only if they begin or end a title.

"**The M**ouse **T**hat **W**on the **R**ace"

Titles of books, magazines, and newspapers are underlined. In print, such titles appear in slanted type called *italics.* (*Washington Post*)

He reads the morning <u>Washington Post</u> on the train.
We started a new magazine called <u>Sport Report</u>.

Titles of short stories, articles, songs, poems, and book chapters should be enclosed in quotation marks.

The poem "This Is My Rock" tells about a special place.
The third chapter is entitled "Planting Your Garden."
My song "Butterflies in the Snow" was not published.

Try It Out

A. Tell how you would write these titles correctly.

1. chicago sun times (newspaper)
2. the necklace (short story)
3. how to be a mime (article)
4. live it up (book)
5. the raven (poem)
6. time (magazine)

B. How would you punctuate and capitalize the titles below?

7. I wrote a poem called outside at recess.
8. A magazine for young writers, cricket, published it.
9. New york times readers live all over the world.
10. I read an article called today's american family.
11. At the school festival, we sang moon river.

The important words and the first and last words in a title are
capitalized.
Titles of books, magazines, and newspapers are underlined.
Titles of short stories, articles, songs, poems, and book chapters
are enclosed in quotation marks.

Written Practice

Copy these sentences, writing the titles correctly.

1. An evening herald reporter interviewed the mayor about his
   article in this month's post.
2. In our card catalog, I found a book called aesop's fables.
3. One of my favorite American short stories is the man without a country.
4. Willie Nelson sang pick up the tempo with Waylon Jennings.
5. I have just discovered the magazine smithsonian.
6. Our social studies teacher read Archibald MacLeish's poem
   voyage to the moon.
7. A new poet, Carol Wenger, read her poem spring pools.
8. In what weekly magazine did the article space shuttle of the
   80's appear?
9. The first chapter of this book is entitled off again.
10. A review of his book appeared in today's chicago tribune.
11. Sharon recited concord hymn, a poem by Ralph Waldo
    Emerson.
12. The last song on the album is the rainbow connection.
13. Charles Dickens edited a magazine called household words.
14. The evening chronicle in London published his articles.
15. Oliver twist, hard times, and a tale of two cities are three
    Dickens novels.

- **Writing Sentences**   Make a list of five of your favorite songs,
  poems, books, magazines, or short stories. Write a sentence for
  each title.

we, us

The pronouns *we* and *us* are often used with nouns.

we sixth-graders   us girls

You use *we* with the subject of a sentence.

<u>We sixth-graders</u> are the state spelling champions.

You also use *we* when it follows a linking verb.

The winning hockey players were <u>we girls</u>.

The object pronoun *us* is used with the object of a verb.

The team needs <u>us fans</u> in the bleachers.

To make sure you are using the right pronoun, ask yourself which pronoun would fit best if it were used alone.

<u>We</u> are the state spelling champions.
The winning hockey players are <u>we</u>.
The team needs <u>us</u> in the bleachers.

To use the pronouns *we* or *us* correctly with a noun in a sentence, first look at the noun.
If the noun is the subject of the sentence or if it follows a linking verb, use the pronoun *we* with it.
If the noun is the object after an action verb, use the pronoun *us* with it.

Practice

A. Choose the correct pronoun for each sentence. If you have trouble, ask yourself which pronoun would fit best if it were used alone.

1. (We, Us) students are learning to program a computer.
2. The demonstrators are (we, us) girls.
3. (We, Us) parents should learn about computers, too.
4. The most confused students were (we, us) boys.
5. Our instructor watched (we, us) students patiently.
6. The central processing unit puzzled (we, us) adults.
7. Ms. Gaal put (we, us) beginners in front of the terminal.
8. The first ones at the keyboard were (we, us) children.
9. (We, Us) students were surprised at its speed.
10. (We, Us) teachers are learning more about data input.

B. Choose the pronoun *we* or *us* to complete each sentence. Write the sentences.

11. ____ tourists saw the Statue of Liberty, a 151-foot statue in New York Harbor.
12. The statue impresses ____ Americans because of its size and its beauty.
13. ____ students learned that the statue's full name is Liberty Enlightening the World.
14. ____ girls took a close-up picture of the torch.
15. Our guide took ____ boys up to the statue's crown.
16. The most excited tourists were ____ students.
17. ____ girls climbed the stairs inside the statue.
18. ____ citizens are proud of our Statue of Liberty.
19. This symbol always welcomes ____ travelers home.
20. ____ Americans have one of the largest and most famous statues in the world.

• **Writing a Paragraph** Write a short paragraph about something you have done. Use *we* with a noun and *us* with a noun at least once.

Homographs and Homophones

Some words look or sound alike but have different meanings: *bear–bear*, *nose–knows*. It is important to remember that words can have identical spellings or pronunciations without having identical meanings.

Homographs are words that are spelled the same but have different meanings and different histories. They may also be pronounced differently: **pres′** ent,   pre **sent.′** What are the homographs in these sentences?

A new conductor will lead the orchestra tonight.
Most new automobiles use gasoline without lead in it.

In order to find the exact meaning of a homograph, you should read the entire sentence. The other words in the sentence will provide clues. A dictionary can also help you. What is the meaning of *lead* in each sentence above?

Homophones are words that are pronounced the same but have different meanings and are spelled differently. Read the following sentences. Which three words are homophones?

I eat a pear with my lunch every day.
Some cooks pare fruits and vegetables with a special knife.
This pair of hiking boots will prevent blisters.

What does the homophone in each sentence mean?

▶ **Homographs** are words that are spelled the same but have different meanings and histories. Homographs are also sometimes pronounced differently.
▶ **Homophones** are words that sound alike but have different meanings and spellings.

Practice

A. Choose the correct homophone in parentheses for each of these sentences. If you need help, check a dictionary.

1. How many rivers flow (threw, through) the (capital, capitol) of Alabama?
2. Fran hurried (passed, past) on her bicycle so fast that her (pedal, peddle) flew off.
3. My brother likes to rush (through, threw) dinner but linger over (desert, dessert).
4. The (principle, principal) suggested that every student (buy, by) a dictionary.
5. (Buy, By) the middle of next month, I will have (passed, past) all my tests.
6. Our mom (led, lead) the Independence Day parade to the front door of the (capitol, capital).
7. If you believe in the basic (principal, principle) of honesty, you will not want to (brake, break) any rules.
8. Daryl tried to patch his broken hand (break, brake) with a strip of (lead, led).
9. The general told the soldiers to (desert, dessert) the fort.
10. We use (coarse, course) sandpaper first on most of our woodworking projects.

B. Write a sentence for each homograph below. Make each sentence show that the homographs have different meanings.

11. post / post
12. duck / duck
13. bowl / bowl
14. patch / patch
15. clear / clear
16. park / park
17. light / light
18. lap / lap
19. maroon / maroon
20. palm / palm

- **Writing Sentences** Create a list of five more pairs of homographs and homophones that you use or hear in everyday speech. Write a sentence for each word. You should have ten sentences in all.

Review

- **Reviewing End Punctuation** *(p. 207)* Write the correct end punctuation mark for each sentence.

    1. Stop at this camping site for the day
    2. What a large bird that is
    3. Did you bring the binoculars
    4. We can use these twigs to start a fire
    5. Do we have time for a hike before dark

- **Commas in a Series** *(pp. 208–209)* Rewrite and correctly punctuate the following sentences.

    6. My cousins have visited Spain Italy and France.
    7. Greg Bob and Cynthia visited us last summer.
    8. We took them to cookouts to the beach and to a TV studio.
    9. Salad barbecued chicken fruit and milk were served.
    10. Their bags held stones shells seaweed and driftwood.

- **More Uses for Commas** *(pp. 210–211)* Rewrite these sentences inserting commas where needed.

    11. Kathleen would you please set the timer?
    12. Yes but how much time do we need?
    13. The directions call for two minutes but we will need six.
    14. The developer a strong-smelling chemical is too cool.
    15. Put the film on this line to dry Jay.

- **Abbreviations** *(pp. 212–213)* Write the correct abbreviation for each of these items.

    16. Registered Nurse
    17. Mount Rushmore
    18. Public Broadcasting Service
    19. P E P Company, Incorporated
    20. Putney, Vermont
    21. 2200 Lake Boulevard
    22. Post Office
    23. Apartment S

- **Punctuating Dialogue** *(pp. 214–215)*   Rewrite each sentence, punctuating and capitalizing the quotations correctly.

24. Our custodian said I'll be glad to help you move.
25. I finally won a race said the runner.
26. I asked have you any ripe oranges?
27. If you do not know the answer she yelled then say so.
28. May I help you the operator asked.

- **Titles** *(pp. 216–217)*   Write each title correctly.

29. My favorite newspaper is the herald traveler.
30. I have just written a story called the revolving door.
31. The poem snow is very short.
32. The book I am reading now is island of the blue dolphins.
33. On our bus trip, we sang found a peanut.

- **Using Words Correctly** *(pp. 218–219)*   Choose the correct subject or object pronoun for each sentence.

34. Mrs. Kennedy lent (we, us) players a new court.
35. (We, Us) teammates helped raise money to build one.
36. (We, Us) parents had a craft and bake sale.
37. The teachers wanted (we, us) workers to have cool drinks.
38. The owners of a new basketball court are (we, us) Stilts.

- **Building Vocabulary** *(pp. 220–221)*   Choose the correct homophones for each sentence.

39. His sense of duty would not let him (desert, dessert) ship.
40. I swam (through, threw) seaweed to reach shore.
41. (Coarse, Course) fabric can never be softened.
42. The candidate was a woman of (principal, principle).
43. Our class (lead, led) the school in math scores.
44. The cheerleaders marched (passed, past) the bleachers.
45. Her sewing machine was run by a foot (pedal, peddle).
46. I expect to be home (buy, by) lunch time.
47. Most drivers use the (brake, break) at a yellow light.

1 | Reviewing Friendly Letters

"Why should I learn to write letters?" you may ask. "I can always call my family and friends on the telephone."

Often, this is true. There are some situations, however, when the pleasure that a letter can bring to your friend or relative is worth the little bit of extra effort it takes to write it.

Suppose that your grandmother is ill. You sit down and write a friendly letter telling her that you hope she feels better soon. You include news about yourself and your family, too. Your grandmother can read and reread the words you wrote especially to her as often as she wants. She can share your letter with others, and she can save it.

Perhaps you receive a birthday present from your uncle. Since he has taken the time to choose a present that you will enjoy, it is important for you to take time to write a thank-you letter that tells him exactly why you like the baseball glove he gave you.

These are just some of the reasons for writing friendly letters. Other reasons might be to invite someone to a party or other event, to accept or refuse someone's invitation to you, or just to say hello to a friend or relative you do not see often and to share with that person news of what you have been doing.

The writing style of a friendly letter is casual and informal. You should write as if you were actually speaking to your friend or relative.

Read the friendly letter on the next page.

54 Ridge Road
Portland, OR 97204
November 1, 1983

Dear Aunt Polly,

    Thank you for inviting me to spend Thanksgiving week-end with you. Mom and Dad said that I can come, and I'm really looking forward to it!

    I've already checked the bus schedule. I can get a bus right after school on Wednesday that will get me to your town at 8 o'clock. I can't wait to see you and to taste your wonderful turkey and stuffing!

Your nephew,

Jonathan

- What was Jonathan's reason for writing this friendly letter?
- What are the five parts of a friendly letter?
- What words are capitalized in the heading? in the greeting? in the closing? What punctuation marks are used in each?
- How many main ideas are discussed in the body of Jonathan's letter? How do you know when a new idea begins?
- Is the style of writing formal or informal?

Practice

Follow the steps below to write a friendly letter.

A. Think of a person you would like to write to. Choose two or three topics that will interest that person.

B. Write a first draft just to get your ideas down on paper.

C. Revise your letter to make it more interesting. Read the letter to someone else, and ask for suggestions.

D. Proofread your work, and check the form of your letter.

E. Make a final copy, address an envelope, and mail it.

2 | Form of a Business Letter

One way in which a business letter is different from a friendly letter is its form. A business letter has one part that a friendly letter does not have. Examine the business letter below. Look at the six parts and the required punctuation in each part.

HEADING	15 Parkside Lane Bakersville, IL 60600 May 25, 1983
INSIDE ADDRESS	Mr. Jacob Stein Director, Summer Extension Program Baker Community College 7 College Avenue Bakersville, IL 60600
GREETING	Dear Mr. Stein:
BODY	Please send me information about Baker Community College's summer program for elementary and junior high school students. I saw your advertisement in Sunday's *Herald,* and I am very interested in registering for a typing class this summer. I am in the sixth grade.
CLOSING	Yours truly,
SIGNATURE	*Catherine Miller*

- What are the six parts of a business letter?
- Which part does not appear in a friendly letter? (Look back at page 226 for help.) What facts does this new part give?
- What words are capitalized in the heading, the inside address, the greeting, and the closing? What punctuation is used in each of these parts?

The form of a business letter also differs in another way. Look back at Catherine's letter on page 227. Notice that the greeting is followed by a colon (:). What punctuation mark follows the greeting in a friendly letter?

Because Catherine had seen a newspaper advertisement giving Mr. Stein's name, she knew that her letter should be addressed to him. Often, however, you will not know the name of the person who will read your business letter. In that case, you may use the title of the person, or simply the name of the company, in the inside address and the greeting. Here are two examples.

INSIDE **ADDRESS**	Personnel Director Apex Insurance Agency 3890 Isherwood Avenue New York, NY 10005	Premium Pet Products 498 Blackstone Drive Oklahoma City, OK 73102
GREETING	Dear Personnel Director:	Dear Premium Pet Products:

Since you usually do not know the person who will read your business letter, the closing should be polite and formal rather than friendly and personal. In a business letter, use closings such as *Sincerely* or *Yours truly,* not *Your friend* or *Love.*

You should use your full name in the signature of a business letter. Can you tell why?

Practice

Write the following business letter on your paper, correcting any errors in business letter form. Add any parts that are missing. Use your own name and address and today's date.

Creamy Yogurt Company
99 sunshine boulevard
Los Angeles Ca 90054

Please send me one Creamy Yogurt beach towel in blue. I am enclosing lids from four cartons of Creamy Yogurt and a check for $3.99.

3 | Style of a Business Letter

Another way in which a business letter is different from a friendly letter is its writing style. The language, or style, of a business letter is formal and polite. The letter should be brief and to the point, including all necessary details but no unnecessary personal information. In other words, it should be **businesslike.**

Parts of two different letters are shown below. Notice that both of them use good businesslike writing.

Please send me one of the plastic rain ponchos that were advertised in the May issue of *Outdoor Life.* I would like a yellow poncho in size small. Enclosed is a check for $12.00 to cover the cost of the poncho, postage, and handling.

On June 12, I ordered a yellow rain poncho, size small, from your company. I enclosed with my order a check for $12.00. The advertisement in *Outdoor Life* said to allow six weeks for delivery. It has been almost twelve weeks since I placed the order, and I have not received the poncho. Please check your records, and let me know if my order was received. Thank you for giving this problem your prompt attention.

- What is the purpose of the first letter? What facts does it include for that purpose? Are any necessary facts missing? If so, which facts? Does the letter include any information not related to its purpose? If so, what information?
- What is the purpose of the second letter? What information does it include for that purpose? Does it include any unnecessary facts? What does this letter request the company to do?
- Is the style of each letter polite? Is it direct and to the point? Give examples.

Notice that, even though the purpose of the second letter is to complain, the writer manages to express this purpose in a polite, businesslike style.

Read Bill Nelson's business letter below. Notice that he uses the proper business-letter form but that he has problems with style.

99 Magnolia Drive
Atlanta, GA 30043
March 19, 1983

Mr. Frank C. Fields
President, Surprise Package Company
444 Madison Avenue
New York, NY 10046

Dear Mr. Fields:

How are you? I am fine. I ordered something that I saw advertised in a magazine. In February I sent your company money. I want you to return my money or send me what I ordered. Two and one half months have passed, and I still have not received what I ordered. What's the matter with your company, anyway? I've ordered lots of things in the mail before and never had any problem.

Sincerely,

Bill Nelson

- What is Bill's main reason or purpose for writing the letter?
- What necessary information has Bill left out?
- What unnecessary information has he included?
- Is the style of his letter businesslike? Give examples.

Practice

Rewrite Bill's letter to the Surprise Package Company. Make up any information necessary for Mr. Fields to satisfy Bill's request. Leave out any unnecessary information. Change any sentences that are not written in a businesslike style.

4 | Addressing an Envelope

No matter how hard you work at writing a friendly letter or business letter, your letter may not be delivered unless you address the envelope clearly and correctly.

The name and address of the person to whom the letter is written go in the center of the envelope. For a business letter, the address on the envelope should be the same as the inside address on the letter. The return address, which is the writer's name and address, goes in the top left-hand corner. Do not forget to put a stamp in the top right-hand corner.

Here is the envelope for Bill Nelson's letter to Surprise Package Company. Notice how he has written each state abbreviation. You can find postal abbreviations like these for all the states in the Zip Code directory of the U.S. Postal Service. Some dictionaries and encyclopedias also list these abbreviations.

RETURN ADDRESS

Bill Nelson
99 Magnolia Drive
Atlanta, GA 30043

Stamp

ADDRESS

Mr. Frank C. Fields
President, Surprise Package Company
444 Madison Avenue
New York, NY 10046

Practice

Draw an envelope on a piece of paper. Address the envelope for Catherine Miller's letter to Baker Community College on page 227.

5 | Getting Started

A business letter is written to do a specific job. It is not intended to entertain, to cheer someone up, or to share news about yourself. Those are jobs for a friendly letter.

You have learned that some typical jobs for a business letter are to order something, to request information, and to request action about a problem.

Think of an example for each of these types of business letters. What have you seen advertised that you would like to order? What do you want to know more about, either for your schoolwork, for a hobby, or just because you are interested? What person or organization can give you that information? Have you had a problem with an item you bought or ordered—a damaged or missing part? something that was not as the advertisement promised? How could writing a business letter help solve the problem?

Practice

A. Choose one of the jobs suggested above. Discuss with a classmate what information a letter should include to do that job.

B. Suppose the label on your new T-shirt says, "Machine wash in warm water." You followed the instructions, and now the T-shirt fits your baby brother! What information about the T-shirt would you include in a business letter to the company? What action would you ask the company to take?

Steps for Writing a Letter   Here are the steps for writing a letter. You will follow these steps to write a business letter.

Step One	Choose a topic.
Step Two	Write your letter.
Step Three	Revise your letter.
Step Four	Proofread your letter.
Step Five	Make a final copy, and mail your letter.

6 | Step One
Choose a Topic

You have learned that business letters can do many different jobs. Jason thought of several reasons he had for writing business letters. This is his list.

-ask for information about tennis lessons given by the town recreation department

-order a model kit that was advertised in <u>Hobby Time</u> magazine

-complain about the last model kit I ordered, which arrived without an instruction sheet

Jason thought about the topics on his list. They were all good reasons for writing business letters. Which one would he do first?

He knew that tennis lessons would not start for several months, so he was in no real hurry to write that letter. He decided that he did not want to order a new model kit until he straightened out the problem with the one he had just received. Therefore Jason decided to write to the Kit 'n' Caboodle Company about the missing instructions.

Assignment
- **Make a List**
- **Choose a Topic**

A. Make a list of some jobs that business letters could do for you. Think of things you would like to order (look at the advertisement section in the back of some magazines if you need ideas), subjects about which you would like information, or problems you need to bring to someone's attention.

B. Look at your list. Which topic is the most important or the one you are most interested in writing about? Circle that topic on your list.

7 | Step Two
Write Your Letter

Jason worked on the first draft of his letter to the Kit 'n' Caboodle Company. He did not know the name or title of anyone there, so he addressed the letter to the company. He did not worry yet about mistakes or about proper business-letter form. He would go back and fix those things later. Right now he was concerned with getting his ideas down on paper.

Jason's first draft

Dear Kit 'n' caboodle company,

My name is Jason Thomas and ~~I am in the sixth~~ I am twelve years old and I ordered a modle spaceship kit from you in febuary. Making models is my favorite hobby. The kit you sent me does not have an instruction sheet how do you expect me to put it together without instructions. ~~Why~~ I wanted to work on the spaceship last night but I couldn't because I didn't have the instructions and I was so mad because there was nothing on TV.

- What is the purpose of Jason's letter?
- Did Jason include all the information necessary for the letter to do its job? If not, what details are missing?
- Did he include any personal information not suitable for a business letter? Give examples.
- Is the letter polite and businesslike? If not, give examples of sentences that could be written in a more businesslike style. How would you change them? Which sentences would you leave out?

Assignment • Write Your First Draft

Write a first draft of your business letter. Remember that this is the time to get your ideas down on paper. You can correct any mistakes later. Concentrate on stating the point of your letter in clear, businesslike language. You may want to skip lines as you write your draft so that you can make changes in it later.

As you write your business letter, try to keep each of these suggestions in mind.

1. Think about the purpose of your letter. Make sure that every sentence you write relates to that purpose.
2. Make sure that you have included all the necessary details for your letter to accomplish its purpose.
3. Do not include personal information.
4. Use language that is polite and businesslike rather than casual and informal.

Write Your Letter 235

8 | Step Three
Revise Your Letter

When he reread his letter, Jason realized he had left out some important details. Kit 'n' Caboodle sells hundreds of different model kits. He had not identified which kit he had ordered. From the side of his kit box, Jason copied down the exact name of the kit and the model number. He added these details to his letter. He also realized that some of the details he had included were not necessary for his purpose. He crossed them out.

Jason still wondered whether his letter sounded polite and businesslike and whether it would do its job. He decided to read it to his friend Chuck and ask for his opinion.

It is often a good idea to read your writing to someone else to make sure your writing is as clear to someone else as it is to you. This is especially important for a letter because your letter will be received and read by someone without your being there to answer questions. Your letter must stand on its own to do its job.

Chuck listened to Jason's letter and then asked, "Do you want them to send you a whole new kit or just the instruction sheet?"

"Just the instructions," said Jason. "The rest of the kit's okay."

"I think you should tell them that," said Chuck. "It wasn't clear to me. I'd change the last sentence, too," he added. "The company doesn't need to know how mad you are or what's on TV."

Together, Jason and Chuck thought of a more businesslike way to make Jason's point. Jason made the changes on his paper.

Jason's revised letter

Dear Kit 'n' caboodle company,
My name is Jason Thomas ~~and I am~~
~~in the sixth~~ I am twelve years old and
I ordered a <ins>an Apollo</ins> ~~modle~~ spaceship kit, <ins>modle 4360</ins> from

> you in febuary. Making models is my
> favorite hobby. The kit you sent me does
> not have an instruction sheet ~~how do you~~
> ~~expect me to put it together without~~
> ~~instructions.~~ ¶ I cannot begin
> ~~Why~~ I wanted to work on
> without the instructions
> the spaceship last night but I couldn't
> please send me an instruction sheet for the model 4360
> ~~because I didn't have the instructions~~
> Apollo spaceship kit as soon as possible
> ~~and I was so mad because there was~~
> ~~nothing on TV.~~

- What details did Jason add? Why? Where did he write them?
- What sentences did Jason cross out? Why?
- How does Jason remind himself that he will need to indent?

Assignment

- **Revise Your Letter**
- **Discuss Your Letter**

A. Read over your letter, and make any changes that you think will improve it. Ask yourself these questions.

1. What is the purpose of my letter? Does every sentence fit that purpose?
2. Have I included all necessary information?
3. Is my letter written in a polite, businesslike style? Have I included personal information not suitable for a business letter?

B. Read your letter to someone else, and ask for suggestions. If your listener's suggestions are helpful or if you think of ideas on your own during the discussion, make those changes on your letter.

9

Step Four
Proofread Your Letter

After working hard to revise his letter, Jason was ready for the next step—proofreading. This is the time to correct mistakes, such as errors in spelling, punctuation, and capitalization, and to check for correct letter form.

Because Jason had made so many changes in the letter, it was hard to read. Jason decided to copy it over before he proofread it. After doing this, he added the heading, the inside address, the closing, and the signature. Then he checked carefully for errors, using a dictionary to help with spelling.

Jason's letter after proofreading

750 Fountain Street
Louisville, K Y 40202
April 16, 1983

Kit 'n' c̄aboodle c̄ompany
1818 Central āvenue
Los Angeles, CA 90054
Dear Kit 'n' c̄aboodle c̄ompany,
    I ordered an Apollo ~~spaceship~~ kit,
^{model} ~~modle~~ 4360, from you in ~~febuary~~ ^{February}. The
kit you sent me does not have an
instruction sheet.

> *I cannot begin to work on the spaceship without the instructions. please send me an instruction sheet for the model 4360 Apollo spaceship kit as soon as possible.*
>
> *Yours Truly,*
> *Jason Thomas*

- What spelling errors did Jason correct?
- What changes did he make in the heading? in the inside address? in the closing?
- What punctuation mark did Jason put after the greeting?
- What punctuation did he add to the body of the letter? Why?
- Why did he correct the word *please* in his last sentence?

Practice

Proofread the letter below. It contains eighteen errors. Use a dictionary to check spelling. Rewrite the letter correctly.

43 stetson street
Buffalo NY 14202
June 23, 1983

Order department
Wildlife Publishing Company
850 Landon Street
Boston Ma 02208

Dear Order department

Please send me one coppy of the book <u>birds of the northeast</u> that was advertised in <u>Feathered friends</u> magizene. I am enclosing a check for $8.95 the price of the book plus postige.

sincerely

Florence Wilder

Assignment • Proofread Your Letter

Add the heading, inside address, closing, and signature to your business letter. Then proofread it. Ask yourself these questions.

1. Have I used proper business-letter form?
2. Are all the words spelled correctly?
3. Is each paragraph indented?

Grammar skills checklist

4. Have I corrected run-on sentences and sentence fragments?
5. Have I used commas correctly to join the parts of a compound sentence and to set off appositives and items in a series?
6. Have I used homophones and homographs correctly?

10 | Step Five
Make a Final Copy

Jason wanted his letter to make a good impression on the person at the Kit 'n' Caboodle Company who would read it. He had been very careful about the form and style of his letter, and he wanted the appearance of his letter to reflect that care. He decided to type the letter in order to make it appear more business-like. Perhaps a professional look would bring a quicker reply, too.

Jason used plain white letter-size paper and a business-size envelope. He also used a sheet of carbon paper since he wanted to keep a copy of his letter.

He placed the sheet of carbon paper, carbon side down, on one sheet of letter paper. Then he placed another sheet of letter paper, for the original, on top. He inserted these sheets in his typewriter and carefully typed the letter.

Before typing his signature, he skipped four lines. Jason removed the paper from the typewriter and signed his name in ink on the original, in the space above his typewritten signature. Then he typed the address and return address on the envelope. At this point, Jason took the time to check his letter and envelope carefully. He wanted to be certain that he had not made any mistakes on his final copy. He put the original letter in the envelope, put a stamp on the envelope, and mailed the letter. He kept the carbon copy with the model kit. If he did not get a reply from Kit 'n' Caboodle in a few weeks, the copy would remind him to write another letter.

Assignment
- **Make a Final Copy**
- **Mail Your Letter**

A. Make a final copy of your business letter, either typed, like Jason's, or written neatly in ink. You might also want to make a carbon copy to keep, as Jason did.

B. Check to make sure you have copied correctly.

C. Address the envelope, put a stamp on it, and mail your letter.

Modifiers

1 | Adjectives

Read the sentences below. How is each one different?

My dog is a <u>young</u> terrier.
My dog is a <u>wire-haired</u> terrier.
My dog is an <u>energetic</u> terrier.

Notice how the underlined adjectives change the meaning of each sentence. An **adjective** modifies a noun or a pronoun. It adds to the meaning. *Young*, *wire-haired*, and *energetic* tell what kind of terrier the dog is. Adjectives can also tell which one and how many.

<u>That</u> retriever runs faster than <u>those</u> dogs.
<u>Some</u> people have <u>two</u> retrievers as pets.

Which of the underlined adjectives above tell which one? Which tell how many? Do these adjectives come before the nouns they modify? Adjectives can also follow nouns. In the following sentences, the adjectives are underlined. The noun they modify is in dark type.

The **campers**, <u>hungry</u> and <u>tired</u>, stumbled home.
They had carried their heavy equipment across twenty miles of **terrain**, <u>treacherous</u> yet <u>beautiful</u>.

As you know, a predicate adjective follows a linking verb. Predicate adjectives modify the noun or pronoun that is the subject of the sentence.

We were <u>anxious</u> for their return.
Alexander feels <u>sleepy</u>.

An adjective may consist of more than one word. When such an adjective precedes a noun, it is usually hyphenated.

The Pentagon is a <u>five-sided</u> **building** near Washington, D.C.
My <u>part-time</u> **job** helped me buy this typewriter.

Try It Out

Identify the adjectives in these sentences. Do they tell what kind, which one, or how many?

1. Gene builds old-fashioned doll houses.
2. They are unusual.
3. That house has three floors.
4. The rooms, small and bright, look empty.
5. Tiny electric lights shine through glass windows.
6. The miniature furniture inside this house includes a fifty-year-old grandfather clock.

> ▸ An **adjective** adds to the meaning of a noun or pronoun.
> An adjective can tell which one, what kind, or how many.

Written Practice

List the adjectives you find in this paragraph. Beside each adjective, write the noun or pronoun it modifies.

Columbia is amazing. It has brought us into a new era of space travel. This spacecraft is an orbital truck. It will carry scientific experiments and maintenance workers into orbit. It is an important pioneer in space development. Do you suppose people will eventually settle in outer space?

- **Writing Sentences**   For each noun below, write one adjective that tells what kind, another that tells how many, and a third that tells which one. Then use each noun in a sentence with one of the adjectives.

  1. suit   3. stars   5. meal   7. parrot
  2. telescope   4. sunset   6. minibike   8. cactus

- **Writing a Paragraph**   Write a paragraph about cars, or use a topic of your choice. Use adjectives to modify nouns and pronouns. Underline each adjective you use.

2 | Articles

The adjectives *a*, *an*, and *the* are called **articles**. An article can come before a noun or before another adjective.

<u>The</u> fly ball hit <u>an</u> old shed and smashed <u>a</u> windowpane.

The refers to a specific item (singular or plural). *A* or *an* refers to any one item of a group or type. Use *a* before words that begin with a consonant sound *(a toe)*. Use *an* before words that begin with a vowel sound *(an ankle, an hour)*.

Try It Out

Choose the correct article(s) to complete each sentence.

1. (A, An) windmill can give energy.
2. (A, The) windmill in our back yard is very old.
3. It once was (an, the) efficient tool.
4. (A, The) blades still turn in (a, an) occasional strong wind.

> ► *A*, *an*, and *the* are special adjectives called **articles**.
> *The* refers to a specific item or items. *A* and *an* refer to any one item in a group.

Written Practice

Write the article that completes each sentence correctly.

1. What is (a, the) news?
2. (A, An) lion had escaped.
3. It found (a, an) open car.
4. (A, The) lion got inside.
5. (A, An) passerby saw it.
6. (An, The) officials got it.
7. It's back at (a, the) zoo.
8. What (a, an) day it had!

- **Writing Sentences**   Write five sentences. Use *a*, *an*, and *the* twice each.

3 | Comparing with Adjectives

You can use adjectives to compare people, places, or things.

> The Washington Monument is a <u>tall</u> structure.
> The Prudential Tower is <u>taller</u>.
> The Empire State Building is the <u>tallest</u> of the three.

To show a difference between two things, you use the **comparative** form of the adjective (*taller*). To show a difference among three or more things, you use the **superlative** form of the adjective (*tallest*). Most one-syllable adjectives form their comparatives by adding *-er*. They form their superlatives by adding *-est*. Most adjectives of two or more syllables use *more* to form the comparative and *most* to form the superlative. Study the chart.

Adjective	Comparative	Superlative
short	shorter	shortest
late	later	latest
plentiful	more plentiful	most plentiful

When you are using comparisons, do not combine *-er* with the word *more* or *-est* with the word *most*.

INCORRECT: Peaches are more sweeter than lemons.
CORRECT: Peaches are sweeter than lemons.
INCORRECT: This is the most shortest rope I have.
CORRECT: This is the shortest rope I have.

Some adjectives change their form completely.

Adjective	Comparative	Superlative
much	more	most
bad	worse	worst
little	less	least

Try It Out

Complete each sentence with the correct form of the adjective.

1. Snorkeling is ____ than water skiing. (difficult)
2. Where is the ____ scenery of all in Florida? (beautiful)
3. Becky was the ____ person in the swimming class. (young)
4. The weather on Tuesday was ____ than today. (bad)
5. Brady is ____ than Becky. (old)
6. What major country has the ____ crime? (little)

Use the **comparative** (*-er* or *more*) form of an adjective to compare two people, places, or things.

Use the **superlative** (*-est* or *most*) form of an adjective to compare three or more people, places, or things.

Some adjectives change completely in the comparative and superlative forms.

Written Practice

Write the correct form of the adjective in parentheses.

1. This year's *Guinness Book of World Records* has ____ facts than last year's. (much)
2. The ____ human bone of all is in the middle ear. (small)
3. Blue whales are ____ than right whales. (large)
4. Is English ____ to learn than Spanish? (difficult)
5. The ____ star we can see is known as the Dog Star. (bright)
6. The ____ word in the English language is *the*. (common)
7. Why is Kauai, Hawaii, the ____ place in the world? (wet)
8. Emeralds are ____ than diamonds. (colorful)
9. America's ____ dog is the poodle. (popular)
10. Is the Library of Congress the world's ____ library? (good)

- **Writing Sentences**　Write five sentences. Use an adjective in the comparative or the superlative form in each one.

4 | Proper Adjectives

An adjective formed from a proper noun is called a **proper adjective**. Like a proper noun, a proper adjective is capitalized.

Mexico produces jewelry. This is a Mexican silver bracelet.

Read both sentences above. Which word in the sentence on the left is a proper noun? Which word in the sentence on the right is a proper adjective? Notice the adjective ending that is added to the proper noun *Mexico* to form the proper adjective *Mexican*. What spelling change has taken place? The endings most often used to change proper nouns into proper adjectives are *-an*, *-ish*, and *-ese*. Often there are other changes in spelling. Study the examples below.

Proper Noun	Proper Adjective
Ireland	Irish (Irish seacoast)
Italy	Italian (Italian painting)
Japan	Japanese (Japanese food)

Try It Out

Form a proper adjective from each underlined noun, and say the phrase. If you need help, you may use a dictionary. The first one has been done for you.

1. bullfighter from <u>Spain</u>
   Spanish bullfighter
2. ruins of <u>Rome</u>
3. pottery from <u>Mexico</u>
4. hotels of <u>Europe</u>
5. imports from <u>China</u>
6. provinces of <u>Canada</u>
7. settlers from <u>England</u>

> ► A **proper adjective** is an adjective formed from a proper noun.
>
> Proper adjectives begin with a capital letter.

Written Practice

A. Write each proper adjective, and capitalize it correctly.

1. Some alaskan dogs are used to pull sleds.
2. The dachshund, a german breed, was used to hunt badgers.
3. An english sheepdog has a long, shaggy coat.
4. Pictures of greyhounds were found in ancient egyptian temples.
5. A mexican dog, the Chihuahua, is a small breed.
6. The pug is a chinese breed that has a snub nose.
7. The australian dingo is a wild dog.
8. Our neighbors own an irish setter pup.
9. Dad built a victorian doghouse for our mutt.
10. This spaniel looks like the dogs pictured on japanese vases.

B. To complete each sentence, write a proper adjective from the noun in parentheses. Use a dictionary if you need help.

11. Sukiyaki is a popular ____ dish. (Japan)
12. Have you ever eaten sweet ____ sausages? (Italy)
13. ____ food is deliciously hot and spicy. (Mexico)
14. My father's favorite cheese is ____ cheddar. (England)
15. We celebrated my birthday at a ____ restaurant. (China)
16. Pineapples are grown on ____ plantations. (Hawaii)
17. The first course of a ____ meal is often fish. (Sweden)

- **Writing Sentences** Write five sentences about animals, styles of dress, or food. Use as many proper adjectives as you can. Look up the correct spelling in a dictionary if necessary.

5 | Adverbs That Modify Verbs

An **adverb** is a word that modifies a verb, an adjective, or another adverb. Adverbs that modify verbs answer the questions, How? Where? When? or To what extent?

HOW: Jackie <u>quickly</u> left.
WHERE: She went <u>downtown</u>.
WHEN: <u>Soon</u> she returned.
TO WHAT EXTENT: She explained <u>thoroughly</u>.

Try It Out

Find the adverbs below. Name the verb each one modifies.

1. Yesterday we packed fast.
2. I really enjoyed the trip.
3. Mom drove carefully.
4. Dad always checked maps.
5. Then we arrived safely.
6. Today I fished alone.

▶ An **adverb** can modify a verb, an adjective, or another adverb.
An adverb that modifies a verb describes how, where, when, or to what extent.

Written Practice

Write the adverbs and the verb each one modifies.

The large-kerneled peanuts develop strangely. First, the flowers wither. Then the stems slowly turn downward. Finally, they enter the ground. There they form seed pods, or shells. Farmers carefully harvest these pods. Then the sun dries the pods naturally, or the farmers dry them artificially.

• **Writing a Paragraph**   Write the four questions adverbs answer. List two adverbs for each. Use your adverbs in a paragraph.

6 | Adverbs That Modify Adjectives

Adverbs can also modify adjectives. They tell how or to what extent.

It is a <u>rather</u> **sad** story.   My aunt is quite comical.
A <u>very</u> **big** bubble burst.   An unusally noisy crowd left.

In the sentences on the left, the adverbs are underlined. They tell how sad or how big. The adjectives they modify are in dark type. Find an adverb in each sentence on the right. What adjectives do they modify?

Try It Out

Identify the adverbs in these phrases.

1. perfectly simple life
2. dreadfully long wait
3. completely safe elevator
4. starkly realistic dreams
5. deliberately rude remark
6. terribly painful sunburn

> Adverbs that modify adjectives tell how or to what extent.

Written Practice

Write the adverbs that modify adjectives in these sentences. Then write the adjective that each one modifies.

1. Even in the unusually dark room, Sue could see Tiffany.
2. On the floor lay the formerly active goldfish.
3. With very tender care, Sue put Tiffany back into the tank.
4. Soon the thoroughly rigid body became surprisingly frisky.

- **Writing Sentences**   Use adverbs to modify adjectives in five sentences.

7 | Comparing with Adverbs

Like adjectives, adverbs can show comparison. To compare two things, use the **comparative** form. To compare more than two things, use the **superlative** form. One-syllable adverbs usually add -*er* for the comparative and -*est* for the superlative.

ADVERB: Donald skated <u>fast</u>.
COMPARATIVE: Sheila skated <u>faster</u> than Donald.
SUPERLATIVE: Of the three of us, Alberto skated <u>fastest</u>.

Many adverbs that end in -*ly* add *more* to form the comparative and *most* to form the superlative.

Adverb	Comparative	Superlative
skillfully	more skillfully	most skillfully
frequently	more frequently	most frequently
heavily	more heavily	most heavily

Some adverbs become completely new words in their comparative and superlative forms.

Adverb	Comparative	Superlative
well	better	best
badly	worse	worst
little	less	least

Do not combine the -*er* ending with the word *more* or the -*est* ending with the word *most*.

INCORRECT: Are you skating more better?
CORRECT: Are you skating <u>better</u>?
INCORRECT: Of all the crew, I worked most hardest.
CORRECT: Of all the crew, I worked <u>hardest</u>.

Try It Out

Which adverb in parentheses is correct for each sentence?

1. Jay makes speeches (better, more better) than Beverly.
2. Beverly speaks (more slowly, most slowly) than Jay.
3. Rudy was the (less, least) interesting of all the speakers.
4. We rehearsed (worse, more worse) today than the day before.
5. Of all the students, Dee worked (hardest, harder).

Many one-syllable adverbs add *-er* to form the comparative, and *-est* to form the superlative.

Many adverbs that end in *-ly* form the comparative by adding *more* and the superlative by adding *most*.

Some adverbs change completely in the comparative and superlative forms.

Written Practice

Complete each sentence by writing the correct comparative or superlative form of the adverb in parentheses.

1. Grandpa tells stories even ＿＿ than Mom. (wonderfully)
2. He visits us ＿＿ now than in the past. (frequently)
3. He speaks ＿＿ than a professional storyteller. (vividly)
4. Of all his stories, I listen ＿＿ to tales of his boyhood adventures. (eagerly)
5. Did his pet frog really jump ＿＿ than Gus's frog? (high)
6. Of all the places he saw, he recalled Iowa ＿＿. (clearly)
7. He builds up the suspense ＿＿ than TV does. (skillfully)
8. His modern stories are ＿＿ interesting of all. (little)
9. Do you learn ＿＿ from a story than from a lecture? (well)
10. Of the four grandchildren, I listen ＿＿. (enthusiastically)

- **Writing Sentences** Write five sentences, using the comparative or superlative forms of five different adverbs.

Comparing with Adverbs 253

8 | Negatives

A **negative** is a word that means "no." Negatives can reverse the meaning of a sentence.

> Lynn is on the basketball team.
> Lynn is <u>not</u> on the basketball team.

Some of the most common negatives are *no, none, not, no one, never, nothing, nowhere,* and *nobody.* Contractions using *not* are also negatives.

> · Don <u>never</u> mows the lawn.   Sid <u>can't</u> go with us.
> <u>Isn't</u> this your coat?   <u>Nowhere</u> else is so sunny.

When two negatives are used in the same sentence, a double negative is the result. Double negatives should be avoided so that your meaning will be clear.

> INCORRECT: Nobody can't lift this box.
> **CORRECT**: <u>Nobody</u> can lift this box.

Often there is more than one way to avoid using a double negative. Study the following examples.

> INCORRECT: I can't find nothing to wear.
> **CORRECT**: I <u>can't</u> find anything to wear.
> **CORRECT**: I can find <u>nothing</u> to wear.

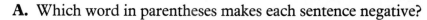

Try It Out

A. Which word in parentheses makes each sentence negative?

1. This flashlight has (no, some) batteries.
2. There are (no, few) batteries in this drawer.
3. (Someone, No one) has gone to the store this week.
4. Batteries were (nowhere, everywhere) to be found.
5. These wax candles (never, always) fail.

B. Choose the word in parentheses that completes each sentence correctly. Avoid double negatives.

6. Kerry didn't have (any, no) trouble on the hike.
7. No one (never, ever) heard him complain.
8. Nothing (ever, never) seemed to bother him.
9. Not even the mosquitoes (couldn't, could) disturb him.
10. Then we discovered he wasn't (nowhere, anywhere) in the camp.

> ▸ A **negative** is a word that is used to reverse the meaning of the sentence.
> Avoid using two negatives together.

Written Practice

Rewrite each sentence correctly to avoid double negatives.

1. The Inca civilization in South America doesn't exist no more.
2. The Incas never had no system of writing.
3. Their group wasn't never very large.
4. Not none of the other Inca cities compared to Cuzco.
5. There weren't no individual landowners.
6. To the Incas, nothing wasn't more important than the clan.
7. There wasn't no unemployment.
8. Children of the poor weren't getting no education.
9. A man from the Inca communes couldn't never change his rank or his occupation.
10. There isn't nothing else in South America today to compare to their empire.

- **Writing a Paragraph**   Write a short paragraph about something you dislike or disagree with. Use at least three negatives, one to a sentence.

9 | Adjective or Adverb?

Sometimes it is easy to confuse adjectives and adverbs. Usually when an adjective and an adverb are similar, the adverb ends in -*ly*. Which word in each pair below is an adverb?

slow — slowly   bad — badly
quick — quickly   sweet — sweetly

How do you know whether to use an adverb or an adjective?

INCORRECT: We drove slow through the fall leaves.
  CORRECT: We drove <u>slowly</u> through the fall leaves.

The word *slow* is an adjective. As you know, adjectives modify nouns, but they never modify verbs. Therefore, the adverb *slowly* is used correctly to modify the verb *drove*.

The words *good* and *well* are often confused. *Good* can modify a noun or a pronoun. The word *good* is never an adverb.

It is a <u>good</u> **day** to take pictures.
Hers are always <u>good</u>.

Well is usually used as an adverb. However, when *well* means "healthy," it is an adjective and modifies a noun or a pronoun.

ADVERB: I **played** baseball <u>well</u>.
ADJECTIVE: **I** didn't feel <u>well</u> when I awoke.

Try It Out

A. Choose the correct word in parentheses for each sentence.

1. The band played (good, well).
2. They were marching (bad, badly), however.
3. Paper streamers waved (wild, wildly) from windows.
4. The hero gave his speech (quick, quickly).
5. He had been praised (great, greatly).
6. Later, hundreds of people departed (slow, slowly) for home.

B. Choose the correct words in parentheses.

    7. Lisa is a (good, well) designer of jewelry.

    8. She turned a potato into a (good, well) bracelet.

    9. She does (good, well) with macaroni and paper clips, too.

    10. I wear my lucky bracelet when I don't feel (well, good).

> Use adjectives to modify nouns and pronouns, but never verbs.
> Use adverbs to modify verbs, adjectives, and other adverbs.
> *Good* is used as an adjective. *Well* is an adjective only when it means "healthy." Otherwise, *well* is an adverb.

Written Practice

Write the adjectives or adverbs from the parentheses to complete this paragraph correctly.

    When Joan of Arc was seventeen, the French army was losing (**1.** slow, slowly) to the English. Joan (**2.** quick, quickly) went to the aid of France. Wearing her white armor, she led and fought (**3.** good, well). Her leadership (**4.** gradual, gradually) united the French people. In the end, she was treated (**5.** bad, badly) by the king she had helped. Joan of Arc defended herself (**6.** good, well), but she was eventually burned at the stake.

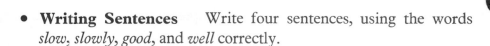

• **Writing Sentences** Write four sentences, using the words *slow, slowly, good,* and *well* correctly.

10 | Expanding Sentences with Modifiers

As you know, a simple subject and predicate make up a sentence.

Stars shine.

Modifiers, such as adjectives and adverbs, can make your writing more vivid and interesting. They also make it clearer.

Countless stars shine brightly tonight.

Try It Out

Use the modifiers given below to expand these sentences.

ADJECTIVES: green   juicy   black   two   huge   lively
ADVERBS: suddenly   here   up   then   overhead   below

1. Crows flew.   3. Leopards leaped.   5. Steak sizzled.
2. Balloons floated. 4. Clouds rumbled.   6. Children played.

> Modifiers add meaning and interest to sentences.

Written Practice

Add at least two modifiers to each sentence. Write the new sentences. Label adjectives *Adj.* and adverbs *Adv.*

1. Plants live.   4. Snow fell.
2. Wheels screeched.   5. Lizards crawl.
3. A boy sang.   6. Soup spilled.

- **Writing Sentences**   Write five simple sentences. Then use adjectives and adverbs to expand each sentence.

Using Words Correctly

Sentences Beginning with *there*

You know that verbs must agree with subjects. A sentence that begins with *there* can be confusing because the subject comes after the verb. What are the subjects and verbs in these sentences?

> There has always been a wasps' nest on our porch.
> Now there are no wasps living in it.

In sentences such as these, you can test whether the verb agrees with the subject by rearranging the sentence. Drop *there*, and put the subject first.

> A wasps' <u>nest</u> **has** always **been** on our porch.
> (singular subject)
> Now no <u>wasps</u> **are living** in it.   (plural subject)

> To find whether the subject and verb agree in a sentence beginning with *there*, drop *there*. Then rearrange the sentence so that the subject is first.

Practice

Is each subject singular or plural? Choose the correct verb.

1. There (is, are) winter clothes in Carol's closet.
2. There once (was, were) a green striped sweater there.
3. There (was, were) tiny pearl buttons on it.
4. Then there (was, were) dozens of hungry moths.
5. Now there (is, are) only pearl buttons left.

- **Writing Sentences**   Write five sentences, each beginning with *there*.

Word Connotations

Look at the cartoon. Which car wash has more cars—the Thrifty Car Wash or the Stingy Car Wash? Both car washes have the same equipment, and both charge the same price. Which car wash would you use? Why?

Even though the words *thrifty* and *stingy* have similar meanings, you may not react to them in the same way. Which word has a positive meaning for you? Would you rather be described as thrifty or stingy?

The words you use or hear can create different feelings and reactions. The positive or negative meaning a word suggests is called its **connotation**. *Thrifty* has a positive connotation, while *stingy* has a negative one.

Read each pair of words below. Which word in each pair has a positive connotation? Which words do you react to negatively?

nosy—curious   tidy—picky   nag—remind   clever—sly

When you write or speak, it is important to know the connotation of the words you use. Choose your words carefully.

> ▸ The negative or positive meaning suggested by a word is its **connotation**.

Practice

A. Which item in each pair do you think has a positive connotation? Which item has a negative connotation?

1. show off *or* perform
2. antique *or* outdated
3. mob *or* crowd
4. vain *or* self-confident
5. comical *or* silly

6. talkative *or* gossipy
7. forceful *or* pushy
8. fragrance *or* smell
9. crafty *or* smart
10. youthful *or* childish

B. Here is a letter Sarah has written to a good friend. For each pair of words in parentheses, write the word that conveys the more positive meaning.

Dear Meg,

Thank you for the (**11.** generous, wasteful) present you sent me. The card was so (**12.** sweet, mushy).

Did you think I looked (**13.** slim, skinny) in the photo? I'm glad you (**14.** encouraged, pushed) me to cut my hair. I love it this way.

Did your aunt tell you that I saw her downtown? She looked as (**15.** flashy, stylish) as I had remembered her. She always seems so (**16.** independent, bossy).

Thank you for the raisin bread you made me. It had a very (**17.** unusual, peculiar) taste. Everything you bake is so (**18.** soggy, moist) and flavorful.

See you soon.

Your (**19.** acquaintance, friend),

Sarah

- **Writing Paragraphs** Write a short paragraph, describing something. Use words with negative connotations. Then write a short paragraph, describing the same thing but using positive words.

Review

- **Adjectives** *(pp. 243-244)* Copy each adjective. (Omit *a*, *an*, and *the*.) Then write the word each adjective modifies.

  1. Edna formed a one-woman band.
  2. She is popular at concerts and parties.
  3. This foot plays a small snare drum.
  4. That foot controls two huge, flat cymbals.

- **Articles** *(p. 245)* Write the correct article.

  5. Do you own (a, an) poodle or (a, an) Irish setter?
  6. I have (a, an) old mutt that is like (a, an) friend to me.
  7. (The, An) gray poodle on the porch is Jo's.
  8. Did it win (a, an) award in (the, a) annual competition?

- **Comparing with Adjectives** *(pp. 246-247)* Write the correct comparative or superlative form of each word in parentheses.

  9. The ____ game was better than the earlier one. (late)
  10. The team's ____ player scored a touchdown. (weak)
  11. It was the ____ game of all. (short)
  12. We were ____ to beat than our challengers. (difficult)

- **Proper Adjectives** *(pp. 248-249)* Rewrite these sentences, capitalizing the proper adjectives.

  13. Jan collects oriental art.   15. She bought a chinese scroll.
  14. She has a korean painting.   16. One japanese vase is blue.

- **Adverbs That Modify Verbs** *(p. 250)* Write each adverb. Next to each one, write the verb it modifies.

  17. The week passed slowly.   19. He often visits the zoo.
  18. Lou waited patiently.   20. Today he ran there.

- **Adverbs That Modify Adjectives** *(p. 251)*   Write each adverb. Beside it, write the adjective it modifies.

  21. Lou watched the unusually playful birds.
  22. A remarkably quiet giraffe kept an eye on Lou.
  23. The gorilla looked quite innocent to the crowd.

- **Comparing with Adverbs** *(pp. 252–253)*   Write the comparative and superlative forms of these adverbs.

  24. casually   **26.** well   **28.** deeply
  25. diligently   **27.** hard   **29.** proudly

- **Negatives** *(pp. 254–255)*   Write each sentence correctly.

  30. Lia didn't see no clouds.   **32.** No warning wasn't given.
  31. A wind didn't never blow.   **33.** No one expected no rain.

- **Adjective or Adverb?** *(pp. 256–257)*   Write the correct word in parentheses. Label adjectives *Adj.* and adverbs *Adv.*

  34. Al likes (good, well) soup.   **36.** He ate too (quick, quickly).
  35. He cooks (good, well).   **37.** He doesn't feel (good, well).

- **Expanding Sentences with Modifiers** *(p. 258)*   Add one adjective and one adverb to each of these sentences.

  38. The dogs dug.   **40.** A bone appeared.
  39. Dirt was thrown.   **41.** The dog growled.

- **Using Words Correctly** *(p. 259)*   Write the correct verbs.

  42. There (is, are) my dime.   **44.** There (was, were) no bats.
  43. There (is, are) two pens.   **45.** There (was, were) the bees.

- **Building Vocabulary** *(pp. 260–261)*   Write a word from each pair that has a positive connotation.

  46. bragged *or* told   **50.** smile *or* smirk
  47. funny *or* ridiculous   **51.** cheap *or* inexpensive
  48. laugh *or* snicker   **52.** take *or* snatch
  49. conceited *or* proud   **53.** lazy *or* relaxed

Writing a Story

1 | Plot, Setting, Character

All the stories you read have at least three things in common. Each beginning below gives you a hint about these elements.

Adventure: As far as Lisa could see, there was nothing but water—flat and gray and lifeless. How long had she been in the rowboat? she wondered.

Mystery: "Most folks around here think the chest is buried at the edge of the cranberry bog," the old fisherman told Tony. "Funny, you're the second person to ask me that question today."

Science Fiction: Lamaar Green adjusted the lenses of his laser glasses. Moments from now, if all went well, he would be in the galaxy Centaur.

What do all stories have in common? (1) Something happens; (2) it happens somewhere; and (3) it happens to someone. What happens is called the **plot.** Where it happens is called the **setting.** The people involved are the **characters.**

Plot

The plot of a story is usually a simple, three-part framework: the **problem,** the **climax,** and the **resolution.** Each of the story beginnings above gives an idea of what the problem will be. How will Lisa find safety? Will Tony find the buried treasure? What will Lamaar Green find in the galaxy?

In each of these stories, there would be many smaller problems as well. What will Lisa do when she gets hungry? Who else is looking for the treasure? What has to go well before Lamaar Green can enter the galaxy?

The climax of a story is the point of greatest suspense. Often, at the climax, it seems that the character may not be able to solve the problem. The resolution comes when the problem is solved one way or another. On the next page, you will see how a familiar story fits this plot framework.

Plot: The Ugly Duckling

Main Problem: The ugly duckling is teased and pushed around by others. What can he do?

Smaller Problems: One egg will not hatch. Should the mother duck keep sitting on it?
Will the strange-looking duckling that hatches from the egg be able to swim?
Will the duckling be shot by hunters?
Will the duckling freeze in the icy pool?

Climax: The duckling expects to be beaten or killed by beautiful swans swimming toward him.

Resolution: The duckling sees his reflection in the water and realizes he has become a beautiful swan.

Practice

Choose one of these activities.

1. Choose a story you know. Use it to make a plot plan like the one above. Write what the main problem or problems are, where the climax comes, and what the resolution is.
2. Make up a plot plan. Use one of the story beginnings on page 265 to start you off, or make up your own story. List at least three problems, the climax, and the resolution.

Setting

The setting is the backdrop against which the story unfolds. Sometimes it is one of the most important parts of the story. How often have you read a book just because of its setting—a ranch in Wyoming, outer space, a whaling ship?

When you are reading, you often take the setting for granted. When you are writing a story, however, you need to make sure that the details of the setting are there to make your story come alive for your reader. What are the sounds? What are the smells?

Does the story take place during a blizzard? on a hot, humid day? Is it morning or evening? spring or fall? All these details help create a rich background that makes the readers believe they are really there in another world, the world of the story.

Practice

Write three short paragraphs describing three different settings. Make one the setting for an adventure story, one for a mystery, and one for a science fiction story. Try to make your reader see and feel what you are describing.

Character

Sometimes the most important part of the story is the characters. Perhaps they learn something new about themselves or about other people. Perhaps they fall in love or lose someone close to them. Characters do not have to be human beings, of course. They can be animals or robots or any creature you make up. Whatever they are, there could be no story without them.

Before you write a story, you should know something about your characters. What do they look like? What do they most enjoy doing? What is their greatest fault? What are their strengths? Knowing about your characters before you start writing will help you make them more real to your readers.

Practice

Choose one of these activities.

1. Describe three characters you have read about recently. Write three sentences about each of them. Include details of how they looked and what they were like.
2. Make up three characters, and write three sentences describing each of them.

2 | Dialogue

When characters speak, they become real, living, breathing, three-dimensional creatures. They step out of the story into the reader's mind. The conversation between characters in a story is called **dialogue.**

Some stories are made up almost entirely of dialogue. Dialogue can show action and tell you something about the characters. How much can you find out from this section of dialogue?

"Good morning, crew," said Gonzalez. "Is everything going according to schedule?"

"So far, so good, sir," said Roger. "We hope to——oh! excuse me, sir; we seem to have lost our picture."

"The stellargast! It's been blown off course!" cried Gonzalez.

"It's off course, sir; that much we can confirm," said Roger.

"Do you know what this means?" said Gonzalez. "There's no hope now of landing on Zapan!"

"I'd like you to take a look at these patterns," said Roger quietly. "It's possible, sir, that all is not lost."

- What problem is faced by the characters?
- Who is Gonzalez? What might his job be?
- Who is Roger? What might his job be?
- What can you tell about the kind of person Gonzalez is?
- What can you tell about the kind of person Roger is?
- What seems to be the setting for the dialogue?

Practice

Write a dialogue that shows both action and character. Choose one of these possibilities.

1. Write more of the dialogue between Gonzalez and Roger.
2. Write a dialogue from a real situation you were involved in.
3. Make up a dialogue between two characters.

3 | Beginnings and Endings

There are many different ways you can start a story to get your reader's interest.

You can give a hint about the plot.

The Jordans never spoke of the exam, not until their son, Dickie, was twelve years old.   –*Henry Slezar*

You can give a hint about the characters.

Almost every afternoon three boys came out to play in the yard. They were all dressed alike, in gray coats and trousers, and identical caps. . . .   –*Maxim Gorky*

You can start with the setting.

The rocket metal cooled in the meadow winds. Its lid gave a bulging *pop*.   –*Ray Bradbury*

You can start with dialogue.

"Isn't it awfully early for you to be up and about?"
"I was thinking the same about you."

In what way are all these beginnings alike? They all leave you with a question: What is the exam, and why is it so important? Who are the boys, and why are they all dressed alike? Who will step out of the rocket? Why did these people get up so early?

A story does not always have to start in the beginning of the action. You can start in the middle, or even at the end of your action and then work backwards.

The queen sat waiting for her subjects to file by.
"I'm an old man and poor. All I have to offer you, honored Queen, is this coin which my grandmother once gave me."
As the old man looked at the piece of gold in his wrinkled hand, he thought of that bright April day many years before.
"Here, Miolanthe," his grandmother had said. "This coin is from your ancestor, the great Omargodden. It is proof of your claim to the throne."

Look back at the story beginning about Miolanthe on page 269. Notice that the story starts with the end of his life and then moves backward quickly to when he received the coin from his grandmother. Many events have taken place between that time and this. You can tell that the following ending wraps up the story and ties the loose ends together.

> The queen fingered the coin. She felt the familiar family seal. Miolanthe's heart pounded. Without a word, the queen handed the gold piece back to him. Her eyes shone with tears.
> "Then *you* are Miolanthe," she whispered.

The best endings, like the best beginnings, use action, setting, or dialogue. Here are three examples.

ACTION: He did not look back, and he did not run until he was a good way down the road. Then suddenly he began to run, and he ran as fast as he could. *–Grant Moss, Jr.*

SETTING: The street lamp flickering opposite shone on a quiet and deserted road. *–W. W. Jacobs*

DIALOGUE: "Charles?" she said. "We don't have any Charles in the kindergarten." *–Shirley Jackson*

Practice

Below is the plot of a story called "The Dinner Party" by Mona Gardner. Read the plot. Then write two possible beginnings and two possible endings.

At a dinner in India, there is an argument about whether or not women can keep calm under pressure. The hostess suddenly calls a servant and asks him to put a bowl of milk outside the doorway. One guest realizes what this means: there is a poisonous snake somewhere in the room. He challenges everyone to keep absolutely still for five minutes, without telling them why. The snake goes over to the milk. Then the hostess admits that the snake had been on her foot.

4 | Getting Started

Stories lurk around almost every corner. What kind of story would you like to write? Are you interested in unsolved mysteries? Mystery story writers often get ideas from newspapers or from television. So do science fiction and adventure writers.

Do you ever imagine yourself in a place or a time that is completely different from yours? Many story ideas come from just letting the imagination run free.

- What might happen if you were marooned alone on a desert island? if you were marooned with someone you disliked?
- What if you turned into an animal or an insect?
- Have you ever imagined yourself at the controls of a spaceship? living in a castle surrounded by miles of deep forest?
- Have you ever wondered what it would be like to be a race-car driver? a horse trainer? an inventor? a zookeeper?

Practice

A. Use ideas from the news or from your imagination to describe two possible story settings and two characters.

B. Choose a classmate as a partner. Use your first setting and your partner's first character. Put the character in the setting, and spend two or three minutes making up a story. Let your imagination run wild. Then do the same thing with one of your characters and one of your partner's settings.

Steps for Writing a Story   Here are the steps for writing a story. You will follow these steps to write your own story.

Step One	Choose a story idea.
Step Two	Write your story.
Step Three	Revise your story.
Step Four	Proofread your story.
Step Five	Make a final copy to share.

5 | Step One
Choose a Story Idea

After thinking about plots, settings, characters, and story beginnings, you probably have a few story ideas in your mind. How do you choose which would make the best story? The one that interests you most may be the one that you cannot think of an ending for. That does not mean that you should not choose that story idea. Stories grow and change in your mind as you work on them, and the final ending might be quite different from the one you planned when you started.

Masako made a story chart to help her think about her story ideas. She made some notes on characters and setting and plot for the three stories she was thinking about. She wrote questions to remind herself of the things she would have to decide on before she started or while she was writing.

---

character: girl like me - black hair, tall

setting: house like mine - square, white, lawn
        town like ours - small

plot: girl gets a letter telling her she can have
      three wishes. Who is letter from? What does
      she pick? How does it turn out?

characters: Jessica, a reporter, sense of adventure
      Brice, her friend, curly brown hair,
      blue eyes, also a reporter

setting: country where there is a revolution - South
      America? What is it like there?

> *plot: Brice is kidnapped, and Jessica finds out where he is on her own and rescues him.*
>
> *characters: my cat, Irving – huge, yellow, with pale brown eyes, very dignified*
> *neighbors – sort of like ours*
>
> *setting: same as first story idea*
>
> *plot: cat decides it's his birthday, looks for place where he can find most scrumptious dinner, visits all the neighbors, decides home is best. Why is it best?*

Masako was excited about all her story ideas. How could she end the first one? If all the wishes worked out perfectly, it would not be a very interesting story. What could go wrong? What could the girl learn from her experience? Masako decided that next summer she would make this a really long story.

She was not very sure about the setting of the story about Jessica and Brice. Masako would have to make up a whole country or do a lot of reading. She decided to save this story for later, too.

She had a lot of ideas about the cat story. Her cat had just had a birthday, and Masako thought he was ready for another one. She was sure she could make up a good story from this idea.

Assignment
- **Make a Story Chart**
- **Choose a Story Idea**

A. Make a story chart like Masako's, using at least two story ideas. Make notes about characters, setting, and plot. Write questions about any missing parts for each story.

B. Put a check mark beside the story you can write best.

6 | Step Two
Write Your Story

Masako began writing her first draft quickly. She just tried to get as much on paper as she could without worrying about whether or not she was making mistakes.

part of Masako's first draft

Irving was feeling very bored. He decided that it must be getting near his birthday. That meant he needed a treat. There ~~sure~~ certinly aren't many treats around here, he thought. Irving thought that chicken livers and cream would be ideal. He was tired of dry cat food and especially of Mrs. Hees skim diet skim milk. Irving went over to the Batesons' and meowed at there door big green door. Mr. Bateson took his time answering the bell. When he saw Irving, he said, "hello, kitty. If you are looking for a mouse, you wont find one here." Irving was very annoyed. He did not like to be called a kitty. He also knew that he <u>could</u> find a mouse there,

> *but his idea of a good birthday dinner was certainly not catching his own dumb mouse.*

Masako wrote about four more of Irving's visits. Here is her last paragraph.

Masako's ending

> *So the big yellow cat with the amber eyes ate his birthday supper of cat food and skim milk and went to sleep in his usual place.*

- How could Masako's beginning be improved?
- How could her ending be improved?
- Where could Masako add dialogue to improve her story?
- What detail helps you see the setting?
- What do you know about the character—Irving—from these two parts of the story?

Assignment • Write Your First Draft

Start writing your story. Try to make your beginning interesting. Look back at page 269 for ideas for beginnings. Add dialogue as you write. Remember, you can change your mind while you are writing about what will happen next. Do not worry at this point about making mistakes. You will have a chance to correct them later. You may want to skip every other line on your paper to give yourself space to make changes later.

7 | Step Three
Revise Your Story

When Masako finished her first draft, she put it away for a day or two. When she came back to it, she tried to read it as though it were someone else's story. Was the story on her paper as interesting as the story in her mind had been? Would someone else enjoy reading it? Would her beginning make a reader want to keep on reading? Masako decided that she wanted to start off with Irving talking to himself. She wrote a new beginning.

Masako's new beginning

> "Its really boring around here," said Irving to himself one summer evening. Let's see. It must be getting near my birthday. That means I deserve a treat but there certinly aren't many treats around here.

Masako taped the new beginning on the side of her paper and drew an arrow to show where it would fit. Then she read her story to Cindy. Cindy liked it a lot. She said, "Why don't you keep on with Irving talking to himself until he goes to the Batesons'?"

Masako decided that was a good idea. She made a note on her paper to help her remember it. She asked Cindy about the ending.

"It really isn't quite as interesting as the rest of the story," said Cindy. "Maybe you could add something. What about having Irving dream about the chicken livers and cream?"

"Thanks!" said Masako. "Your ideas are really good." Masako made the changes on her first draft right away. She got an even better idea for the ending, she thought, and she used hers instead of Cindy's. On the next page, read the changes Masako made.

Masako's revisions

(New beginning goes here.)

"C
that chicken livers and cream would be
Irving thought. "I've had enough
ideal." ∧He was tired of dry cat food and
enough   for a lifetime.
especially of Mrs. Hees ~~skim diet~~ skim milk.
¶Irving went over to the Batesons' and meowed
" They certinly take
at there ~~door~~ big green door. Mr. Bateson
their time comming." he ∧thought. Finlly Mr. Bateson came to the door.
~~took his time answering the bell.~~ When he
saw Irving, he said," hello, kitty. If you
are looking for a mouse, you wont find
one here. "

So the big yellow cat with the amber eyes
ate his birthday supper of cat food and skim
milk and went to sleep in his usual place.
When he woke up early the next morning,
Irving found himself thinking about fish.
"Now there's an idea," said Irving. "Where——"

- What changes did Masako make in order to show Irving talking to himself?
- Where did she start a new paragraph? Why?
- Which do you think makes a better ending—Cindy's idea of Irving dreaming of chicken livers and cream or Masako's new ending? Why?

Assignment

- Revise Your Story
- Discuss Your Story

A. Read over your first draft with these questions in mind.

1. Does the plot make sense? Does one event lead to another? If you changed your mind as you wrote about what was going to happen next, it is especially important to go back and check for sense.
2. Have you described the setting so that your readers can see it clearly? Where could you add more details about setting?
3. Do your characters seem real? Where could you add details that would help them to come alive for your readers?
4. Have you used dialogue to make your story and characters more vivid? Where in your story could you use dialogue instead of explanation to show what is happening?

B. Write two new beginnings for your story. Do this even if you like the beginning you already have. Use the ideas on page 269 to help you.

C. Write a new ending, even if you like the ending you have. Use the ideas on page 270 to help you.

D. Make all the changes you thought of as you read over your draft, asking yourself the four questions in part A. Improve the plot, if you need to. Add details about setting and characters. Add dialogue. Use the best of your beginnings and endings.

E. Read your story to someone else—a classmate or your teacher. Ask your listener to think about the four questions in part A, as you read. Discuss your story, and make any changes that come out of the discussion. The changes can come from your listener's ideas and from new ideas of your own.

8 | Step Four
Proofread Your Story

Proofreading gives you the chance to check for errors like misspelled words and mistakes in capitalization and punctuation. When you are writing and revising your story, you concentrate on what you want to say and how you want to say it. When you are ready for other people to read it, however, you need to make sure that your story is neat and correct.

Masako had made so many changes that she decided to copy her story over. She had been thinking about a title all along. She now wrote her title at the top of the page. Then she proofread her story.

Masako's first paragraph after proofreading

> *Irving Makes the Rounds*
>
> "It's really boring around here," said Irving to himself one summer evening. "Let's see. It must be getting near my birthday. That means I deserve a treat, but there certinly aren't many treats around here."

- Where did Masako add an apostrophe? Why?
- Where did she add quotation marks? Why?
- Why did she add a comma after *treat*?
- Which word did Masako misspell? What proofreading mark did she use to show the spelling change?
- Do you think that the title Masako wrote fits the story? Why or why not?

Practice

Here are Masako's next two paragraphs. There are ten errors. Copy the paragraphs over correctly. Check page 357 in the Handbook if you need to review how to use quotation marks with punctuation marks.

"Chicken livers and cream would be ideal." Irving thought. "I've had enough dry cat food and enough of Mrs. Hees diet skim milk for a lifetime.

Irving went over to the Batesons' and meowed at there big green door. "They certinly take their time comming." he thought. Finlly Mr. Bateson came to the door. When he saw Irving, he said, "hello, kitty. If you are looking for a mouse, you wont find one here."

Assignment • Proofread Your Story

Use the checklist below to help you proofread your own story.

1. Are all my words spelled correctly? Have I checked any words I am not sure about?
2. Did I begin a new paragraph every time there was a new speaker in dialogue?
3. Have I indented to show where new paragraphs begin?

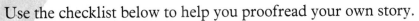

Grammar skills checklist

4. Does each sentence express a complete thought?
5. Have I used possessive nouns correctly?
6. Have I used commas between the parts of compound sentences and in appositives?
7. Have I used quotation marks correctly?

9 | Step Five
Make a Final Copy

Now Masako was ready to make the final copy of her story. She was good at drawing cats, so she decided to make an illustrated story booklet with a cover made of heavy paper.

Masako put two sheets of typing paper together and folded them in half. This gave her eight pages to work with. On the first page, she wrote the title of the story and her name. On the second page, she made a drawing of Irving thinking. She put the third page in a typewriter and very carefully typed as much of her story as fit well on that page. She left half of the next page blank for another drawing.

Before she took each page out of the typewriter, Masako read it over carefully. She erased mistakes and typed the corrections over them. Then she took the page out of the typewriter.

Masako made a cover from a piece of heavy colored paper. She sewed it onto the folded sheets and gave her booklet to Cindy to read. She wanted Cindy to see how her suggestions had helped. Then she put the booklet on the bookshelf with other classmates' stories. By the end of the week, everybody had read them all.

Assignment
- **Make a Final Copy**
- **Share Your Story**

A. Write or type your story as neatly as you can. Look at the suggestions below before you do this—you may want to use a special size paper.

B. Check to be sure you have copied your story correctly.

C. Give your story a title, if you have not yet done so.

D. Think of a special way to share your story.

- You could make a story booklet like Masako's.
- You could read your story to the class.
- You could tape your story for class members to listen to.
- Your class could put all your stories together in a class story collection.

1 | Prepositions

You often use prepositions like the underlined ones below.

> We placed the chairs <u>under</u> the table.
> We placed the chairs <u>on</u> the table.
> We placed the chairs <u>by</u> the table.

A **preposition** is a word that shows the relationship between a noun or pronoun and some other word in a sentence. It also tells direction. Notice how the prepositions *under*, *on*, and *by* show the changes in position between the chairs and the table.

The following chart shows many common prepositions.

about	before	during	past
above	behind	for	through
across	below	from	throughout
after	beneath	in	to
against	beside	into	toward
along	between	near	under
around	beyond	of	until
as	by	on	up
at	down	over	with

Try It Out

A. Find the prepositions in these sentences.

1. Joe rode the bus across town.
2. He walked into the museum.
3. He waited for his brother.
4. They studied the skeleton of a dinosaur in one gallery.
5. Several people stood around a huge statue.
6. Its parts had been discovered by a historian.
7. The brothers took a guided tour through the museum.

B. Choose a preposition from the chart on page 283 to complete each sentence.

8. Doris left school ——— her brother.
9. We ate lunch ——— the park bench.
10. I heard band music ——— the auditorium.
11. The volleyball went ——— the net.
12. Volleyball is played ——— both hands.

> ▶ A **preposition** is a word that relates a noun or pronoun to some other word in the sentence.

Written Practice

A. Write the prepositions in these sentences.

1. The discovery of King Tut's tomb was a real adventure.
2. Howard Carter had searched for a long time.
3. He believed that the tomb was in the Egyptian valley.
4. A worker uncovered a rock step beside an old hut.
5. Diggers found a door with an unbroken seal.
6. Behind it was a long dark passage.
7. An unbelievable treasure lay beyond it.
8. The tomb was filled with prized items.
9. This treasure has been exhibited by many museums.
10. Carter's discovery became famous throughout the world.

B. Rewrite the sentences below, replacing each preposition with another one that changes the meaning of the sentence.

11. Crop dusters fly planes over huge fields.
12. Some animals see better after dark.
13. Beside the mountain lies a famous lake.
14. I am rooting for your team before halftime.

- **Writing a Paragraph**   Write a paragraph about a discovery. Use as many prepositions as you can. Underline them.

2 | Prepositional Phrases

Each group of underlined words below begins with a preposition and ends with a noun or a pronoun.

I went <u>to a football **game**</u> <u>with **her**</u>.

The noun or pronoun that follows the preposition is called its **object**. The preposition, its object, and the words that modify the object make up a **prepositional phrase**.

Try It Out

Identify the prepositional phrases in these sentences.

1. Our trip began in Iowa.
2. We skated across the lake.
3. Others stood by the shore.
4. The lights shone above us.
5. At midnight everyone left.
6. Night on the lake was calm.

> ▸ A **prepositional phrase** is made up of a preposition, its object, and the object's modifiers.

Written Practice

Write each prepositional phrase. Circle the object in each one.

1. Supreme Court Justice Sandra Day O'Connor was the first woman on this court.
2. She was appointed by President Reagan in 1981.
3. She was raised on a cattle ranch without electricity.
4. She and her sister did heavy work around the ranch.
5. At sixteen she was graduated from high school.
6. Her Supreme Court appointment is for life.

- **Writing Sentences**   Write five sentences about your ideas for your future. Use a prepositional phrase in each sentence.

3 | Prepositional Phrases as Adjectives

You have learned that an adjective modifies a noun or a pronoun. Can you find the adjective in each of these sentences?

Mary bought a sweater <u>with a V-neck</u>.
The door <u>to the apartment</u> is locked.

In the first sentence, the prepositional phrase, *with a V-neck*, works as an adjective. It modifies the noun *sweater* and tells what kind. The prepositional phrase in the second sentence tells which one. What noun does it modify?

Look at the placement of the prepositional phrases. Unlike most adjectives, prepositional phrases come after the words they modify.

One-word Adjectives	**Prepositional Phrases as Adjectives**
wild lion	lion <u>in the wild</u>
neighborhood dogs	dogs <u>of the neighborhood</u>

Try It Out

A. The prepositional phrases are underlined. Tell which noun or pronoun each prepositional phrase modifies.

1. Nancy built a model railroad <u>with many cars</u>.
2. A control panel <u>in the center</u> supplies the power.
3. Toy locomotives <u>with electricity</u> seem real.
4. The signal switches <u>on the track</u> are automatic.
5. The builder <u>in overalls</u> likes her conductor's cap.

B. Identify the prepositional phrase in each sentence. Tell which noun each phrase modifies.

6. We gave a party for our visiting Polish relatives.
7. Many guests with government jobs attended.
8. Old snapshots of friends and family members were circulated.
9. Some guests in traditional costume sang folk songs.
10. The fireplace with its roaring fire was a gathering spot.

> A prepositional phrase can act as an adjective and modify a noun or a pronoun.

Written Practice

Write the prepositional phrases in these sentences. Beside each phrase, write the noun it modifies.

1. The guitar with the broken string is mine.
2. Several members of our group play professionally.
3. The girl in the purple shirt is the most talented.
4. Her music lessons at the college were helpful.
5. Their trips to outdoor concerts are the most fun.
6. Tanglewood in the Berkshire Mountains has the best setting.
7. Twenty-seven musicians in casual clothes played brass and string instruments.
8. Visitors from everywhere walked, talked, and listened.
9. The conductor of the group was Andre Previn.
10. The music on the stage was played masterfully.
11. Many visitors with small children played games.
12. The musicians behind the stage talked quietly.

• **Writing Sentences**   Write five sentences about a musical event you have attended, heard, or wanted to attend. Use a prepositional phrase in each one.

Prepositional Phrases as Adjectives   **287**

4 | Prepositional Phrases as Adverbs

A prepositional phrase can also work as an adverb. Adverb phrases modify verbs, adjectives, or other adverbs. They tell how, where, or when.

> Sue ran toward the lake.
> Ted was eager for the race.
> Melanie swims early in the morning.

In the first sentence, the prepositional phrase modifies the verb *ran*. In the second sentence, it modifies the adjective *eager*. In the third sentence, it modifies the adverb *early*.

Try It Out

Identify the prepositional phrase that acts as an adverb in each sentence, and tell which word it modifies. Some sentences have more than one prepositional phrase.

1. I swam in the pool for an hour.
2. The jogger leaped over several deep puddles.
3. Animals perform for television audiences.
4. On weekends my sister works until noon.
5. We left late in the afternoon.
6. After school we waited beside the car.
7. A black bear sat beneath the gently swaying branches.
8. I am ready for my trip.
9. She spoke in a loud voice.
10. Along the shore stood some seagulls.

> A prepositional phrase can work as an adverb. It can modify a verb, an adjective, or another adverb. Adverb phrases tell how, when, or where.

Written Practice

Write each prepositional phrase. Then write the word each phrase modifies.

1. Sir Winston Churchill served Great Britain during World War II.
2. He was Prime Minister and led his country bravely through the war.
3. He became friendly with President Roosevelt.
4. They worked closely during difficult times.
5. Churchill's speeches appeared in newspapers and books.
6. People cheered loudly during his radio speeches.
7. His appearances brought hope to the war-weary nation.
8. Memorial statues and buildings stand in his honor.
9. Students still read intently from his memoirs.
10. Some world leaders today govern by Churchill's principles.
11. During quiet moments, Churchill enjoyed oil painting.
12. He often painted by a rippling stream.
13. On his head, he wore an old floppy hat.
14. Both Winston Churchill and Grandma Moses painted late in their lives.
15. Their popularity endures over the years.

- **Writing a Paragraph**   Think of some qualities you think a good leader should have. Write a paragraph. Use some prepositional phrases, and underline them.

5 | Expanding Sentences with Prepositional Phrases

You can use prepositional phrases to make your sentences more descriptive. When you expand your sentences with prepositional phrases, you not only give your reader more information but you also make your writing more interesting. First, look at the sentence below.

Ken played.

Where did Ken play? When? For how long? We can answer these questions with prepositional phrases.

After school Ken played on stage for an hour.

What prepositional phrases were used to expand this sentence? In the sentences below, notice how the meaning of the original sentence was changed by adding different prepositional phrases.

During the snowstorm, Ken played with his trains on the floor.
Ken played on the softball team for three years.

Try It Out

Find the prepositional phrases in the paragraph below. Then read the paragraph without the phrases. Notice the difference.

Phillis Wheatley filled her life with poetry. She was a slave from Senegal in West Africa. She served as a companion for the wife of a tailor, John Wheatley. Phillis learned English from the Wheatleys. She wrote poetry about her life. When she was a teen-ager, one of her poems was published. In later years, her first collection of poems came off the press in London. People showered her with praises. Phillis Wheatley died at thirty-one.

> Prepositional phrases expand the meaning of a basic sentence.

Written Practice

Use the prepositional phrases in these lists to expand the sentences below. Some phrases can be used more than once. Write each expanded sentence.

during the night	without my knowledge
under my window	from little dark spots
through the leaves	inside their helmets
without any noise	before my eyes
about their funny cars	after the landing
behind tall buildings	through the streets

1. The wind blew.
2. They talked.
3. Clouds formed.
4. Spaceships landed.
5. My feet flew.
6. Trumpets played.
7. The children laughed.
8. The fire alarm rang.

- **Writing Sentences**   Choose five of the sentences from the exercise above. Expand these sentences by using your own prepositional phrases as modifiers. Write the sentences.

6 Using Words Correctly

Choosing Prepositions

Some prepositions are very similar in meaning. However, if you use them correctly, the slight difference can make your meaning clearer. Notice how *in* and *into* are used below.

> We waited <u>in</u> the dark room.
> The guide led us <u>into</u> the tomb's deepest chamber.

The preposition *in* means "located within." When you are in a place, you are already there, not moving toward it. The preposition *into* means "movement from the outside to the inside."

The preposition *of* can also be confusing. You should use *of* only as a preposition. Do not use *of* as a helping verb.

> INCORRECT: We could of gone to the movies.
> **CORRECT**: We could have gone to the movies.

The preposition *in* means "located within."
Into means "movement from the outside to the inside."
Always use *of* as a preposition. It is not a helping verb.

Practice

Write each sentence, choosing the correct word(s) in parentheses.

1. John James Audubon (might of, might have) been a noble.
2. Audubon painted birds (in, into) natural settings.
3. He would go (in, into) the woods to look for them.
4. His pictures (could have, could of) almost come to life.
5. Audubon died famous (in, into) his house beside the Hudson.

- **Writing Sentences**   Write five sentences, using *in*, *into*, and *of* correctly.

Blended and Clipped Words

We often put parts of two words together to make a new word. When we do this, some letters are dropped. The new word is called a **blend**. What blends can you form from these words?

breakfast + lunch   motor + hotel   television + marathon

Did you form *brunch*, *motel*, and *telethon* from the word pairs?

Another way we create new words is by cutting off parts of words when we talk casually. A word shortened in this way is a **clipped** form of the original word. What clipped words are used instead of these longer words?

influenza   dormitory   delicatessen

Practice

A. Match the word pairs on the left with the blends on the right.

1. news + broadcast   **a.** smog
2. smoke + fog   **b.** cheeseburger
3. cheese + hamburger   **c.** newscast
4. helicopter + airport **d.** motorcade
5. motor + cavalcade   **e.** heliport

B. Write a clipped word for each of these words.

6. advertisement   8. submarine   10. automobile
7. mathematics   9. telephone   11. fanatic

- **Writing Sentences**   Write the blended or clipped form for each item below. Then write a sentence using each word.

12. cable + telegram   14. sports + broadcast
13. stereophonic   15. gymnasium

Review

- **Prepositions** *(pp. 283–284)* Write the prepositions in these sentences.

    1. Young people across the country earn money at unusual jobs of all kinds.
    2. In Maine Barry catches lobsters in wooden traps.
    3. During vacations from school, Linda baby-sits for lab mice in her home.
    4. Larry and a few of his friends in the neighborhood raise and sell worms by the handful.
    5. Chris walks dogs to the city park before dinner.

- **Prepositional Phrases** *(p. 285)* Write each prepositional phrase in these sentences. Underline the prepositions once and the objects of the prepositions twice.

    6. Tim visits his aunt during the summer.
    7. Her house is by a pond.
    8. Sometimes, after breakfast Tim and his aunt go fishing at the pond near the border of her property.
    9. They sit beside the weeds and bait their hooks.
    10. They throw their lines into the water.

- **Prepositional Phrases as Adjectives** *(pp. 286–287)* Write each prepositional phrase that is used as an adjective. Then write the word it modifies.

    11. Masks of papier-mâché are easily made if you are a person with some artistic ability.
    12. Make sure the bag is the size of your head.
    13. The newspaper in the bag is crumpled.
    14. Features for your mask can then be shaped.
    15. Make strips of wet, pasted paper.

- **Prepositional Phrases as Adverbs** *(pp. 288–289)*   Write each prepositional phrase that is used as an adverb. Then write the word or words it modifies.

16. Your fingers will be sticky during this activity.
17. Features can be cut from cardboard.
18. Paper strips are placed over the mask.
19. Strips should be wet on both sides.
20. Masks can be changed in every possible way throughout this entire process.

- **Expanding Sentences with Prepositional Phrases** *(pp. 290–291)*   Add one or two prepositional phrases to each sentence. Write each expanded sentence. Underline prepositions once and objects of prepositions twice.

21. Jan shoots baskets.
22. Her shots hit.
23. She practices.
24. Her foul shooting is the best.
25. She made eleven points.

- **Using Words Correctly** *(p. 292)*   Write the correct word or words from those in parentheses.

26. Val's family built a windmill (in, into) their yard.
27. They built it (in, into) an open field, but they (could of, could have) built it on a hill.
28. Val's neighbors (in, into) Charleston watch the windmill quietly produce energy.
29. Tourists coming (in, into) Charleston enjoy the sight, too.
30. The windmill (in, into) Val's yard is among the most interesting sights (in, into) Vermont.
31. The wind blows (in, into) the propeller wheel.
32. What else (could have, could of) turned the wheel so fast?
33. Val's windmill (must of, must have) converted wind into electricity and transported it (in, into) her house.

Maintain

- **End Punctuation and Commas** *(pp. 207–211)* Rewrite each sentence with correct end punctuation and commas.

    1. Jason my cousin in Boston got a great summer job
    2. He pedals a swan boat in the park and he answers questions
    3. Ask him about trees birds statues and buildings
    4. Jason how old are the swan boats

- **Quotations and Abbreviations** *(pp. 212–215)* Write this paragraph, correctly punctuating the dialogue. Abbreviate the underlined words. If you need help, check a dictionary.

    > My mother is a stage and <u>television</u> actress. Last <u>December</u> she became a member of the Screen Actors Guild. Will you be in commercials all over the <u>United</u> <u>States</u> and Canada I asked.
    >
    > Yes, she said. I am filming one at the <u>United</u> <u>Nations</u>.

- **Titles** *(pp. 216–217)* Rewrite the following titles correctly.

    5. jingle bells (song)
    6. to james (poem)
    7. black beauty (book)
    8. the gift of corn (article)

- **Adjectives** *(pp. 243–244, 248–249)* Write each adjective and the noun it modifies. Then underline each proper adjective.

    9. Canadian cities are fun.
    10. The French language is spoken in Montreal.
    11. Ottawa is the capital city.
    12. *Ottawa* is the English version of an Algonquin word.

- **Articles** *(p. 245)* Write the correct article.

    13. (a, an) high waterfall
    14. (an, the) vast ocean
    15. (a, an) empty nest
    16. (a, the) underwater cave

- **Comparing with Adjectives** *(pp. 246–247)*   Write the comparative and superlative forms of these adjectives.

  17. helpful   **18.** curious   **19.** precious   **20.** warm

- **Adverbs** *(pp. 250–253)*   Write each adverb and the word it modifies. Then write its comparative and superlative forms.

  21. Ellen walked quickly.   **23.** She recently bought them.
  22. She held the flowers tightly.   **24.** They are nicely arranged.

- **Negatives** *(pp. 254–255)*   Write the correct word.

  25. Joe didn't take (no, any) map on his hike.
  26. He didn't have (anything, nothing) but a compass.
  27. Luckily, there weren't (any, no) hidden paths.
  28. He hadn't (never, ever) been on a hike.

- **Prepositions** *(pp. 283–291)*   Write each prepositional phrase. Then write *adjective* or *adverb* after it to tell how it is used. Circle the object of the preposition.

  29. A boat was full of salmon.   **31.** He called to his crew.
  30. A violent storm blew over   **32.** A sailor on the bow was
    the bay.   frightened.

- **Using Words Correctly** *(pp. 218–219, 259, 292)*   Write the correct word or words.

  33. Lee (could of, could have) sat between two famous TV personalities on the podium (in, into) the high school auditorium.
  34. (We, Us) players saw Willie Graham in the sports shop.
  35. We began to whisper when he walked (in, into) the shop.
  36. There (was, were) several more customers in the shop.

- **Building Vocabulary** *(pp. 220–221)*   Write the correct word.

  37. She played a (chord, cord) on the guitar, and we all sang.
  38. The wind filled our (sail, sale).
  39. I have (grown, groan) taller.
  40. The (principal, principle) of our school is Mr. Anastas.

1 | Story

Has a friend or someone you know ever been your rival? Rivals are persons who try to equal or outdo one another in any number of ways. Read this story to find out about the experiences of two cousins who were rivals.

Rivals

That summer on my grandfather's farm, I more than half-tried to be a better farmer than my cousin Cassy. I tried at least one hundred per cent. But I might just as well not have tried, for all I got done. Cassy was thinner, meaner, and luckier than I was. I will give examples of each.

THINNER: Because Cassy was so skinny, she was more athletic than I, although I hate to say it. Hanging from the great beams of the barn were long ropes. And on them, she could swing from one end of the hayloft to the other. Being heavier, or fatter, as she put it, I could not get as fast a running start. Most of the time, I would just dangle and fall off with an "oof," like an apple that was wormy and too ripe.

MEANER: Every day we walked down the gravel county road to the main highway to get the mail from the rural mailbox. On the way, big insects often buzzed near our heads. One day when one of them hovered before my face, Cassy suddenly screamed at me to run, run, run because it was a darning needle. If you didn't hurry, she added, it would sew up your lips, and you could never say another word. I was terrified. I knew nothing about wildlife and insects. Holding my hand over my mouth, I dashed all the way back to the house and nearly fainted. When she told our grandfather, G.B., how she had fooled me, he did a little dance of delight.

LUCKIER: For a treat, G.B. took us fishing on the three joined lakes. If there is anything I am good at, it is fishing. Sure enough, I caught six bluegills and a sunfish compared to Cassy's two bluegills. My grandfather and I were just bragging about our fishing

QUEEN MARY

ability, when Cassy got a bite and started to pull in a sunfish the size of a minnow. All at once, there was a huge splash, and a pickerel two feet long grabbed at her sunfish, thinking it was bait. She quickly pulled the pickerel into the rowboat and sat on it, shrieking her triumph. G.B. said it was the best fish he had seen taken in those lakes in years. I was so mad I could have torn a telephone book in two—a New York telephone book. You may be able to equal experience, but you can't beat luck.

To keep up my spirits, I would sometimes make a list in my mind of the ways in which I was better than Cassy Rubbins. It went like this:

1. More imagination
2. Better vocabulary
3. Better manners
4. Musically gifted

The only trouble was, I couldn't see that any of these had much to do with good farming.

Oh, yes, I forgot, Cassy had another advantage.

TRICKIER: One day G.B. hired a dipper to dip his sheep to kill their ticks. Ticks are tiny bitey bugs that live in the sheeps' wool and drive them sort of nutty, the way mosquitoes do people. The dipper brought a big rustproof iron tank and placed it in the barnyard. Then he filled it with water and mixed in a terrible-smelling solution. This would kill the ticks when the sheep were dumped into it. Now all was ready. The flock was in the orchard. G.B. asked which one of us, Cassy or me, would bring the sheep into the barnyard by persuading the ram to lead them. That was the way you moved the flock: If you could get the ram to start, the ewes and lambs would follow him. I piped up that I would, which was a fearful mistake. G.B. said "Brave lad." So I went into the orchard, and Cassy came along to see the fun.

Now the ram was a large animal with great curling horns and a stuck-up look on his face. His name was Pasha of Constantinople III. He had won several prizes at the county fair and was very conscious of it. I walked up to him carefully and put my hand on his back and tried to start him. He wouldn't move. He was chewing grass.

"C'mon, Pasha, old pal," I said. "Let's go and take a nice perfumey bath. And let's bring all the family too."

He refused to move. I stepped in front of him and tugged on his horns until I was leaning west and he was leaning east. He could be very stubborn when he wanted to.

"What you should do," Cassy advised, "is wet your finger in the tank and let him smell it. Then he'll want to have a bath."

"Really?" I asked.

"Sure," she said nodding wisely.

So I went back to the barnyard and wet my finger in the solution. I suspected nothing. G.B. was talking to the dipper and paid no attention. Then I returned to Pasha and put my finger to his nose. Little did I know that giving him a single whiff of that awful stuff would be like waving a red flag in front of a bull. He had been dipped before, many times probably, and he must have sworn a kingly oath he never would be again.

"PPFFEEWW!" he cried. He backed up, lowered his head and horns like a battering-ram, and charged at me!

I ran. I ran as fast as my legs would take me, into the barnyard, then round and round the fence in a crazy game of tag with that savage beast at my heels. Following him was the whole yammering flock! Laughter rang in my ears, but I was running so fast that I couldn't find the gate. I knew that just one butt of those great horns would blast me off like a rocket. When I was close to complete exhaustion, when I could just about feel Pasha's hot breath burning my neck, I finally did the only thing I could. To escape, I took a headlong dive into the dipping tank.

I was pulled out of the tank and helped, coughing and dripping, up the hill. But my grandmother, Nola, would not even allow me in the house. I stunk like a skunk. My pal Pasha beat me after all. He had to take only one bath. I had to take four in a row, outdoors, in a washtub, with about half the world looking on and holding its nose.

That's what I meant about Cassy being trickier.

Glendon and Kathryn Swartout

For Discussion

1. What are some of the ways the boy names in which Cassy has an advantage over him?
2. What does the boy's reaction to the darning needle story tell you about where he is from? Do you think Cassy was from a similar place? Explain your answer.
3. How did Cassy manage to trick her cousin?
4. How do you think the cousins really felt about each other?
5. The **setting** of a story is the time and place in which it takes place. What is the setting of this story? Why is the setting important in "Rivals"?

Activities

1. Write a new version of "Rivals" in which the setting of the story is a large city. Include the same characters. In your story, Cassy is visiting her big-city cousin, and he manages to outdo her at whatever they do. Make the incidents in your story fit a big city setting. Share your story with the class.
2. Choose one incident in "Rivals" to illustrate or illustrate something that happens in your version of the story.

2 | Haiku

Haiku is a Japanese form of poetry usually about nature. Notice, as you read, how much feeling is created in so few words.

A tree frog trilling
Softly, the first drop of rain
Slips down the new leaves.

Rogetsu

That duck, bobbing up
From the green deeps of a pond
Has seen something strange . . .

Joso

Now a spring rain falls
Gently . . . the world grows greener
And more beautiful.

Chiyo

For Discussion

Haiku are poems of images, or word pictures. Most haiku have a set form of five syllables in the first and third lines and seven in the second line. One image in the first haiku is of spring when leaves are new. One feeling created by this image is of peacefulness. What images and feelings are created in the other haiku?

Activity

Write some haiku of your own. Close your eyes and let a picture come into your mind. Jot down some notes about your picture, and turn it into a three line poem. Then, correct your syllable count. If you have trouble starting, use these suggestions: a song bird chirping; a blanket of snow; footprints in the sand.

3 | Free Verse

In this poem, the poet writes about a joyful time in the snow. How do you think the speaker in the poem felt when the snow turned to rain?

WINTER POEM

once a snowflake fell
on my brow and i loved
it so much and i kissed
it and it was very happy and
     called its cousins   5
and brothers and a web
of snow engulfed me then
i reached to love them all
and i squeezed them and they
     became   10
a spring rain and i stood
     perfectly
still and was a flower

Nikki Giovanni

For Discussion

1. How can you tell that the speaker in the poem enjoyed the snow? What words tell how she or he felt?

2. Try to imagine how a light snowfall looks. How would you describe a heavy snowfall? What did the poet mean when she wrote in lines 4-6, the snowflake "was very happy and /called its cousins / and brothers"?

3. How do you think a flower feels in the rain? What did the poet mean when she wrote she was a flower in the rain?

4. Some poems follow a set pattern of **rhyme** and **rhythm.** For example, every other line in a poem may rhyme. If the rhythm follows a set pattern, you can tap out the number of beats in each line. Poetry that is written in **free verse** does not follow a set rhyme or rhythm pattern. Although free verse poems do not rhyme, they do have a rhythm. Their rhythm is more like speech which does not repeat a pattern of regular beats. Poets may use free verse because they feel it allows them to focus more on meaning and less on following a strict pattern.

    Do any of the lines in "Winter Poem" rhyme? How do you think the poem would be different if it had a regular rhyme and rhythm?

Activities

1. Close your eyes and think about one of the following: snow, hail, wind, rain, thunder, sleet, lightning. Relax and let your imagination go. What pictures come to mind? Write a poem about your mind-pictures. Write your poem in free verse if you like.

2. Think of your favorite or least favorite time of year. Write down sense words—sight, smell, sound, taste, touch—that come to mind when you think of this time. Then make a drawing or a collage that reflects your feelings about the time of year you selected.

4 | Fable

While you are laughing at the Scotty's predicament in this story, look for the writer's serious message.

The Scotty Who Knew Too Much

Several summers ago there was a Scotty who went to the country for a visit. He decided that all the farm dogs were cowards, because they were afraid of a certain animal that had a white stripe down its back.

"You are a pussy-cat and I can lick you," the Scotty said to the farm dog who lived in the house where the Scotty was visiting. "I can lick the animal with the white stripe, too. Show him to me."

"Don't you want to ask any questions about him?" said the farm dog.

"Naw," said the Scotty. "*You* ask the questions."

So the farm dog took the Scotty into the woods and showed him the white-striped animal and the Scotty closed in on him, growling and slashing. It was all over in a moment and the Scotty lay on his back. When he came to, the farm dog said, "What happened?"

"He threw vitriol," said the Scotty, "but he never laid a glove on me."

A few days later the farm dog told the Scotty there was another animal all the farm dogs were afraid of. "Lead me to him," said the Scotty. "I can lick anything that doesn't wear horseshoes."

"Don't you want to ask any questions about him?" said the farm dog.'

"Naw," said the Scotty. "Just show me where he hangs out."

So the farm dog led him to a place in the woods and pointed out the little animal when he came along. "A clown," said the Scotty, "a pushover," and he closed in, leading with his left and exhibiting some mighty fancy footwork. In less than a second the Scotty was flat on his back, and when he woke up the farm dog was pulling quills out of him.

"What happened?" said the farm dog.

"He pulled a knife on me," said the Scotty, "but at least I have learned how you fight out here in the country, and now I am going to beat *you* up."

So he closed in on the farm dog, holding his nose with one front paw to ward off the vitriol and covering his eyes with the other front paw to keep out the knives. The Scotty couldn't see his opponent and he couldn't smell his opponent and he was so badly beaten that he had to be taken back to the city and put in a nursing home.

Moral: It is better to ask some of the questions than to know all the answers.

James Thurber

For Discussion

1. What two animals did all the farm dogs fear? Why was the Scotty not afraid of them?
2. A **fable** is a very old story form in which a moral, or lesson, is revealed at the end. The characters in a fable are often animals who behave as people might. The lesson to be learned is usually how *not* to behave. In the modern fable "The Scotty Who Knew Too Much," the Scotty has many human faults. What are they? What does the moral of the fable mean?

Activities

1. Think of a saying that expresses a lesson or use one of these.

   Don't judge a book by its cover.
   Don't cry over spilt milk.

   Then make up a fable that illustrates the meaning of your saying. Include the moral at the end, as Thurber did in his fable.

2. If you were asked to rewrite "The Scotty Who Knew Too Much" without any animal characters, what kind of people would you substitute? Write a short description of each character from the fable, explaining how they would look or act if they were humans instead of animals.

5 | Simile

There is something mysterious about all living creatures, even a little frog.

FROG

The spotted frog
Sits quite still
On a wet stone;

He is green
With a luster   5
Of water on his skin;

His back is mossy
With spots, and green
Like moss on a stone;

His gold-circled eyes   10
Stare hard
Like bright metal rings;

When he leaps
He is like a stone
Thrown into the pond   15

Water rings spread
After him, bright circles
of green, circles of gold.

Valerie Worth

For Discussion

1. In the first stanza (lines 1–3), the poet emphasizes stillness. What besides the frog is still?
2. In the sixth stanza, the poet describes rings spreading in the water after the frog. What besides a frog makes rings on contact with water?
3. A **simile** is a comparison between two unlike objects or things. The comparison is always made by using the words *like* or *as*. For example, in the third stanza, the poet compares the frog's mossy back with the moss on a stone. Although moss on a stone and a frog's mossy back are different, the poet stresses their similarities in texture and color. What is the simile that describes the frog's eyes? What other simile is there in this poem? What comparison is made in it?

Activities

1. Write a short poem about an animal that interests you. Think about how it looks, sounds, feels, and moves. Try to include at least one simile in your poem.
2. Write four sentences in which you use similes. Remember that a simile compares two things in a new or unusual way. Look at the example below.

   The red balloon looked like an apple in the sky.

6 | Metaphor

A vivid imagination can turn a walk down the street into an unexpected adventure involving a dinosaur.

The dinosaurs are not all dead.
I saw one raise its iron head
To watch me walking down the road
Beyond our house today.
Its jaws were dripping with a load   5
Of earth and grass that it had cropped.
It must have heard me where I stopped,
Snorted white steam my way,
And stretched its long neck out to see,
And chewed, and grinned quite amiably.   10

Charles Malam

For Discussion

1. Was the person in the poem afraid of the dinosaur? What line in the poem, in particular, shows this?

2. The entire poem "Steam Shovel" is a metaphor. A **metaphor** compares two unlike things not by using the words *like* or *as* as a simile does, but by saying that one thing *is* the other. A dinosaur and a steam shovel are very different, but the poet sees similarities in them. One similarity the poet stresses is their giant size. In what other ways are they alike?

Activities

1. Make up a list of five everyday items. Next to each item, list qualities that describe the way this item looks, feels, tastes, smells, and sounds. Then think of something else that shares at least one of these qualities. Write a poem or a paragraph describing how the two objects are similar.

2. Pair up with a classmate. Decide which of the following lines are metaphors and which are not.
   a. My best friend is a dream come true.
   b. The golden leaf shimmers like a ray of the sun.
   c. The ship is a whale rising on the crest of a wave.
   d. The whale dives like a submarine.
   e. The fog is a mysterious friend.
   f. The buzz of the bee was persistent.

Interviewing a Book Character

Lucy had really enjoyed reading *Mrs. Frisby and the Rats of NIMH* by Robert C. O'Brien. She decided to share her book with her classmates by interviewing Nicodemus, an important character in the book. She asked a classmate to be the interviewer, and she was Nicodemus. Here is the interview that she presented.

INTERVIEWER: This is Nicodemus from the book *Mrs. Frisby and the Rats of NIMH* by Robert C. O'Brien. Nicodemus, just what is NIMH?

NICODEMUS: NIMH is the National Institute of Mental Health. It's a government agency that does psychological research.

INTERVIEWER: What is psychological research?

NICODEMUS: As I understand it, psychologists are people who study the mind, emotions, and behavior of different animals in order to understand people. Researching is gathering information and facts.

INTERVIEWER: What was your life like at NIMH?

NICODEMUS: We lived in cages in a large room. We were fed every day, and we learned some tricks.

INTERVIEWER: What kinds of tricks?

NICODEMUS: It seems that we were part of an experiment. We were put into something called a maze, and we were supposed to get from one end of it to the other. If we went one way, we would feel an unbearable pain. We soon learned how to avoid that.

INTERVIEWER: Is it really true that you learned to read?

NICODEMUS: It certainly is. We are probably the first rats to do so. At first, I had no idea what the letters meant, but eventually I caught on. In fact, reading saved our lives.

INTERVIEWER: How could reading save your life?

NICODEMUS: Well, there were about twenty of us in one group. Jenner and I had become friendly with Justin, who was a very

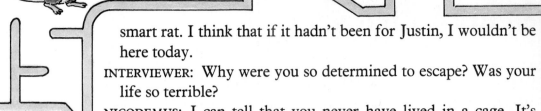

smart rat. I think that if it hadn't been for Justin, I wouldn't be here today.

INTERVIEWER: Why were you so determined to escape? Was your life so terrible?

NICODEMUS: I can tell that you never have lived in a cage. It's true that we had food and a place to sleep, but we couldn't run around or do anything when we wanted to. We were not free!

INTERVIEWER: Tell us how reading helped you to escape.

NICODEMUS: I think it was Justin who first read the sign on our cages. It said: To release door, pull knob forward and slide right. Once Justin got out, and he was the first to get out, he found the air duct that led to our freedom. So reading really did save us.

INTERVIEWER: To find out more about Nicodemus and his remarkable friends, read the book *Mrs. Frisby and the Rats of NIMH.*

- Who are some of the characters in the book?
- What did you find out about the characters?
- Why is this a good way to share a book?

Follow these steps to share a book by interviewing a character.

1. Decide which character in the book to interview. Choose an important character who knows what happens in the story.

2. Decide which parts of the book you will tell about. Choose exciting or interesting incidents that will interest your classmates. Ask your character questions about those parts of the book. Before asking a question, you may want to tell some background information.

3. Write down what the interviewer and the character will say. Ask a classmate to read the part of the interviewer, and you be the book character. Be careful not to tell too much of the story.

4. Start your interview by having the interviewer introduce the character to the class. Tell the title and author of your book.

Activities

1. Interview a character in your book, following the instructions on page 314.

2. Interview the author of your book. The questions you ask should provide information about the book, not the author. You might ask the author who his or her favorite character in the book is and why. You might also ask the author what his or her favorite part of the story is. Write what the interviewer and the author will say. Then with a classmate, present your interview.

3. Interview the illustrator of your book. Ask the illustrator how he or she decided which parts of the story to illustrate. You might also ask how he or she decided what to draw on the cover.

More Books to Read

Here are some other books that you might enjoy about animals.

Arabel's Raven by Joan Aiken   The Jones family is kept on their toes by Mortimer, a curious bird, who wings his way destructively through London.

Time Cat by Lloyd Alexander   Gareth is a remarkable cat who needs only to blink an eye to transport himself and his owner, Jason, back into time.

The Yearling by Marjorie Rawlings   Jody must make a difficult decision about the life of the wild deer he has raised.

2 | Making a Comic Strip

Carol has just finished reading the play *Blind Sunday* by Arthur Barron. She decided to share it with her classmates by making a comic strip about one part of the play. This is how her comic strip looks.

Blind Sunday by Arthur Barron

- Why do you think Carol shared this section of her play?
- How do you find out about the characters?
- What do you discover about the characters?

Follow these steps to share a book by making a comic strip.

1. Decide which part of the book you will share. Choose a part that you think is interesting and that you can illustrate.
2. Decide how many frames or sections you will need. Divide a large sheet of drawing paper into that many frames.
3. Draw the picture for each frame, leaving enough room for the dialogue bubbles. Write in the bubbles what each character says. You do not have to use the exact words from your story.
4. Include the title and author of your book.

Activities

Here are some ways you can share a book using art.

1. Make a cartoon strip, using the instructions above.
2. Imagine that you are a portrait painter. Draw several of the important characters from your book. Include each character's name and the title and author of the book on each drawing.
3. Make a mobile of the important characters in your book. Draw your characters on heavy paper, and cut them out. Write the characters' names on the drawings. Attach the cutouts to a wire clothes hanger with pieces of string. Somewhere on the hanger, attach the title and author of the book.

More Books to Read

You may enjoy reading these other books about people with physical limitations.

The Story of Stevie Wonder by James Haskins   Here is an inside look at how this singer, pianist, and composer became a superstar.

It Can't Hurt Forever by Marilyn Singer   Eleven-year-old Ellie tells the sometimes funny and often moving experiences of her hospitalization for heart surgery.

3 | Writing to an Author

Eliot shared the book *Run for the Blue Ribbon* by writing to Rafe Gibbs, the author of the book. Here is the letter he wrote.

4632 Samsoa Street
Everett, Washington 98203
April 15, 1983

Dear Mr. Gibbs,

   I am a boy about the age of Dave Telford, the main character in Run for the Blue Ribbon. I was really involved in the story. In fact, my hands began to sweat when Dave was racing. And when Dave runs to flag down the train, he seems to regain the confidence he had lost during the 440 race.

   Did you make up this story or did someone you know run a race and lose? I don't know how you made Dave and old, blind Mr. Johnson seem so real, but I feel as if I know them. I have the feeling that Dave will never give up at anything he tries. I really liked him. I hope you write another story like this one.

Sincerely,
Eliot Casidy

- What do you find out about the story and the main character in Eliot's letter?
- Why is this a good way to share a book?

Follow these steps to share a book by writing to the author.

1. Think about two or three incidents in the book you especially liked that would make someone else interested in the book.

Refer to these incidents in your letter. Tell enough about what happened without giving away the story.

2. Tell the author why you liked the book.

3. You may ask a question or two about how the author decides something in the story. You may even guess why the author created a certain kind of character or decided how the story would end.

4. Write your letter in correct friendly letter form. Be sure you include the author's name and the title of the book somewhere in the letter.

5. Display your letter on a bulletin board in your classroom. If you want to mail your letter to the author, send it in care of the publisher and ask that they forward it.

Activities

Here are some ways to share a book using letters.

1. Write a letter to the author of your book, following the instructions above.

2. Write a letter to the main character in your book. Tell the character why you liked or did not like him or her. Remember not to tell too much of the story and to include the title and author of the book.

More Books to Read

Here are some other sports stories you may enjoy.

The Rascals from Haskell's Gym by Frank Bonham   In order to win the gymnastics competition, Sissy and her team have to overcome inexperience, injury, and dirty tricks played by their rivals, the Rascals.

The Goof That Won the Pennant by Jonah Kalb   The Blazers are a baseball team who take advantage of a once-in-a-lifetime error and develop a taste for winning.

4 | Making a Television Commercial

After reading *Island of the Blue Dolphins* by Scott O'Dell, Angela decided to share this book with her class. She thought she could interest her classmates in the book by making a television commercial for it. She had only one minute to get them curious about the book. Here is the commercial she made.

This is Angela Ferrilli from WRTD Channel 3 bringing you the news. But first, here is a message that will interest those of you with unusual appetites.

Start a special diet today—a reading diet that is guaranteed to beautify your brain! Start by devouring the juicy adventure *Island of the Blue Dolphins* by Scott O'Dell. In this award winning book, you will share in the adventures of Karana, a young Indian girl, who was stranded on an uninhabited island. Learn how she survives among savage wild dogs and tames one of them to be her companion. Her battle with a giant devilfish will take your breath away! Since you have good taste, I'm sure you will want to head for your nearest library to get a copy of Scott O'Dell's *Island of the Blue Dolphins*. Don't hesitate. A feast awaits you!

- How does Angela try to interest her classmates in reading this book?
- What do you learn about the book from this commercial?
- Why does Angela try to interest her listeners quickly in her television commercial?

Follow these steps to make a commercial for your book.

1. Think of a way to get your listeners' attention quickly. Since many people are interested in eating and good food, Angela used this technique to catch her listeners' attention.
2. Tell your listeners that the book is a mystery, biography, adventure, romance, or some other kind of book.

3. Tell the name of the book, the author, who the main character or characters are, and something interesting or exciting that happens in the book.
4. You may want to write your commercial on note cards that you can glance at while you present your commercial.
5. Give yourself a one-minute time limit.
6. Show a copy of the book, and tell where it can be found.

Activities

Here are some ways to use advertisements to share a book.

1. Make a television commercial for your book, using the instructions above.
2. Make a billboard advertisement for your book. On a large sheet of paper, draw a picture of an exciting part of your book that will interest people. Think of words that describe your book that will catch people's attention. These might be words such as *thrilling, spellbinding, heartwarming,* and *fascinating.* Include such words and the title and author of your book in large letters in your billboard.
3. Create a magazine advertisement for your book. Think of an exciting or interesting passage to include in your ad. Then, retell this section and draw a picture to illustrate it. Be sure the title and author's name are clearly visible.

More Books to Read

Here are other exciting stories you might enjoy reading.

Zia by Scott O'Dell   Meeting her Aunt Karana, who lives alone on an island for many years, has a powerful effect on young Zia.

Trapped on a Golden Flyer by Susan Fleming   Alone and nervous about his first long train trip, Paul is courageous and helpful to stranded passengers when an avalanche blocks the tracks and isolates the train.

5 | Making a Book Jacket

Julian really liked reading *The Phantom Tollbooth* by Norton Juster. He decided to share his book by making a book jacket. On one side of his paper, he drew a picture for the cover. On the other side, he wrote about the book. Here is how the book jacket looked when he finished.

The Phantom Tollbooth
Norton Juster

Milo and his friends, Tock and Humbug, are heading for the Valley of Sound in their electric automobile. They are astonished that when they arrive they hear not one sound. They learn that after Rhyme and Reason were banished,

people started making ugly sounds. As a result the Soundkeeper decreed that since sound was no longer valued, it would be abolished and locked away. Milo volunteers to free sound. He visits the Soundkeeper and discovers that she is not as fond of silence as she pretends.

- What have you found out about this story?
- Who are some of the characters in the story?

Follow these steps to share a book by making a book jacket.

1. Fold down a flap about two inches wide on each end of a large piece of drawing paper. Paste lined paper on each flap.
2. On the left flap, print the title and author of your book. Below this tell about some of the characters in the book and what happens to them. Include information that you think will make someone want to read the story. Continue telling about the book on the right flap.

3. Decide how you will illustrate the cover of the book. Draw a picture using crayons and markers on the side of the paper without the flaps. Include the title and author of the book on this side also.
4. Share your book jacket with your class by showing the illustration and reading the information you have written about the book.

Activities

Here are some ways of using art to share a book.

1. Make a book jacket for your book, following the instructions above.
2. Make a collage that represents your book. From magazines and newspapers, cut out pictures and words that capture an exciting part of the story. Try to include pictures of people and places that represent the characters and setting of your story. Paste your pictures on a large piece of drawing paper. Leave room for the title and author of your book.
3. Imagine that you are the illustrator of your book. Draw pictures of some of the interesting or exciting incidents in the story. Include the important characters in some of your illustrations. Write the title and author's name on the pictures.

More Books to Read

The Cat-King's Daughter by Lloyd Alexander Margot, a talking cat, helps Princess Elena convince her father, the King, to let her marry her true love.

The First Two Lives of Lukas-Kasha by Lloyd Alexander When Lukas volunteers to take part in a magician's trick, he finds himself in a strange land where he has many adventures.

Stoneflight by Georgess McHargue Jamie is unhappy about being in New York for the summer until she discovers that she can fly around the city on a stone griffin that decorates her apartment building.

End-of-Book Test

- **Sentences** Write each sentence, adding end punctuation. Then write *declarative, interrogative, imperative,* or *exclamatory* to identify each type of sentence.

    1. Show me that photograph of the moon's surface
    2. Wouldn't you like to go there
    3. How far away it is
    4. The moon actually reflects light from the sun

- **Subjects and Predicates** Write each sentence. Draw a line between the complete subject and complete predicate. Underline each simple subject once and each simple predicate twice.

    5. Two thousand people waited along the parade route.
    6. The brass band was playing some lively marches.
    7. Horses with riders pranced proudly past the spectators.

- **Finding the Subject** Write the subject for each sentence.

    8. Here is the road to Iona.
    9. Are you tired of driving?
    10. Rest for a while.
    11. Will the engine overheat?

- **Compound Subjects and Predicates** Write each compound subject and predicate.

    12. The dachshund and the sheepdog trotted down the road.
    13. The plane stopped at Caracas and refueled.
    14. Uncle Ned planted the seeds and watered them every day.

- **Compound Sentences** From each pair of sentences below, form one compound sentence. Write the new sentences, using correct punctuation.

    15. Frances did not hear the bell. She did hear a knock.
    16. The delivery person smiled. He handed her a package.
    17. Should Frances tear off the wrapping now? Should she wait?

- **Fragments and Run-ons**   Correct each fragment or run-on.

   18. Tossing pebbles into a brook.
   19. When I first saw you at the station.
   20. The rabbit hopped across the green lawn then it disappeared under the grape vines.
   21. Laura dialed the number she let the phone ring ten times.

- **Nouns**   Write each noun. Label it *common* or *proper*.

   22. Norman Rockwell lived in Stockbridge, Massachusetts.
   23. This artist painted scenes of life in America.
   24. The *Saturday Evening Post* sometimes featured his work.

- **Plural Nouns**   Write the plural form of each noun below.

   25. tornado   27. patch   29. life   31. scarf   33. fly
   26. goose   28. solo   30. waltz 32. man   34. moose

- **Possessive Nouns**   Write the possessive form of the noun in parentheses.

   35. The ____ old trunk is in the attic. (Higginses)
   36. ____ wedding dress is in the trunk. (Aunt Doris)
   37. Their ____ table linens are in the trunk, too. (grandparents)

- **Appositives**   Rewrite each pair of sentences into a single sentence containing an appositive. Punctuate it correctly.

   38. The Doves were the strongest team. The Doves won the game.
   39. Willis is the team's best hitter. He hit two home runs.
   40. The fans are an enthusiastic group of people. The fans filled the stadium.

- **Verbs**   Write *action* or *being* for each verb below.

   41. Dolphins are marine animals.
   42. They sometimes help other dolphins in difficulty.
   43. Dolphins eat fish and other marine life.

- **Direct Objects**   In exercises 41–43, write each direct object.

- **Linking Verbs** Copy these sentences. Underline the linking verbs. Label predicate nouns *PN* and predicate adjectives *PA*.

    44. Deserts are unsuitable for many life forms.
    45. The desert atmosphere is dry.
    46. Death Valley is the hottest area in the United States.
    47. The Sahara is the largest desert in the world.

- **Main Verbs and Auxiliaries** Write each verb phrase. Underline the auxiliary once and the main verb twice.

    48. The Eiffel Tower is located in Paris, France.
    49. It was built for the International Exposition in 1889.
    50. Can the three elevators carry us all to the top?

- **Principal Parts of Verbs** Write the correct form of the verb for each sentence. Then write its past participle.

    51. Last Sunday Gina ——— to Baltimore. (fly)
    52. She ——— to Baltimore often. (travel)
    53. She ——— to Baltimore a month ago, too. (go)
    54. She ——— the city next Friday. (leave)

- **Irregular Verbs** In exercises 51–54, label each of the irregular verbs *IR*.

- **Subject-Verb Agreement** Write the verb that agrees with each subject.

    55. Ted and his sisters (has, have) planted flowers.
    56. Neither vegetables nor parsley (is, are) in the garden.
    57. Neither Ted nor his neighbors (plant, plants) them.
    58. Either herbs or spices (are, is) too delicate.

- **Pronouns** Copy each pronoun in the following sentences. Then write its antecedent.

    59. Wendy told the teachers, "I will be absent on Thursday."
    60. They gave her a homework assignment.
    61. She handed it to them on Friday morning.

- **Subject and Object Pronouns**   Write *S* above each subject pronoun in exercises 59–61. Write *O* above each object pronoun.

- **Possessive Pronouns**   Write the correct pronoun.

  62. Is (your, you're) birthday in July?
  63. (Who's, Whose) birthday is on (their, they're) calendar?
  64. The bird spread (it's, its) great wings and flew away.

- **Pronouns in Compounds and After Linking Verbs**   Write the correct word or words to complete each sentence.

  65. Mom will drive (Jay and I, Jay and me) to the movies.
  66. That is (she, her) in the driveway now.
  67. (Jay and I, Jay and me) saw a movie about runners.

- **End Marks**   Copy each sentence. Punctuate it correctly.

  68. Ride the elevator to the top of the building
  69. What sights we can see
  70. Is that the Milltown water tower over there
  71. We can see for miles in every direction

- **Commas**   Write these sentences, adding commas as needed.

  72. Kate would you bring the shovel rake and hoe?
  73. Yes I know where are they.
  74. They were in the barn but now they are gone Kate.

- **Abbreviations**   Write the abbreviation for each item.

  75. Mount Hood   **77.** Apartment 342
  76. Rocky Hill Road   **78.** Public Broadcasting Service

- **Punctuating Dialogue**   Punctuate and capitalize each sentence.

  79. Please turn the volume of the radio down said Miranda.
  80. Scott called wait for me!
  81. If you follow me replied Donna we can take a shortcut.

End-of-Book Test   327

- **Titles** Write these titles correctly.

   82. the new york times (newspaper)   **84.** fog (poem)

   83. the story of my life (book)   **85.** the leopard (article)

- **Adjectives** Write each adjective and the word it modifies. Underline the proper adjective.

   86. Ted has a Japanese car.   **88.** Ted will drive the new

   87. The two-door car is red.   car to an Italian villa.

- **Articles** Write the correct article.

   89. Has (the, an) captain ever eaten (a, an) oyster?

   90. I ate (a, an) raw oyster in (the, an) seafood restaurant.

- **Comparing with Adjectives** Write the comparative and superlative forms of these adjectives.

   91. ridiculous   **92.** proud   **93.** beautiful   **94.** noisy

- **Adverbs** Write each adverb and the word it modifies. Then write the comparative and superlative form of each adverb.

   95. That is a remarkably tall building.

   96. They built it well.

   97. The cranes blocked traffic badly.

- **Negatives** Write the correct word. Remember to avoid using double negatives.

   98. Mr. Gilmore didn't have (no, any) suitcase.

   99. The airline couldn't find it (nowhere, anywhere).

   100. He hadn't (never, ever) lost a suitcase before.

- **Adjective or Adverb?** Write the word from the parentheses that will complete each of the following sentences correctly. Then label it *adj.* or *adv.*

   101. Anna can sing (good, well).

   102. She is a (good, well) pianist, too.

   103. Ride your bicycle (slow, slowly) in the park.

   104. You may need to make a (quick, quickly) stop.

- **Prepositions** Write each prepositional phrase. Underline the prepositions. Write the word each phrase modifies.

    105. The tropical fish in a glass tank are John's.
    106. Bubbles float to the surface.
    107. We watched a fish with a bright red tail.

- **Using Words Correctly** Write the word in parentheses that completes each sentence correctly.

    108. Joel needs to (lend, borrow) your slide projector.
    109. He will (sit, set) it on the table in the meeting hall.
    110. Joel will (lend, borrow) me his slides later.
    111. Bring extra chairs for people to (sit, set) on.
    112. Joel will (teach, learn) the audience about Egypt.
    113. Fertile banks (lay, lie) along the Nile River.
    114. The desert becomes hot after the sun (rises, raises).
    115. The Suez Canal fascinates (we, us) newcomers.
    116. There (is, are) oil tankers among the ships.
    117. (We, Us) people in the audience asked Joel questions.
    118. (Who, Whom) will travel with Joel on his next trip?
    119. I hope he will (let, leave) me go with him.
    120. Joel waved before he stepped (in, into) the plane.
    121. Joel (could of, could have) shown many other slides.
    122. We can (let, leave) anytime now.

- **Building Vocabulary** Write a synonym and an antonym for each of the words below.

    123. dirty   **124.** far   **125.** funny   **126.** many

    Add a prefix or a suffix or both to each of these words. Write the new word.

    127. climb   **128.** agree   **129.** fold   **130.** employ

    Write the correct homophone for each sentence.

    131. I need to (buy, by) a rain slicker.
    132. Perhaps I can find one on (sale, sail).
    133. Will you (lone, loan) me yours?

Language Handbook

Parts of Speech

Nouns

Definition   A **noun** names a person, place, thing, or idea.

What <u>energy</u> <u>Captain Carl</u> had for this <u>double-header</u>!

Practice   Copy each sentence, and underline each noun.

1. The beauty of the sunset attracted the artist.
2. Doctor Bae visited the pyramids in Egypt.
3. Never stand under a tree during a thunderstorm.
4. More teen-agers were absent from school this week.
5. Drive with caution on the snowy roads of New England.

Singular and Plural Nouns   To form most plurals, add *-s*.

cart – carts   dinner – dinners   turkey – turkeys

To form the plural of most nouns ending in *-s, -ss, -ch, -sh, -x, -z,* and *-o,* add *-es.*

glass – glasses   brush – brushes   potato – potatoes

To form the plural of a noun ending in a consonant and *-y,* change the *y* to *i* and add *-es.*

story – stories   lobby – lobbies   penny – pennies

To form the plural of a noun ending in *-f* or *-fe,* change the *f* to *v* and add *-es.*

scarf – scarves   calf – calves   knife – knives

Practice   Write the plural form of each noun.

1. tomato	**3.** pirate	**5.** union	**7.** crutch
2. half	**4.** monkey	**6.** diary	**8.** melody

Common and Proper Nouns A **common noun** names any person, place, thing, or idea. A **proper noun** names a particular person, place, thing, or idea. Always capitalize proper nouns.

holiday	street	man	(common)
Fourth of July	Michigan Avenue	Mr. Goldman	(proper)

Practice Copy each proper noun. Beside it, write the common noun that matches it best.

1. Wednesday   **a.** holiday
2. Venus   **b.** month
3. Lexington Avenue   **c.** day
4. Abraham Lincoln   **d.** waterway
5. March   **e.** street
6. Halloween   **f.** president
7. Suez Canal   **g.** planet

Possessive Nouns Possessive nouns show ownership. To form the possessive of most singular nouns, add *'s*.

apron belonging to Chris   Chris's apron

To form the possessive of a plural noun that ends in *-s,* add *'*.

camera belonging to the Zukroffs   the Zukroffs' camera

To form the possessive of a plural noun not ending in *-s,* add *'s*.

suits of the women   women's suits

Practice Rewrite each item, using a possessive noun.

1. shoes belonging to the boys   **6.** book of Betsy
2. hats belonging to the men   **7.** flights of a pilot
3. meeting of the stockbrokers   **8.** toys of the child
4. car belonging to the Grahams   **9.** manes of the horses
5. speeches of the candidates   **10.** kite belonging to Iris

Appositives An **appositive** is a word or a group of words that tells more about the noun it follows. An appositive is usually set off from the rest of the sentence by commas.

The gazelle, a very graceful animal, can run at high speeds.

Practice Combine each pair of sentences into a single sentence that contains an appositive. Use commas correctly.

1. Uncle Fred is a brick layer. Uncle Fred came to dinner.
2. Martin is my other uncle. He flew to Seattle on business.
3. Kathy is a good swimmer. She competes in many races.
4. She wore a sari. A sari is a long garment made of silk or cotton.
5. I lost my favorite book. The book is called *Hornet Cove*.

Verbs

Definition A **verb** can show action or a state of being.

The students <u>voted</u> in the school election.   (action verb)
The day <u>became</u> sunny and warm.   (being verb)

Practice Write the verb in each sentence. Beside it, write *action verb* or *being verb*.

1. The mayor appointed her to the committee.
2. The chairperson asked for my opinion.
3. Public speaking upsets Harry.
4. That dinner looks delicious.
5. Several of her friends planned the surprise.

Direct Objects The **direct object** receives the action of the verb. Some direct objects are compound. To find the direct object, find the action verb. Ask who or what receives the action.

Our plan will raise <u>money</u> for the sports program.
We asked <u>Bob</u> and the <u>girls</u> for some help.

Practice Write the action verb and the direct object in each sentence.

1. He bought a jacket and a shirt at the store.
2. The consultant helped the mayor and her staff.
3. We exported grain to those countries.
4. The committee greeted the special guests.
5. The politician's speech won many votes and much applause.
6. The lecturer held the attention of the audience.

Linking Verbs   A **linking verb** joins the subject with a related noun or adjective in the predicate.

The dog <u>was</u> happy with its new toy.

A **predicate noun** is a noun that follows a linking verb and names the same person or thing as the subject.

Her uncle from Chicago was a <u>firefighter</u>.

A **predicate adjective** is an adjective that follows a linking verb and describes the subject.

Some green grapes taste <u>sour</u> to me.

Practice   Copy each sentence. Underline the verb. Draw an arrow from the subject to the predicate noun or adjective.

1. Those diamonds are priceless.
2. The sunset over the mountains looked glorious.
3. Everyone was ready for the beginning of the movie.
4. Abraham Lincoln was a famous president.
5. His eyeglasses seemed too big for his face.

Main Verbs and Auxiliaries   A **verb phrase** is made up of one or more auxiliary verbs plus a main verb.

A new shop <u>is opening</u> today.   <u>Have</u> you <u>been</u> there?

The **main verb** is the last word in a verb phrase.

Dad must have <u>arrived</u> early.

Auxiliary verbs (helping verbs) can be used in contractions.

I have read = I've read   I could not go = I couldn't go

Practice   Copy each incomplete sentence. Underline the main verb once and the auxiliary verb(s) twice. Complete the sentence.

1. Have you seen _____?
2. Tim could have been running _____.
3. She didn't hear _____.
4. Now he'll dance _____.
5. Would you help _____?

Verb Tenses   The **tense** of a verb tells when the action or state of being takes place. The **present tense** tells that something is happening now. The **past tense** tells that something has already happened. The **future tense** tells that something is going to happen.

> Sam <u>cooks</u> dinner outdoors.   (present tense)
> We all <u>watched</u> a television program.   (past tense)
> Sara <u>will read</u> the poem aloud.   (future tense)

Practice   Copy this chart. Fill in the past and future tenses.

Present Tense	Past Tense	Future Tense
1. calculate		
2. memorize		
3. expect		
4. satisfy		

Principal Parts of Verbs   The **principal parts** of a verb include the verb itself, the past, and the past participle. The past participle is used with the auxiliary *has, have,* or *had.*

> ask   asked   (has, have, had) asked

When the past and the past participle of a verb are formed by adding *-d* or *-ed,* the verb is **regular.**

> smile   smiled   (has, have, had) smiled
> fold   folded   (has, have, had) folded

When the past and the past participle are formed in some other way, the verb is **irregular.**

> buy   bought   (has, have, had) bought
> bite   bit   (has, have, had) bitten

Practice   Write each verb. Label it *regular* or *irregular.*

1. No one knew the correct answer.
2. The two sisters have caught cold.
3. Suddenly thunder boomed in the distance.
4. Four hours later, the storm had ended.
5. My uncle has given us tickets to the game on Saturday.

Irregular Verbs The principal parts of many verbs are irregular. The best way to learn the principal parts of an irregular verb is to memorize them.

Here are the principal parts of some common irregular verbs. Remember that the past participle is used with *has, have,* or *had.*

Verb	Past	Past Participle	Verb	Past	Past Participle
begin	began	begun	ride	rode	ridden
blow	blew	blown	ring	rang	rung
break	broke	broken	run	ran	run
bring	brought	brought	say	said	said
choose	chose	chosen	see	saw	seen
come	came	come	shrink	shrank	shrunk
do	did	done	sing	sang	sung
drink	drank	drunk	sit	sat	sat
drive	drove	driven	speak	spoke	spoken
eat	ate	eaten	steal	stole	stolen
fly	flew	flown	swim	swam	swum
freeze	froze	frozen	take	took	taken
give	gave	given	tear	tore	torn
go	went	gone	think	thought	thought
grow	grew	grown	throw	threw	thrown
know	knew	known	wear	wore	worn
lend	lent	lent	write	wrote	written
make	made	made			

Practice Copy each verb. Label it *past* or *past participle.*

1. The students have chosen teams for the game.
2. They wrote a book report every Friday.
3. The family always ate dinner at seven o'clock.
4. I took my notebook to school.
5. The senator had gone to Minneapolis.
6. Birds had flown southward in formation.
7. The child rode her bike to the park.
8. The weather forecaster said, "Snow tonight."
9. We had swum in the pond every day.
10. Michelle often lent me her bike.

Subject-Verb Agreement   The subject of a sentence must agree with its verb.

>   The white **horses** <u>pull</u> the carriage with ease.

If a compound subject is joined by *and,* use a plural verb.

>   **Michael** and **Tom** <u>are</u> good friends.

If the parts of a compound subject are joined by *or, either . . . or,* or *neither . . . nor,* the verb agrees with the part of the subject that is closer to it.

>   **Sal** or her **sisters** <u>paint</u> well.
>   Either the **manager** or the **workers** <u>have</u> the solution.
>   Neither your **cats** nor our **dog** <u>makes</u> a sound.

Practice   Write each sentence, choosing the correct verb or verb phrase from the parentheses.

1. Neither the train nor the buses (is running, are running).
2. The snowstorm (have stopped, has stopped) all transportation.
3. Either my cousins or I (shovel, shovels) the snow.
4. Mandy, her sisters, and Tomas (watch, watches) closely.
5. Kate or Pete (clear, clears) snow from the path.
6. Neither his dogs nor his cat (like, likes) the game.
7. In autumn Carlos and Chris (rake, rakes) leaves.
8. Neither my pens nor my notebook (is, are) here.

Pronouns

Pronouns and Antecedents   A **pronoun** is a word that takes the place of a noun. The words *I, you, she, he, it, we,* and *they* are pronouns. An **antecedent** is the noun or nouns that a pronoun refers to. Every pronoun should have a clear antecedent.

>   Zeb and Ron wrote a letter to Grandmother Simms. <u>She</u> never received <u>it</u>. <u>They</u> had forgotten to put a stamp on <u>it</u>.

Grandmother Simms is the antecedent of the pronoun *She. Letter* is the antecedent of *it. Zeb* and *Ron* are the antecedents of the pronoun *They.*

Practice   Write the pronouns in each group of sentences. Beside each pronoun, write its antecedent(s).

1. Shelly and Max have a dog. They named it Ruff.
2. I am named Pete, and here is Karl. We built a go-cart and painted it blue.
3. This report belongs to Irene. She deserves an *A* on it.
4. The cellar was flooded. The water was three inches deep. Dad and Bill mopped it up from the floor. They worked all night.
5. José and Pam listened to the librarian. He pointed to the card catalogue and explained that it is arranged alphabetically. They can find books easily now.
6. I am named Judith. My friend is Henrietta. She drew a map, and I painted it.

Pronouns as Subjects and Objects   A pronoun can be the subject of a sentence. A pronoun can be a direct object.

The subject pronouns are *I, he, she, we,* and *they.*

This year I want to go to summer camp.

The object pronouns are *me, him, her, us,* and *them.*

The director interviewed me.

You and *it* can be either subjects or objects.

It is a gift for you.   You gave it away.

Practice   Write the correct pronoun to complete each sentence. Then write *S* if it is a subject or *O* if it is a direct object.

1. (We, Us) heard the bell ring.
2. These books are heavy, but (I, me) can carry (they, them).
3. You can see (they, them) through this telescope.
4. Sometimes (I, me) like to swim in the lake.
5. Harry's dad brought (he, him) to a horse show.
6. (He, Him) likes the colors purple and orange.
7. (She, Her) and I picked some flowers and gave (they, them) to our friend.
8. (They, Them) should eat some fresh vegetables.

Possessive Pronouns   A possessive pronoun is a pronoun that shows ownership. *My, your, his, her, its, our, their* and *whose* can come before nouns. *Mine, yours, his, hers, ours, theirs,* and *whose* can stand alone.

Did you see <u>my</u> coat?   <u>Whose</u> is that parka?

The possessive pronouns *its, your, their,* and *whose* should not be confused with the contractions *it's* (it is), *you're* (you are), *they're* (they are) and *who's* (who is).

<u>Your</u> locker is open.   (possessive pronoun)
<u>You're</u> the only mountain climber I know.   (contraction)

Practice   Write each sentence, using the correct pronoun.

1. I think that the kite is (her, hers).
2. Is that paper (my, mine)?
3. (Who's, Whose) glasses are those?
4. Please help (your, you're) sisters.
5. I think these cars are (their's, theirs).
6. No one knows if that sandwich is (your, yours).
7. I believe this tent is (ours, our's).
8. This is (their, they're) home.

Pronouns After Linking Verbs   Use the subject form for pronouns that follow linking verbs.

The only one on key was <u>I</u>.   My favorite TV star is <u>he</u>.

Practice   Write these sentences, using a pronoun for the words in parentheses. The first one has been done for you.

1. The best swimmer on the team is ——. (a girl)
   The best swimmer on the team is she.
2. It was —— who painted that picture. (a woman)
3. The speakers at the meeting were ——. (two people)
4. It is —— who helped us most. (a boy)
5. It was —— who played the flute. (a girl)
6. The performer with the guitar is ——. (a man)
7. The newly-elected president is ——. (a woman)

Compound Subjects and Objects   When you include your-self as part of a compound subject or object, it is always polite to mention yourself last. A pronoun in a compound subject must be a subject pronoun (*I, you, she, he, it, we, they*). A pronoun in a compound object must be an object pronoun (*me, you, her, him, it, us, them*).

> <u>Mark and I</u> knew the answer.   (compound subject)
> Their prices surprised <u>him and me</u>.   (compound object)

Practice   Choose the correct compound subjects and objects from the parentheses. Write each sentence.

1. (Bill and me, Bill and I) like to talk on the telephone.
2. Grandma called (she and I, her and me).
3. (I and Sue, Sue and I) saw (Grandpa and her, Grandpa and she) last week.
4. Fran told (George and I, George and me) about the fire.
5. (James and me, James and I) invited (Carla and him, he and Carla) to the party.
6. Who visited (me and Jill, Jill and me) during vacation?
7. (Ramon and me, Ramon and I) planted some rose bushes.
8. Dad praised (me and Nancy, Nancy and me).

Adjectives

Definition   An **adjective** adds to the meaning of a noun or pronoun. Adjectives tell which one, what kind, or how many.

> <u>That</u> ant is a <u>busy</u> insect.   I see <u>twenty-one</u> stars.

Practice   Copy each sentence. Underline each adjective, and then draw an arrow to the noun or pronoun it modifies.

1. Ninety-two passengers boarded the small aircraft.
2. Scientific experiments are performed with great care.
3. She looked healthy after her long vacation.
4. The weather, hot and humid, was uncomfortable.
5. He is upset because the homework is hard.
6. This dog is friendly, even though it has a loud bark.

Articles   *A, an,* and *the* are special adjectives called **articles.** *The* refers to a specific item or items. *A* and *an* refer to any one item in a group.

The hat is wet.   A guide showed us an interesting exhibit.

Practice   Write the correct article for each sentence.

1. (A, An) police officer gave us directions.
2. (A, The) usher showed us to our seats.
3. Let's see if there is (a, the) ballgame on TV.
4. (An, The) star of the team gave us (a, an) autograph.
5. The teacher explained (a, the) homework to us.

Comparing with Adjectives   Use the **comparative** (*-er* or *more*) form of an adjective to compare two people, places, or things.

She is taller than he.
That kitten is more playful than this one.

Use the **superlative** (*-est* or *most*) form of an adjective to compare three or more people, places, or things.

He is the tallest student in our class.
That is the most playful kitten I have ever seen.

Some adjectives change their forms completely.

much, more, most   bad, worse, worst   little, less, least

Practice   Write the correct form of the adjective in parentheses.

1. Of all our field days, this year's was the ____ fun. (much)
2. Today Karen is ____ than Jan is. (cheerful)
3. Our ____ idea of all was the bake sale. (successful)
4. Is this towel ____ than that one? (wet)
5. That was the ____ movie I have ever seen. (bad)
6. Of the four boys, Grover tells the ____ jokes. (silly)
7. That story is ____ than this one. (suspenseful)
8. Of the four problems, which one is ____? (easy)
9. Is Rhode Island the ____ state in the nation? (small)
10. Your car has ____ rust than mine does. (little)

Proper Adjectives   A **proper adjective** is an adjective formed from a proper noun. Proper adjectives begin with a capital letter.

Sean is an <u>Irish</u> name.   Who was that <u>Spanish</u> writer?

Practice   Write each proper adjective correctly.

1. Bullfighting is a popular mexican spectator sport.
2. Last night we ate at our favorite japanese restaurant.
3. We visited all of the canadian provinces.
4. That is an italian painting from the fifteenth century.
5. That is a siamese cat.
6. This volume is a translation of a french novel.
7. The building on the hill is a chinese pagoda.
8. My sweater is woven from irish wool.
9. Many european countries agreed to the treaty.

Adverbs

Definition   An **adverb** can modify a verb, an adjective, or another adverb. An adverb that modifies a verb describes how, where, when, or to what extent.

The horse runs <u>quickly</u>.

<u>Slowly</u> the car turns into the driveway.

He pointed <u>upward</u> at the airplane.

Practice   Write each adverb and the verb it modifies.

1. Soon Maggie carefully tied the package.
2. The roots of the plant grow downward.
3. Everyone cheered noisily for the actors.
4. Yesterday rain fell heavily, and the river soon overflowed.
5. Gradually winter turned into spring.

Adverbs That Modify Adjectives   Adverbs that modify adjectives tell how or to what extent.

The room was <u>surprisingly</u> quiet.

The climbers are <u>thoroughly</u> aware of the danger.

Practice   Write the adverbs that modify adjectives in these sentences. Then write the adjective that each one modifies.

1. The weather has been unusually cold this winter.
2. That jacket is rather dirty.
3. The gloriously warm sun appeared after three rainy days.
4. Very small children can learn quickly.
5. Marcie drew an extremely colorful picture of a forest.

Comparing with Adverbs   Many one-syllable adverbs add *-er* to form the comparative and *-est* to form the superlative.

Henry's dog ran **faster** than Lou's.
Of the three dogs, Biff ran **fastest.**

Many adverbs that end in *-ly* form the comparative by adding *more* and the superlative by adding *most*.

Grandma calls **more frequently** than Aunt Sue does.
Grandpa calls **most frequently** of all.

Some adverbs change completely in the comparative and superlative forms.

well, better, best   badly, worse, worst   little, less, least

Practice   Complete each sentence by writing the correct comparative or superlative form of the adverb in parentheses.

1. This bus stops ——— than the Upsala bus. (frequently)
2. It rained ——— in June than in April. (heavily)
3. Did you really run ——— of all the racers? (fast)
4. Bill reads ——— than Mike does. (little)
5. You can do that job ——— than I did. (well)

Negatives   A **negative** is a word that reverses the meaning of the sentence. Some common negatives are *no, none, not, no one, never, nothing, nowhere,* and *nobody*. Contractions using *not* (*-n't*) are also negatives. Avoid using two negatives together.

That tape recorder <u>doesn't</u> work.   We are getting <u>nowhere</u>.
<u>No one</u> has any more   I <u>never</u> saw anything.

Practice   Rewrite each sentence to avoid double negatives.

1. Jamie hasn't never seen an elephant.
2. The rancher cannot find none of the cattle.
3. He couldn't never imagine a space colony.
4. There isn't nothing in the world as tasty as mushrooms.
5. There weren't no pencils left.

Adjective or Adverb?   Use adjectives to modify nouns and pronouns, but never verbs.

My original report is complete.   It sounds scientific.

Use adverbs to modify verbs, adjectives, and other adverbs.

The train moves slowly.   The cars are almost empty.

Good is used as an adjective. *Well* is an adjective only when it means "healthy." Otherwise, *well* is an adverb.

Isn't this apple good?   Sue feels well. (adjective)
He reads well. (adverb)

Practice   Write the correct word. Label it *Adj.* or *Adv.*

1. She was ill yesterday, but she is (good, well) today.
2. The rain (thorough, thoroughly) soaked my flower beds.
3. He is a (competent, competently) swimmer.
4. After much practice, she became a (good, well) pitcher.
5. Clouds gathered (slow, slowly) on the horizon.
6. The room looks (bright, brightly) with a new coat of paint.
7. He finished his work (easy, easily).
8. Philip speaks French (good, well).

Prepositions

Definition   A **preposition** is a word that relates a noun or pronoun to some other word in the sentence.

Everyone at the play applauded.
Do not pick the flowers in the park.
My socks and shoes were under the bed.

Sentences

The Sentence

Kinds of Sentences A **sentence** expresses a complete thought. A **declarative sentence** makes a statement and ends with a period. An **interrogative sentence** asks a question and ends with a question mark. An **imperative sentence** gives a command or makes a request and ends with a period. An **exclamatory sentence** shows excitement or strong feeling and ends with an exclamation mark.

Fourteen children signed up for the contest. (declarative)
Did you enter the track meet? (interrogative)
Give this note to your grandmother. (imperative)
What a thoughtless remark that was! (exclamatory)

Practice Copy each sentence. Add the correct punctuation, and label what kind of sentence it is.

1. Pick out the records you want to buy
2. You may buy three records or two tapes
3. Don't you already have that album
4. What a great song this is
5. You must pay before you leave the store
6. Is a tape more expensive than a record
7. Listen closely to the lyrics
8. The flute reminds me of a bird in flight
9. How smoothly the notes rise
10. How do you judge a piece of music

Compound Sentences A **compound sentence** contains two or more simple sentences that are related. The sentences are usually joined by a comma and a connecting word such as *and, or,* or *but.*

He is a good athlete, and he is also an excellent student.
Put on your glasses, or stop watching television.
The mayor wanted to win the election, but he lost.

Practice Write compound sentences by joining each pair of simple sentences with a connecting word. Use commas correctly.

1. The dog must be fed once a day. The kittens should be fed twice a day.
2. Some fish need a heated tank. Others can live in water at room temperature.
3. Wednesday it rained. We postponed our trip until Thursday.
4. You may rake the yard now. You may wait until later.
5. A few students signed up for the newspaper. Most students wanted to learn photography.

Correcting Fragments and Run-ons A sentence **fragment** is a group of words that does not express a complete thought. A **run-on sentence** strings together sentences that should be written separately. Avoid fragments and run-ons in your writing.

> Running to catch the leader.   (fragment)
> Jennifer designed the new car, she worked for at least seven months.   (run-on)

Practice Change the sentence fragments into complete sentences. Write the run-on sentences correctly.

1. John had a hamburger then he had an apple and a banana he felt sick because he ate too much.
2. Everyone standing in front of the display window.
3. I wish you had been there with us the circus was great.
4. That cheese is made from goat's milk it's very good.
5. Since the public library is closed on Sundays.

Subjects and Predicates

Simple Subjects and Complete Subjects The **simple subject** in a sentence tells who or what the sentence is about. The **complete subject** contains the simple subject and all the words that tell more about it.

> The big shaggy **dog** barked at them.   (simple subject)
> **The big shaggy dog** barked at them.   (complete subject)

Practice   Write these sentences. Circle the simple subject. Draw one line under the complete subject.

1. The people in our department lost their jobs.
2. Her briefcase was found by the taxi driver.
3. Ten-year-old Betsy won the prize.
4. The farmer's sheep were in the pen.
5. The two children have been late every day this week.
6. Customers with coupons get a discount.
7. The easiest step is the first one.
8. Microscopic animals moved through the liquid.

Simple Predicates and Complete Predicates   The **simple predicate,** the verb, tells what the subject is or does. The **complete predicate** contains the simple predicate (the verb) and all the words that tell more about it.

Timothy is waiting for his brother.   (simple predicate)
Timothy is waiting for his brother.   (complete predicate)

Practice   Write these sentences. Circle the simple predicate. Draw one line under the complete predicate.

1. The girls are going to ballet class.
2. No one has seen Marty's dog.
3. The puppy is yelping loudly.
4. All of the children do their homework.
5. Everyone wants a turn on the swing.
6. The three boys skate well.
7. Evie won the race by three meters.
8. Eleven-year-old Molly has written a letter to her uncle.

Subjects in Imperative and Interrogative Sentences   The subject of an imperative sentence is usually understood to be *you.*

(You) Don't let the cat out.   (You) Keep quiet.

To find the subject of an interrogative sentence, rearrange the question into a statement. Then ask who or what the verb talks about.

Did Harold finish his work?   Harold did finish his work.

Practice   Write *interrogative* or *imperative* to name the kinds of sentences below. Then write each simple subject.

1. Wait until eight o'clock.
2. Will they accept the invitation?
3. Did the lawmakers pass that bill?
4. Cool the bread for ten minutes.
5. Would you turn on the lamp please?

Subjects in Sentences with *here* and *there*   If a sentence begins with *here* or *there,* you can find the simple subject by asking either, Who or what is here? or Who or what is there?

Here is the <u>test</u>.   (*What is here?* Test.)

Practice   Write the simple subject of each sentence.

1. There are the two quarters.
2. Here is your notebook.
3. There was a beautiful sunset.
4. There are my two friends.
5. Here are the reports.
6. Here is your ticket.

Compound Subjects and Predicates   A **compound subject** has two or more subjects joined by a connecting word such as *and* or *or.*

The <u>children</u>, the <u>teachers</u>, and the <u>principal</u> left the school.
<u>Joe</u> or <u>Sarah</u> will lead the parade.

A **compound predicate** has two or more predicates joined by a connecting word such as *and* or *or.*

Brad <u>has seen</u> a bluebird and <u>photographed</u> it.
We'll <u>write</u> these reports or <u>type</u> our notes tonight.

Practice   Write the compound subject and the compound predicates in the sentences below. Label them *CS* or *CP.*

1. The mayor or the city councilor will make a speech.
2. You may draw a chart or make a graph for art class.
3. The boy caught a frog and drew a picture of it.
4. Mason, Laura, and Ramon are the class monitors.
5. That author has written and published ten novels.

Using Words Correctly

borrow, lend; let, leave   *Borrow* means "to take." *Lend* means "to give." *Let* means "to allow." *Leave* means "to go away from."

> May I borrow that eraser?
> I will lend you my eraser.
> Jason will let us ride his bike.
> They leave the house at seven o'clock.

Practice   Choose a word from the parentheses to complete each sentence correctly.

1. Will Dad (leave, let) us go to the movies?
2. Kate wants to (lend, borrow) me the scissors.
3. (Let, Leave) Jackson use the book now.
4. Roger promised to (lend, borrow) Syd a dollar.
5. Please do not (let, leave) until I get home.
6. I will (lend, borrow) two eggs from my neighbor.

rise, raise; teach, learn   Use *rise* when you mean "to get up or go up." Use *raise* when you mean "to move something up, to increase something, or to grow something." Use *teach* when you mean "to give instruction." Use *learn* when you mean "to receive instruction."

> The sun will rise at six o'clock.
> A crane can raise the steel beams.
> Deborah will teach me how to crochet.
> We learn about animals by observing them.

Practice   Write each sentence, choosing the correct word in parentheses.

1. Mark will (teach, learn) Michael how to water-ski.
2. The farmers (rise, raise) barley and oats.
3. Please (rise, raise) your hand before you speak.
4. This summer she will (teach, learn) us history.
5. Helium-filled balloon (rise, raise) in the air.
6. Does she want to (teach, learn) to swim?

sit, set; lie, lay   Use the verbs *sit* and *lie* when referring to a resting position. Use the verbs *set* and *lay* to mean putting an object somewhere.

    Please <u>sit</u> in a chair.   <u>Set</u> the glasses on a shelf.
    Don't <u>lie</u> on the floor.   <u>Lay</u> the papers on a table.

Practice   Write the correct word from the parentheses.

1. Mom likes to (sit, set) in her favorite chair.
2. I will (lie, lay) the towels on the counter.
3. You should (sit, set) that plant in a sunny window.
4. (Sit, Set) the radio here.
5. The dog is not allowed to (lie, lay) on the sofa.

who, whom   The pronoun *who* is the correct form to use as subject. *Whom* is the correct form for direct object.

    <u>Who</u> is knocking at the door?
    <u>Whom</u> did you see at the show? (*You did see* whom?)

Practice   Write the correct pronoun for each sentence.

1. (Who, Whom) will fix this fan?
2. (Who, Whom) is the owner of the red car?
3. (Who, Whom) did you telephone?
4. (Who, Whom) did he see at the skating rink?

we, us   To use the pronouns *we* or *us* correctly with a noun in a sentence, first look at the noun. If the noun is the subject of the sentence or if it follows a linking verb, use the pronoun *we* with it. If the noun is the object after an action verb, use *us* with it.

    <u>We</u> students are active.   The busiest people are <u>we</u> teachers.
    Please help <u>us</u> volunteers.

Practice   Choose the correct pronoun for each sentence.

1. (We, Us) students need help with math.
2. The oldest students are (we, us) sixth-graders.
3. Will Ms. McCarthy help (we, us) after school?
4. The teachers will congratulate (we, us) students.

there   To find whether the subject and verb agree in a sentence beginning with *there*, drop *there*. Then rearrange the sentence so that the subject is first.

There **are** two <u>birds</u> in the tree. (Two <u>birds</u> **are** in the tree.)

Practice   Write each sentence, choosing the correct verb.

1. There (was, were) two holes in my jacket.
2. There (is, are) a good movie at the theatre.
3. Now there (is, are) three people in line.
4. There (is, are) two storms in the forecast.
5. There (was, were) more shirts in the closet.
6. Soon there (was, were) butterflies everywhere.
7. There (is, are) a tennis court behind the school.
8. There (was, were) some extra copies here.

in, into, of   The preposition *in* means "located within." *Into* means "movement from the outside to the inside."

Dad is waiting for you <u>in</u> the car.
Please go <u>into</u> the house.

Always use *of* as a preposition. It is not a helping verb.

Fran <u>should have</u> been here by now. (*not* should of)

Practice   Write each sentence, choosing the correct word(s) in parentheses.

1. We (would have, would of) been earlier, but the bus was late.
2. Put the trash bags (in, into) the garbage can.
3. Jan is (in, into) the library.
4. You (might of, might have) been seriously hurt.
5. Let's go (in, into) the classroom.
6. Everyone is (in, into) the swimming pool.
7. I (should of, should have) known better.
8. The cat slipped (in, into) the garage.
9. The train (must have, must of) broken down.
10. Your photographs are (in, into) my album.

Punctuation and Capitalization

Abbreviations   Abbreviations are shortened forms of words. Most abbreviations begin with a capital letter and end with a period.

Titles

Mr. (Mister) Mr. Ed Lane   Sr. (Senior) Paul Haley, Sr.
Mrs. (Mistress) Mrs. Ida Lu   Jr. (Junior) Paul Haley, Jr.
Dr. (Doctor) Dr. Ella Solt

Days of the Week

Mon. (Monday)   Thurs. (Thursday)   Sat. (Saturday)
Tues. (Tuesday)   Fri. (Friday)   Sun. (Sunday)
Wed. (Wednesday)

Months of the Year

Jan. (January)   Apr. (April)   Oct. (October)
Feb. (February)   Aug. (August)   Nov. (November)
Mar. (March)   Sept. (September)   Dec. (December)

May, June, and *July* are usually not abbreviated.

Words Used in Addresses

St. (Street)   Blvd. (Boulevard)   Pkwy. (Parkway)
Rd. (Road)   Rte. (Route)   Mt. (Mount or Mountain)
Ave. (Avenue)   Apt. (Apartment)   Expy. (Expressway)
Dr. (Drive)

Words Used in Business

Co. (Company)   Corp. (Corporation)   Inc. (Incorporated)

Some abbreviations are written in all capital letters, with a letter standing for each important word. A period follows each letter in this type of abbreviation.

P.D. (Police Department)   P.O. (Post Office)
M.P. (Member of Parliament)   R.N. (Registered Nurse)
J.P. (Justice of the Peace)   U.K. (United Kingdom)

Some abbreviations have neither capital letters nor periods.

mph (miles per hour)   hp (horsepower)   ft (feet)

Abbreviations of government agencies or national organizations do not usually have periods.

SBA (Small Business Administration)
OAS (Organization of American States)
PBS (Public Broadcasting Service)
NATO (North Atlantic Treaty Organization)

The United States Postal Service uses two capital letters and no period in each of its state abbreviations.

CA (California)   OH (Ohio)   NJ (New Jersey)
IN (Indiana)   SC (South Carolina)

Practice   Write abbreviations where you can for each item.

1. Mount Rushmore
2. Post Office Box 54
3. Sure Goods, Incorporated
4. Wednesday, April 22
5. Nat Inge, Registered Nurse
6. 12 feet
7. Mister Al Tribe
8. 43 Maple Boulevard

Titles   The important words and the first and last words in a title are capitalized. Titles of books, magazines, and newspapers are underlined.

<u>Great Expectations</u>   <u>Journal of Photography</u>   <u>Daily News</u>

Titles of short stories, articles, songs, poems, and book chapters are enclosed in quotation marks.

"How to Redecorate for Pennies"   "What Is Orange?"
"Yellow Rose of Texas"

Practice   Copy these sentences, writing the titles correctly.

1. The rally is described in this morning's phoenix gazette.
2. The article cutting food costs in this month's modern consumer is very interesting.
3. She sings home on the range whenever she is bored.
4. Have you read bleak house, a novel by Charles Dickens?
5. Jorge Luis Borges wrote the story streetcorner man.

Punctuation

End Punctuation   There are three end marks. A period (**.**) ends
a statement or a command. A question mark (**?**) follows a question. An exclamation mark (**!**) follows an exclamation of strong
feeling.

> Seattle is in the state of Washington. (statement)
> Put these dishes away. (command)
> What time is lunch served? (question)
> How cold it is! (exclamation)

Practice   Write these sentences, adding end punctuation.

1. Is the dog in the kennel

2. Please close the door

3. Who is responsible for this mess

4. What a fierce storm that was

5. We'll begin the spelling lesson in ten minutes

Apostrophe   Use an apostrophe in the following ways.

1. Use an apostrophe to show possession.

> Doug's rabbit   girls' shoes   women's talents

2. Use an apostrophe in contractions in place of one or more
dropped letters.

> isn't (is not)   wasn't (was not)   I'm (I am)
> can't (cannot)   we're (we are)   they've (they have)
> won't (will not)   it's (it is)   they'll (they will)

Practice   Write a contraction or a possessive for each item.

1. cage of the mice   **3.** I have   **5.** is not
2. you are   **4.** books of the boys **6.** he is

Colon   Use a colon after the greeting in a business letter.

> Dear Mrs. Trimby: Dear Realty Homes:

Practice   Write two possible greetings for a business letter to
the Palmer Doorbell Company.

Commas   A comma tells the reader to pause between the words it separates. Use commas in the following ways.

1. Use a comma to separate words in a series.

   We'll go to the zoo on Monday, Wednesday, or Friday.

2. Use a comma to separate simple sentences in a compound sentence.

   Some students were at lunch, and others were studying.

3. Use commas to set off an appositive from the rest of the sentence.

   Margaret Reilly, Nan's aunt, is a newspaper reporter.

4. Use a comma after the introductory word *yes, no, oh,* or *well.*

   Well, it's too cold out.   No, it isn't six yet.

5. Use a comma to separate a noun in direct address.

   Jean, help me fix this tire.   How was your trip, Grandpa?

6. Use a comma to separate the month and day from the year and to separate the year from the rest of the sentence.

   On July 4, 1776, our nation was born.

7. Use a comma between the names of a city and a state.

   Chicago, Illinois   Miami, Florida

8. Use a comma after the greeting in a friendly letter.

   Dear Deena,   Dear Uncle Rudolph,

9. Use a comma after the closing in a letter.

   Your nephew,   Sincerely yours,

10. Use a comma after a statement or command in a direct quotation when the speaker's name is at the end. Use a comma after the speaker's name when it begins a sentence containing a direct quotation.

    "Bring a map," said Eli.   Joyce said, "I must go."

11. Use a comma to set off the word *too* when it means "also."

Michael has a new haircut, too.

Practice   Write each item. Add commas as needed.

1. Well Nancy your report is due on October 20 1983.
2. Edwin Ames, Jr. a well-respected judge tried the case.
3. Combine the flour raisins and milk and mix thoroughly.
4. "Please pass the salad" said Mrs. Falcone.
5. Gerald asked "Are the chairs lamps and rugs on sale?"
6. Dear Mugsie
7. Yours truly
8. You can mow the lawn clean your room or relax.
9. The parchment is finished but the ink is still wet.
10. With your help Liz we will be ready before April 1 1984.

Punctuating Dialogue   **Dialogue** is written conversation. **Quotation marks** are used to set dialogue apart from the rest of the sentence. The first word of a quotation begins with a capital letter when it begins a new sentence. Punctuation belongs inside the closing quotation marks. Commas separate a quotation from the rest of the sentence.

"That novel," explained the teacher, "was written in 1852."
"I need a break," said Ann. "The undertow is very strong."
Fran asked, "Did you tell anyone the secret?"

Practice   Write these sentences, punctuating and capitalizing the quotations correctly.

1. She shouted save me a place, too
2. What a great painting it is exclaimed the critic
3. Look at the sun said Irene it sparkles on the water
4. Her supervisor said you'll receive a raise in salary
5. Where is room 202 asked Fred
6. I'm sure said Morgan that we'll be late
7. Patience is better than wisdom said Isaac
8. Madeline Ling asked what are floppy disks
9. The best actor replied Mom is on now

Capitalization

1. Capitalize the first word of every sentence.

   <u>W</u>hat an unusual color the roses are!

2. Capitalize the pronoun *I*.

   On April 14, <u>I</u> will fly to London.

3. Capitalize every important word in the names of particular people, places, or things.

Emily <u>G</u>. <u>S</u>henk	<u>E</u>don, <u>O</u>hio	<u>G</u>ateway <u>A</u>rch
<u>T</u>homas <u>J</u>akups	<u>T</u>odd's <u>G</u>rocery	<u>L</u>incoln <u>M</u>emorial
<u>L</u>ake <u>M</u>ilton	<u>S</u>tatue of <u>L</u>iberty	<u>G</u>olden <u>G</u>ate <u>B</u>ridge
<u>I</u>reland		

4. Capitalize titles or their abbreviations when used with a person's name.

<u>G</u>overnor <u>B</u>radford	<u>M</u>s. <u>I</u>da <u>L</u>ee	<u>M</u>r. <u>M</u>ax <u>S</u>ouda

5. Capitalize the names of months and days.

   My birthday is on the last <u>M</u>onday in <u>M</u>arch.

6. Capitalize the names of businesses.

<u>M</u>oore <u>P</u>ower <u>T</u>ools, <u>I</u>ncorporated	<u>T</u>he <u>S</u>tatus <u>C</u>ompany

7. Capitalize names of holidays and other special events.

<u>F</u>lag <u>D</u>ay	<u>H</u>alloween	<u>F</u>ourth of <u>J</u>uly

8. Capitalize the first word of a direct quotation.

   David shouted, "<u>B</u>uckle your seat belts!"

9. Capitalize the first and last word and all important words in the titles of books, magazines, newspapers, stories, songs, poems, reports, and outlines.

<u>From the Earth to the Moon</u>	"<u>The Rainbow Connection</u>"
<u>The New York Times</u>	"<u>Growing Up</u>"
<u>The Luckiest of All</u>	"<u>How to Write a Story</u>"

10. Capitalize the first word of each main topic and subtopic in an outline.

    I. Types of libraries
       A. Large public library
       B. Bookmobile

11. Capitalize the first word in the greeting and closing of a letter.

Dear Marcia,   Yours truly,
Dear Olson Mills: Sincerely,

Practice   Write each sentence. Use capital letters correctly.

1. have you read the wind in the willows?
2. we visited the eiffel tower in paris, france.
3. karen asked, "where is the empire state building?"
4. i read an article called "a journey to alaska."
5. president franklin d. roosevelt came here on june 3.
6. chuck wrote to the patchwork prints company.
7. doctor donavan said, "eddie has no cavities."
8. "what a good time we will have!" exclaimed david.
9. my favorite book is little house on the prairie.
10. fenway park is one of the oldest baseball parks.
11. our meeting is scheduled for valentine's day, february 14.
12. last monday ms. ide saw the metropolitan museum of art.
13. monica works at the jamestown columnns restaurant.
14. this toy catalog comes from elk grove village, illinois.
15. mr. john w. willis has said, "if you see vermont from burke mountain, you've seen it all."
16. jessica asked captain douglas, "how many more miles before we reach bermuda?"
17. i wrote a short story called, "beyond the yellow stripes."
18. on september 18 i plan to go on a whale watch.
19. please open the door for me, paula.
20. "you must be mistaken," said sharon. "i don't have your apartment keys."

More Practice

- **Kinds of Sentences** Copy each sentence. Capitalize and punctuate it correctly. Then label what kind of sentence it is.

  1. the sky was threatening
  2. what a dark cloud that was
  3. was a twister approaching
  4. our family found shelter
  5. listen to the wind
  6. has the storm passed
  7. a tree hit our barn
  8. help me with the repairs

- **Subjects and Predicates** Copy each sentence. Draw a line between the complete subject and the complete predicate. Underline the simple subject once and the simple predicate twice.

  9. Deena and Carlotta wandered into the city park.
  10. Paddle boats on the pond were shaped like swans.
  11. Several passengers smiled and waved at their friends on shore.
  12. Carlotta relaxed and took pictures of flowers.

- **Finding the Subject** Write the subject of each sentence.

  13. Read this travel folder about Jamaica.
  14. Is the Rocklands Bird Feeding Station on the island?
  15. Ride a bamboo raft down the Martha Brae River.
  16. There are craft shops in Montego Bay.

- **Compound Sentences** Copy only the compound sentences. Add commas. Underline the simple sentences that make up each compound. Circle the connecting word.

  17. Mild Virginia breezes blow and spring is in the air.
  18. You can see and smell cherry blossoms everywhere.
  19. The Capitol runs tours on Saturdays but the FBI is closed.
  20. Did I. M. Pei design the new wing of the National Gallery of Art or was it some other architect's work?

Write a compound sentence from each pair of sentences.

21. The sea was calm. The merchant ship was in grave danger.
22. Another ship appeared. It raised a pirate flag.
23. They could outrun the pirates. They could fight.
24. The captain grabbed the helm. The crew worked the sails.
25. The pirates pursued. The merchant ship escaped.

- **Correcting Run-ons and Fragments**   Write a complete sentence from each fragment below. Write the run-ons correctly.

26. Waiting in her dressing room for the start of the show.
27. Laced both of Page's skates carefully.
28. The performers skated across the ice and they danced in a line and music accompanied their routine.
29. The audience cheered wildly Page had glided around the rink and leaped into the air.

- **Using Words Correctly**   Write the word *lend, borrow, let,* or *leave* to complete each sentence.

30. _____ the building immediately after school.
31. Will you _____ me a lawn chair?
32. _____ a piece of paper from the person next to you.
33. Dad, can I _____ this fish go free?

Enrichment

A. Write the word *IMPERATIVE* down the left side of your paper. Use each letter to begin the first word of a sentence. Make all ten sentences imperative. Now follow these same steps, using the word *DECLARATIVE*.
B. The paragraph below is about sentence fragments. However, none of the sentences in the paragraph are complete. Change each fragment into a sentence.

When you write a sentence fragment. No matter how many words. Any group of words that does not form a sentence. Without expressing a complete thought. Because the subject or predicate or both are missing.

More Practice

- **Nouns**   Write the nouns in these sentences.

    1. Jerry and Bill spend the summer at a ranch in Arizona.
    2. The herd of cattle is treated with care.
    3. The ranchers eat in a kitchen next to the bunkhouse.
    4. Jerry will compete in two events at the rodeo.

- **Singular and Plural Nouns**   Write each sentence, using the plural form of the nouns in parentheses.

    5. The wind rustled through the autumn ____. (leaf)
    6. ____ honked on the ____ of the lake. (Goose, shore)
    7. The ____ watched the ____. (man, deer)
    8. The ____ harvested ____. (farmer, potato)
    9. ____ ripened and fell from the ____. (Berry, bush)

- **Common and Proper Nouns**   Write a proper noun for each common noun below.

10. country	12. holiday	14. president	16. car
11. building	13. river	15. city	17. bank

- **Possessive Nouns**   Rewrite each item. Use possessive nouns.

18. sketch the artist has	22. book of Chris
19. quiz for the student	23. dog owned by the Harrises
20. hoof of the horse	24. squeal of the mice
21. antler of the moose	25. smile of Luis

- **Appositives**   Combine each pair of sentences into a single sentence with an appositive. Use commas correctly.

    26. Clara is my neighbor. She plays in a jazz band.
    27. She plays the piccolo. A piccolo is a small flute.

28. The band is the Ivory Coast. It will perform tonight.

29. Soon the band will appear at the Somerville Jamboree. It is the biggest jazz competition in the state.

- **Using Words Correctly**   Write the correct word in parentheses to complete each sentence.

30. Will you (teach, learn) me to change a tire?

31. I can (teach, learn) the safest method from you.

32. Your owner's manual will (teach, learn) you, too.

33. The car will (raise, rise) slowly under the jack.

34. (Rise, Raise) the spare tire up onto the wheel.

- **Building Vocabulary**   For each word below, write a synonym and an antonym.

35. screamed	**37.** rapidly	**39.** strong	**41.** grin
36. careful	**38.** clean	**40.** break	**42.** icy

──**Enrichment**────────────

Copy the chart below, including the letters from the word *SINGULAR* for the boxes on the left. For each box, write a noun that fits the column heading and begins with the letter shown in the first box of each row. The first row of answers has been done for you.

	PERSON	PLACE	THING	IDEA
S	secretary	Seattle	sand	sadness
I				
N				
G				
U				
L				
A				
R				

More Practice

- **Main Idea of a Paragraph**   Read the two groups of sentences below. Then write the answers to the questions that follow.

    Movie special effects experts can build miniature ships that would fit into a bathtub. Then they photograph them so that, on screen, they appear to be enormous ocean liners. Thanks to these experts, huge spaceships can seem to soar between planets across a movie-studio galaxy. With great skill, they can turn ordinary human actors into believable characters from science fiction. The make-up from one recent film took seven hours to apply each day! There is really nothing that a screenwriter can imagine that a movie technician cannot make happen on the screen.

    Lighting and sound are not the only areas for special effects. To create the effect of an earthquake, a camera person can simply rock the camera. Thin wires can make a bicycle appear to move by itself. How do special effects make an actress fly over rooftops? Some actors do their own stunts.

    1. Which group of sentences is a paragraph?
    2. What is the main idea of the paragraph?
    3. Which sentence does not belong in the paragraph?
    4. Why is the other group of sentences not a paragraph?

- **Topic Sentences and Supporting Details**   Using the two groups of sentences from the previous exercise, answer the following questions.

    1. What is the topic sentence of the paragraph above?
    2. Reread the group of sentences that is not a paragraph. Draw the sentences together by writing a topic sentence for them and turning them into a paragraph with a main idea. Add or delete details as needed.

Below are four possible topic sentences. Choose two of them to develop into paragraphs. For each topic sentence you choose, write two or three sentences that give supporting details.

1. The automobile of the future will be nothing like the car of today.
2. That was the funniest thing that ever happened to me.
3. There are many different ways to cook an egg.
4. Cleaning out my desk can be a great adventure.

- **Order in Paragraphs** If the sentences below were in a different order, they would be a paragraph of instructions. Read over the sentences carefully. Then write them in the correct order. Add order words to make the paragraph clear.

> Press the shutter.
> Taking a good photograph can be easy.
> Look through the view-finder at your subject.
> You may want to ask your subject to smile.
> Be sure you have loaded your camera with film.
> Hold the camera steady.

- **Proofreading** Proofread the following paragraph, and find the fourteen errors. You may use a dictionary to help you check for spelling mistakes. Then copy the paragraph correctly on your paper.

> Here is one trick that dieters use to loose weight. They eat selery. Selery ackually has very few caloreys. it takes more caloreys to chew on and swalow a peace of selery than the selery has to begin with?

Now proofread this paragraph, and find ten errors. Write the paragraph correctly.

> There is more then one way to buy a concert ticket You can call and charge you're tickets to your credit card account. You can right a letter to the music directer. Be sure to lists the number of seats, the price the date, and the time of the preformance. You can also by your tickets in person at the box office.

More Practice

- **Action Verbs and Being Verbs**   Write each verb. Label it *action* or *being*.

    1. The air smelled fresh.
    2. Waves rocked the tiny boats in the harbor.
    3. A thick mist covers the wharves.
    4. The sailors seem tired of the sea.
    5. They will repair their heavy nets.

- **Direct Objects**   Write the direct objects in exercises 1–5.

- **Linking Verbs**   Copy each sentence. Underline the linking verb. Label predicate nouns *PN* and predicate adjectives *PA*.

    6. A sea gull is a hearty creature.
    7. The early morning wind is damp.
    8. José became sleepy after sunset.
    9. My granddaughter is the only good pitcher on the team.

- **Main Verbs and Auxiliaries**   Write each verb phrase. Underline main verbs once and auxiliaries twice.

    10. Two scientists have removed the bottles from the shelf.
    11. They're mixing the chemicals together carefully.
    12. The scientists shouldn't add too much to the acid.
    13. The test tube may explode.
    14. Have they finished their experiments?

- **Verb Tenses**   Write the past and future tenses of these verbs.

    15. bake   17. fold   19. reply   21. erase
    16. fill   18. attend   20. invite   22. try

    Label each verb in exercises 1–5 *present*, *past*, or *future*.

- **Principal Parts of Verbs**   Copy each verb. Circle the irregular verbs. Write the past and past participle for each verb.

  23. glance   **25.** swim   **27.** soar   **29.** ring
  24. write   **26.** conquer   **28.** steal   **30.** freeze

- **Irregular Verbs**   Write a sentence, using the past participle of each verb. Underline each verb.

  31. take   **32.** drive   **33.** speak   **34.** throw

- **Subject-Verb Agreement**   Write each sentence, choosing the correct verb or verb phrase from the parentheses.

  35. Nicole and her cousins (work, works) in the barn.
  36. Neither Ida nor the boys (has ridden, have ridden) a plow.
  37. Either Nicole or Al (has broken, have broken) the ladder.

- **Using Words Correctly**   Write the word from the parentheses that completes each sentence correctly.

  38. I (set, sit) in the middle row of the theatre.
  39. A tall man (set, sit) a package on the seat in front of me.
  40. "Why don't you (lie, lay) your box on the floor?" I asked.
  41. He said, "Then where will my dog (lie, lay)?"

- **Building Vocabulary**   Add a prefix, a suffix, or both to each word. Write as many new words as you can.

  42. agree   **43.** content   **44.** amuse   **45.** fold

Enrichment

Form two teams of players. Each player writes an irregular verb on an index card. (You may use pages 100–101 for help.) Then play Verb Charades by acting out a verb from one of your opponents' cards. The other members of your team try to figure out the word. The player who guesses your verb must give its principal parts before a point is scored. Set a three-minute time limit for each turn. Alternate turns between the two teams.

More Practice

- **Using Your Senses** Pretend that you are writing to a pen pal who lives in a distant place. Because she lives so far away, she will probably never be able to visit you. However, she has written you a letter wanting to know all about where you live. Use your five senses—seeing, hearing, tasting, smelling, and touching—to describe some of your environment to her. Write at least one sentence for each topic below. You may use one or more than one sense in each description.

  1. A kind of flower that grows nearby
  2. What your playground is like during recess
  3. A type of animal that you see often
  4. What it is like to ride a bike around your neighborhood
  5. How summer feels
  6. Your favorite lunch
  7. What your classroom is like during a test
  8. The school cafeteria at lunchtime

- **Using Exact Words** Rewrite each sentence below in two ways. In each, try to make an exact picture with your words. The first sentence has been done for you.

  1. His cat is big and orange.
     His fat cat has fur that reminds me of a golden marble.
     His cat stands tall and arches her back of amber fur.
  2. I can skate fast.
  3. Her room is a mess.
  4. I heard a sound.
  5. Martha walked to her office.
  6. A man closed the book.
  7. Every nurse was nice to the girl.
  8. A little rain fell.

- **Choosing Details** Below is a list of eight possible story characters. Each has one outstanding personality trait. Without naming any traits, write a two- or three-sentence description of five of the characters. Choose details carefully to show what each character is like.

1. an extremely intelligent five year old
2. a lazy dog
3. an athletic young woman
4. a proud giraffe
5. a stingy grocer
6. a sympathetic doctor
7. a selfish older brother
8. an angry customer

Remember, the details you include in a description will depend on your purpose in writing it. Look over the list of items below. Choose three of them. For each one, write two descriptive sentences, each with a different purpose. The first topic has been done for you.

1. a rabbit

   (to give facts about how a rabbit feels) **The rabbit's fur was smooth, but there was a toughness in its thick winter growth.**

   (to tell how charming a rabbit can be) **A fluffy ball of fur wiggled its pink nose into the newly cut grass.**

2. a bicycle
3. a towel
4. a pencil

5. a tomato
6. a pair of sneakers
7. a baby

- **Proofreading** Find eleven mistakes in the paragraph below. Use a dictionary to check spelling. Write the paragraph correctly.

   The spidder about the size of a sesame seed or a freckle sat in the very scenter of her webb It seamed to be waiting. it sat on a butiful netlike trap for some tiny inset to become it's pray.

More Practice

- **Pronouns and Antecedents** Copy the pronouns in these sentences. Beside each pronoun, write its antecedent(s).

  1. When Ina and Sal had enough money, they gave a party.
  2. It was a costume party.
  3. Marion and I dressed up as lobsters. I am Oscar.
  4. We wore red shells, claws, and small dark eyes.

- **Pronouns as Subjects and Objects** Write the correct pronoun for each sentence. Label subject pronouns *S* and object pronouns *O*.

  5. Dad drove (we, us) to the apple orchards.
  6. (They, Them) are near Lake Fairlee.
  7. Two apples hit (me, I) on the shoulder.
  8. I put (they, them) in a big wooden basket.

- **Possessive Pronouns** Write the word that correctly completes each sentence.

  9. (My, Mine) sand castle is bigger than (your, yours).
  10. (They're, Their) castles have more windows than (our's, ours).
  11. (Her, Hers) has three drawbridges and a moat.
  12. (Who's, Whose) castle was destroyed by the tide?
  13. The waves knocked down (its, it's) towers.

- **Pronouns After Linking Verbs** Write each sentence, choosing the correct pronoun from those in parentheses.

  14. The woman who built the space rocket was (she, her).
  15. The astronauts who operate the controls are (them, they).
  16. It was (he, him) who landed the craft safely.
  17. The first reporters on the scene were (he, him) and (I, me).

- **Compound Subjects and Objects**   Write the correct compound subjects and objects from the parentheses. Label subjects *S* and objects *O*.

  18. (Sue and her, Sue and she) showed slides of London.

  19. (He and I, I and he) watched carefully.

  20. The Tower of London fascinated (they and I, them and me).

  21. Big Ben impressed (him and me, me and him), too.

- **Using Words Correctly**   Write *who* or *whom* to complete each sentence. Label your answer *S* for subject or *O* for object.

  22. _____ can I trust?

  23. _____ lost this wallet?

  24. _____ saw the flashlight in the car?

  25. _____ should I thank for this gift?

  26. _____ did you meet?

  27. _____ was the first person at the scene of the crash?

  28. _____ began the conversation with a joke?

  29. _____ should I call for help?

  30. _____ crawled around the lobby on her hands and knees?

  31. _____ are you watching?

  32. _____ is polite, intelligent, and healthy?

  33. _____ will you inform of your plans?

Enrichment

Write the word that completes each sentence correctly. Draw a box around each letter that is boxed here. Unscramble the eleven boxed letters to form the word that answers this silly pronoun question.

Who is married to Uncle Cedents?

1. Use the subject form for pronouns □ _ □ □ _ linking verbs.

2. A pronoun takes the _ _ _ □ □ of a noun.

3. *I, he, she, it, we,* and *they* are always □ _ _ _ □ _ □ pronouns.

4. A possessive pronoun shows _ _ □ _ _ _ _ _ _ .

5. Either _ _ _ □ _ _ _ _ _ nouns, adjectives, or _ _ _ □ _ _ _ _
can be linked to the subject of a sentence.

More Practice

- **Writing a Good Beginning** The following paragraph is the second paragraph in a story. Write a good beginning of four or five sentences to come before it. Try to draw your readers into the story and leave them curious about what will happen.

    I froze in my tracks and stared at the shadowy figure standing before me. What mysterious intruder was lurking there? Slowly I raised my hand. The visitor did exactly the same thing. Suddenly I knew who my threatening stranger was. I had been frightened by my own reflection in the full-length mirror on the far wall!

- **Telling Enough** Rewrite the following paragraph. Add enough details to make a vivid scene that comes alive for your reader. Do not try to tell everything, but tell enough to hold a reader's interest.

    Maurice had worked all day preparing the meal for them. They sat down and ate the food. They ate everything, but they looked disappointed. Maurice knew something must have gone wrong. He went back into the kitchen and studied his cookbooks. Then he realized he had left out one of the key ingredients in the recipe. He understood why they had not been pleased.

- **Writing Dialogue** Change at least three sentences below to dialogue. Try to reflect the speaker's feelings.

    Jane told Mom that Rusty was the best dog in the world. Mom said she loved Rusty, too, but that he had to stop chasing children in the neighborhood and barking at them. Jane explained that Rusty did it only because he wanted to play with the children. Mom asked her if she thought that reason would satisfy the children's angry, frightened parents.

- **Improving Your Sentences**   Rewrite both of the following paragraphs so that some of the sentences are long and some of them are short.

> We wanted to fix up the old shed. We bought some white paint. We also bought some red paint. Judy found some old paint brushes. We painted the walls white. The doors and trim were painted bright red. We worked all day. The shack looked like new when we were done. It would be a great clubhouse.

> I needed to think of a subject for my short-story assignment, but I could not think of anything, and the story was due in three days. Then I came up with the idea of keeping a diary because I thought that, possibly, the events in the average day of a sixth grader might be made into an interesting story. I walked around with a notebook for a whole day, taking notes of everything I did and what I said and what people said to me. When I sat down to write my story, I found that I had more than enough material for a really unusual description about the good, bad, funny, and serious things that happened in my day-to-day life. Everyone in my class liked my story, and the teacher decided to make a class project of having us keep diaries and write stories based on them.

- **Proofreading**   Proofread the following paragraph to find the ten errors in spelling, punctuation, and grammar. Use a dictionary whenever you are unsure of the spelling of a word or confused about the meaning of a homophone. Then write the paragraph correctly on your paper.

> I could not understand why Jill had not answered my question I was looking rigt at her. I kept starring at her and repeted what I had said, but she just looked off into space and did not speak. then I noticed something strange about her ears. After a careful look, I spotted the tiny radio headphones hiden by her thick hair. I new she could not here me because she was listening to hers favrite music.

More Practice

- **Getting Meaning from Context** Write the word(s) closest in meaning to the underlined word in each sentence.

  1. Herds of caribou moved slowly across the cold, empty <u>tundra</u>.
     kind of metal   treeless plain   gentle
  2. We rowed out to the sailboat in our <u>dinghy</u>.
     motorboat   wild dog   rowboat
  3. As the mystery grew, her face took on a <u>quizzical</u> look.
     puzzled   happy   sad
  4. Rob is so <u>maladroit</u> that he trips on the sidewalk.
     active   intelligent   clumsy

- **Finding Words in a Dictionary** Write these words in alphabetical order. For each word, tell whether you would find it before, after, or on the page with the guide words *jester/jitter*.

  jitney   jetty   jeer   jocular   juvenile   jinx
  jiggle   jibe   jaguar   jewelry   jingle   jounce

- **Using Dictionary Definitions** Read the dictionary entry for *opening*. For each sentence, write the part of speech and the number of the meaning for *opening*.

  o·pen·ing |ō pə nĭng| *n.* **1.** The act of becoming open: *the opening of the West.* **2.** An open space or clearing: *an opening in the woods.* **3.** The first occasion of something, especially of a play. **4.** A favorable opportunity: *motorists vying for an opening.* **5.** An unfilled job; a vacancy: *an opening on the teaching staff.*

  5. Raul invited us to the <u>opening</u> of his exhibit at the museum.
  6. There are several summer job <u>openings</u> at my mom's office.
  7. Through an <u>opening</u> in the trees, we saw the mountain.
  8. At the first <u>opening</u>, I'll ask Dad for five dollars.

- **Using a Dictionary for Pronunciation**   Use these special spellings to answer the following questions.

cortege |kôr **tĕzh′**| vulgarity |vŭl **găr′** ĭ tē|
oscillate |**ŏs′** ə lāt′| melancholy |**mĕl′** ən **kŏl′** ē|

9. Which syllables in *oscillate* and *melancholy* have the same vowel sound? What is the symbol for that sound called?
10. Which syllable of *cortege* is spoken with more stress?
11. Which syllable of *vulgarity* is given the most stress?

- **Using an Encyclopedia**   Imagine that your encyclopedia has one volume for each letter of the alphabet. Write the letter of the volume you would use to answer each question below. Then look up the answers in an encyclopedia.

12. Who was James K. Polk?   14. What do gibbons eat?
13. How high is Longs Peak?   15. Where is Algiers?

- **The Newspaper**   Use the newspaper index below. Write the letters and page numbers for the sections or features to which you would turn to answer these questions.

Business C1–8   Editorials A12–13   Sports B9–14
Classified D6–15   Letters A14   TV/Radio C13
Comics C12   Real Estate D16–20   Weather D11

16. Will High-Tech Electronics merge with Computers, Inc.?
17. Are any houses for sale on the South Side?
18. When is that snowstorm expected to reach our area?
19. How do readers feel about plans for the new high school?

- **Choosing Reference Aids**   Write *encyclopedia*, *almanac*, *atlas*, or *newspaper* to tell where to find answers to these questions.

20. Which baseball team won the World Series in 1963?
21. What highway runs from Washington, D.C., to Richmond, Virginia?
22. What is tungsten, and what are its uses?
23. What did the President say in his speech last night?

More Practice

• **Taking Notes** Read the paragraph below, and take notes to answer the question *What is the food value of bread?* Write only the key words that will help you recall the facts.

> The nutritional content of different types of bread varies greatly. Carefully baked bread containing natural, wholesome ingredients is of very high food value. The milk used in bread contains proteins and calcium. Good bread also contains vitamins, minerals, protein, and carbohydrates. Whole-wheat and soybean flour breads are believed to have higher nutritional value than refined white bread, even though extra vitamins are often added to refined bread before baking.

• **Making an Outline** Use the notes below to complete the outline at the top of the next page. Write a title. Then turn the questions in the notes into main topics. Write the facts in the notes that support the main topics as subtopics. Write the facts that tell about a subtopic as details under that subtopic.

What are the main kinds of bread, and what are they like?
    —two main kinds of bread—leavened, unleavened
    —leavened—can be fermented with yeast
    —leavened—can be fermented with baking powder or soda
    —unleavened bread—not fermented

What is the early history of bread?
    —early humans made bread from grass
    —early humans learned to grind grain
    —early humans cooked grain and water
    —Egyptians made first oven
    —Egyptians made bread rise
    —Native Americans made cornbread

I. Main kinds of bread
   A. Leavened bread
      1.
      2.
   B.
II.
   A. Early humans
      1.
      2.
      3. Learned to cook grain and water
   B.
      1.
      2.
   C.

- **Writing a Paragraph from an Outline** Read the section from an outline below. Write a topic sentence for it. Then write an interesting paragraph for it.

Alexander Graham Bell

I. Childhood
   A. Born in Scotland
   B. Grandfather taught speech, father taught deaf-mutes
      1. Alexander was interested in speech, hearing
      2. Alexander learned public speaking skills
   C. Studied at Edinburgh, London
      1. studied speech
      2. studied acoustics (hearing)

- **Proofreading** Proofread the following paragraph to find ten errors. Use a dictionary to check spelling. Write the paragraph correctly on your paper.

    Bacteria are really microscopic plants that our so small that they are invisibel to the human eye They arenot green because they do not contain any chlorophyll. Bacteria our made up of protoplasm they have only one sell. Their are four main types of bacterai.

More Practice

- **Reviewing End Punctuation**   Write these sentences, adding correct end punctuation.

  1. Is the mountain rumbling   **3.** Watch for the smoke

  2. What a strange noise it is   **4.** A volcano can erupt

- **Commas**   Write these sentences, inserting commas as needed.

  5. Morris Frank attended college, worked as an insurance salesman and led an active social life.

  6. Yes Morris was blind.

  7. His friends guided him around town but Morris was not content.

  8. He learned of the work of Dorothy Eustis a dog trainer.

  9. She believed that dogs could lead the blind down busy streets around obstacles and through unfamiliar places.

  10. Morris wrote to Dorothy and she invited him to visit her.

  11. Morris Frank Dorothy Eustis and Willi Ebeling founded a school to train guide dogs in New Jersey.

- **Abbreviations**   Write abbreviations where you can for these items.

  12. New York   **14.** Main Street   **16.** Post Office

  13. 20 feet   **15.** the Knot Company   **17.** Apartment 16

- **Punctuating Dialogue**   Copy these sentences. Capitalize and punctuate each quotation.

  18. where did you learn to drive shouted the taxi driver.

  19. What lovely roses you sell exclaimed a customer.

  20. The newspaper vendor hollered get the late edition here

  21. this train said the conductor goes to Park Street

  22. take two tokens now said the commuter you will save time

- **Titles**   Write each title correctly.

23. david copperfield (book)   **26.** the birthmark (story)
24. daily star (newspaper)   **27.** sailor's lullabye (song)
25. pacific weekly (magazine)   **28.** song at sunset (poem)

- **Using Words Correctly**   Write the pronoun *we* or *us*.

29. ____ students had never heard of Georges Mélies.
30. Arthur told ____ movie fans that Mélies was an inventor.
31. ____ boys read about the special effects Mélies developed.
32. Special sound effects interest ____ women the most.

- **Building Vocabulary**   Write the correct homophone.

33. Our pencils are filled with (lead, led).
34. The (principal, principle) teaches our art (course, coarse).
35. Before you eat (dessert, desert), take a (brake, break).

Write a sentence for each homograph. Make each sentence show
that the homographs have different meanings.

36. service / service   **39.** express / express
37. quarter / quarter   **40.** fair / fair
38. content / content   **41.** fit / fit

Enrichment

None of these sentences have punctuation. Write them correctly.

42. Senator Louise Scrima a lawmaker from Milford spoke to us
43. She said I highly recommend a book called Voting Laws
44. Zeke would you like Congress to let sixteen-year-olds vote
45. We asked parents students and teachers the same question
46. Yes the question was interesting but it was a new idea

Write a paragraph of your own. Leave out all the punctuation.
Make two copies. Give each one to a classmate. Ask each person
to work alone, inserting the missing marks. Then compare the
two punctuated paragraphs. Do both classmates have the same
answers? Can two different answers both be right?

More Practice

- **Reviewing Friendly Letters** Write the following friendly letter on a piece of paper. Put it into the correct form, and add any parts that are missing. Remember to use the correct punctuation for the five parts of a friendly letter. Beside each part, write the label *heading, greeting, body, closing,* or *signature.*

  > 380 Eastwood
  > Rome, NY 13340
  > Thanks so much for the wonderful birthday present. I know I'm going to get a lot of use out of my new racket. My old one was so worn out that it was beyond repair!
  >
  > I can hardly wait for your visit here in October, Aunt Kate. You and I can play tennis together every morning. Let us know what day you'll be arriving.
  >
  > Fred

- **Form of a Business Letter** Write the following business letter to Pat Brown, Director, Camp Sun, Carver, MA 02330 on a piece of paper. Put the letter into the correct business form. Add any parts that have been left out. (Use your own name and address and today's date.) Remember to punctuate and capitalize the six parts of the business letter correctly. Then label the six parts *heading, inside address, greeting, body, closing,* and *signature.*

  > I am interested in applying for a job as a counselor's aide at Camp Sun this summer. I am 12 years old and have worked with little children. Would you please send me an application form and some information about Camp Sun?

- **Style of a Business Letter** Rewrite the business letter shown at the top of the next page. Change any parts that are not in a businesslike style. Leave out any unnecessary information. Make up the information missing from the letter.

4917 Fremont Street
Decatur, IL 62526
June 9, 1983

James Green
Head Librarian
Midtown Public Library
9 Main Street
Decatur, IL 62523

Dear James:

    I can't believe what happened. Yesterday in the mail I got an overdue notice from your library for a book called Beginning Mechanics. I've never even heard of this book. I haven't been to the library since March, and this book was supposedly taken out just last April. What's going on?

Hope to see you soon,
Johnny Adams

- **Addressing an Envelope**   Draw an envelope, and address it to Ms. Rona Gary, Publisher, Jogging Digest, 909 Madison Ave., New York, NY 10021. Use your own return address.

- **Proofreading**   Proofread this business letter. Find ten errors. Write the letter correctly.

P.O. Box 932
Red Bank, NJ 07701
April 19 1983

Milton Bean
Host, Morning Show
TV Station WBCS
Los Angeles, CA 90004

Dear mr. Bean

    Please send me a copy of the recipey for sesame chicken you preparred on your April 18th show. I unclose a stampt, self-addressed envlope for this purpose.

Sincerly yours
Lisa Devon

More Practice

- **Adjectives**   Write the adjectives and the word each adjective modifies. List the articles separately.

   1. The five-year-old coat hung loosely around her.
   2. A salesperson, aggressive and loud, recited the prices.
   3. These soldiers seem loyal.
   4. Three weary joggers moved up a hill.

- **Comparing with Adjectives**   Write the comparative or superlative form of each adjective in parentheses.

   5. The Mardi Gras parade was the _____ I have seen. (grand)
   6. The costumes were _____ than they were last year. (elaborate)
   7. The end of the parade had _____ confusion than the beginning. (much)

- **Proper Adjectives**   Write a proper adjective for each noun.

   8. France   **9.** Japan   **10.** Mexico   **11.** Ireland

- **Adverbs**   Write each adverb. Then find the word it modifies, write it, and label it *V* (verb) or *Adj.* (adjective).

   12. Soon a ten-speed bike moved quickly into the lead.
   13. One photograph had especially bright colors.
   14. With a perfectly innocent smile, he walked away.

- **Comparing with Adverbs**   Write the comparative or superlative form of each adverb in parentheses.

   15. Each mountain ridge rose _____ than the one before it. (high)
   16. The actors dressed the _____ of all. (outrageously)
   17. Albert danced _____ than his sister. (energetically)
   18. Judy bruises the _____ of all my children. (badly)

- **Negatives**   Rewrite each sentence to avoid double negatives.

19. Natalie didn't see no grocery store.
20. Nobody wasn't paying attention.
21. Your store isn't nothing like my store.
22. The aisles of food didn't exist no longer.

- **Adjective or Adverb?**   Write the correct word.

23. George did not feel (good, well).
24. We could see home plate (good, well).
25. The weather turned out (good, well).
26. She improved her grades (slow, slowly).

- **Using Words Correctly**   Write the correct verbs.

27. There (is, are) no clocks.   29. There (were, was) silence.
28. There (is, are) a ticking noise. 30. There (is, are) some mice.

- **Building Vocabulary**   Write *negative* or *positive* to identify each word's connotation.

31. moist / soggy   32. cook / chef   33. take / grab

Enrichment

A. Make tongue twisters by adding modifiers to these simple sentences. The first one has been done for you.

1. Swans swim.

   Soon seven soft slim swans slowly swam southward.

2. Buses beep.   4. Trees tremble.   6. Hares hopped.
3. Sue sang.   5. Roberta reported.   7. Whales watch.

B. Form a new adjective by changing one letter of each word. Use the clues in parentheses for help. The first one has been done for you.

1. c <u>o l</u> <u>d</u>(icy)   2. m _ _ _ _ (stale)   3. b _ _ (evil)
   <u>b</u> <u>o l</u> <u>d</u>(brave)   _ _ _ _ _ (foggy)   _ _ _ (angry)

More Practice

- **Plot** Along the right-hand side of your paper, copy the four headings for a plot plan. Fit the sentences given below into the correct category by writing them beside the appropriate headings. Or, if you prefer, write sentences of your own to complete the chart.

  Main Problem: Climax:
  Smaller Problems: (at least 3)   Resolution:

  > Midas found that he could not eat because all the food that he touched turned to gold.

  > King Midas realized that there were many things more valuable than gold. When the stranger returned, Midas requested that the golden touch be taken from him. His wish was granted.

  > King Midas's glasses turned to gold, and he could no longer see through them.

  > Although King Midas loved his daughter dearly, he began to love gold more. One day a stranger visited him and granted his wish that everything he touched would be turned to gold. Midas became concerned about how he would keep all his gold safe.

  > Before he could stop her, King Midas's daughter reached up to kiss him. She was changed from a living child into a golden statue.

- **Setting** Write a short paragraph describing the setting from each of two kinds of stories listed below. Try to describe what you see and feel so that a reader could share your vision of the setting.

  a talking animal fantasy
  a present-day realistic story
  a fairy tale

- **Character**   Make up one character to fit into each type of story described in the previous exercise (Setting). Write two or three sentences to describe each character.

- **Dialogue**   Write dialogue that will let a reader know what kind of person each speaker is. Make up two characters of your own, or choose from the pairs listed below.

  > a sixth-grade girl and a robot in a computer center
  > a brother and sister entering an old, deserted house
  > a lifeguard and a swimmer at a beach

- **Beginnings and Endings**   Below is the plot of a story called "The Standard of Living" by Dorothy Parker. Read the plot. Then write two possible beginnings and two possible endings.

  > Two young working women play a game while they are window shopping on their day off. They pretend that a rich person has just left them a million dollars with the condition that they must spend every penny of it on themselves. As they peer into windows in shops along the street, they pick out items they would buy with their fortunes. One day they see a double-strand pearl necklace in a window. They decide that they would want such a pearl necklace if they were rich. On an impulse, they enter the shop to ask its price. When an icy clerk informs them that the price of the necklace is two-hundred and fifty thousand dollars, the women return to the street outside, dazed at the enormous price—a quarter of their million-dollar fortune! They begin to look at shop windows again. Then one woman asks the other what she would buy if someone suddenly left her <u>ten</u> million dollars.

- **Proofreading**   Proofread the following paragraph. Find the fifteen errors. Copy the paragraph over correctly.

  > "Noone has to no about are little seckret, said Mr Taylor. he looked up too see if the pirate was still stairing at the jewels in the chest "i can promis you that ill never breath a word of it"

More Practice

- **Prepositions**   Write the prepositions in these sentences. Some sentences have more than one preposition.

    1. Lori Beth explored the attic above her aunt's house.
    2. A curtain of cobwebs covered the windows from inside.
    3. She made footprints in the dust on the floor.
    4. Lori Beth moved between the two bicycles.
    5. In a trunk she found letters to her grandfather.

- **Prepositional Phrases**   Write each prepositional phrase. Circle the object in each one.

    6. She examined the old clothes beneath the letters.
    7. A blue silk dress with velvet trim caught her eye.
    8. Lori Beth turned to the old mirror behind her.
    9. How lovely Grandma must have looked in this dress!
    10. Is there a photograph of it in this album?

- **Prepositional Phrases as Adjectives**   Write each prepositional phrase. Beside it, write the noun it modifies.

    11. The picture frame on the wall was empty.
    12. There were hat boxes from Denholm's department store.
    13. The straw hat with the wide brim is Grandpa's.
    14. She saw a dressing table with no drawers.
    15. She discovered a small book for autographs.

- **Prepositional Phrases as Adverbs**   Write each prepositional phrase. Then write the word it modifies.

    16. She thumbed through the pages patiently.
    17. A poem or a joke appeared on each page.
    18. Lori Beth marveled at the handwriting styles.

19. Each signature sparkled on the page.
20. Late in the afternoon, she noticed the time.
21. She felt happy about her attic visit.

- **Using Words Correctly** Write each sentence, choosing the correct word(s) in parentheses.

22. Jed waited (in, into) the reception room.
23. The manager asked him to come (in, into) her office.
24. Jed (must of, must have) seen the notice on the bulletin board.
25. She hired him as a programmer (in, into) the computer department.
26. His salary (could have, could of) been higher.

- **Building Vocabulary** Write the blended form from each word pair.

27. sports + broadcast   **29.** motor + hotel
28. breakfast + lunch   **30.** smoke + fog

Write a clipped word for each of these words.

31. laboratory   **33.** delicatessen
32. gymnasium   **34.** telephone

Enrichment

Each set of numbers below is a preposition. Use the code in the boxes to change each number to a letter. Write the prepositions, and use each one in a sentence. Then use the code to write some prepositions of your own. Ask a partner to decode them.

a	b	c	d	e	f	g	h	i	j	k	l	m	n	o	p	q	r	s	t	u	v	w	x	y	z
2	25	4	23	6	21	8	19	10	17	12	15	14	13	16	11	18	9	20	7	22	5	24	3	26	1

1. 25•6•7•24•6•6•13   **4.** 2•9•16•22•13•23
2. 7•19•9•16•22•8•19   **5.** 25•6•26•16•13•23
3. 23•22•9•10•13•8   **6.** 22•13•7•10•15

INDEX

Numbers in **bold type** indicate pages where
   item is introduced.
Numbers in *italic* indicate further practice.

Acknowledgments *(continued from page 2)*

Table of contents and Index from *Around Our World (Houghton Mifflin Social Studies Program).* Copyright © 1980 by Houghton Mifflin Company. Reprinted by permission.

"The Boys Next Door" (excerpt), from *My Childhood,* by Maxim Gorky. Translated by Isidor Schneider, 1953, Elek Books Ltd., London. Used by permission of Lyle Stuart, Inc.

"The Californian" (excerpt), by Jesse Hutchinson. Reprinted by permission of Harvard University Press from *Argonauts of '49* by O. T. Howe, copyright 1923.

"The Great Lover" (excerpt), by Rupert Brooke, from *The Collected Poems of Rupert Brooke.* Reprinted by permission of Dodd, Mead & Company, Inc., McClelland and Stewart Limited, Toronto, and Sidgwick and Jackson Ltd., London.

"The Monkey's Paw," from *The Lady and the Barge,* by W. W. Jacobs. Published by Dodd, Mead & Company, Inc. Reprinted by permission of The Society of Authors as the literary representative of the Estate of W. W. Jacobs.

"Winter Poem 3 Feb 72," from *My House* by Nikki Giovanni. Copyright © 1972 by Nikki Giovanni. Reprinted by permission of William Morrow & Company.

Credits

Cover and Title Page Photography by Olmsted Studio

Illustration

Laura Beatty: pp. 33, 35, 36, 38, 41, 47, 48–49, 160, 163, 164, 166, 168, 169, 171, 175, 177.

Carol Bjork: p. 198.

Dave Blanchette: pp. 300, 302.

Kristine Bollinger: pp. 314, 315, 320.

Kevin Callahan: pp. 306, 307.

Linda Chen: pp. 73, 75, 78, 79, 81, 84.

Laura Cornell: p. 303.

Jon Goodell: pp. 111, 112, 116, 118.

David Kelley: pp. 119, 157, 316.

Diana Magnuson: pp. 225, 228, 232, 233, 235, 239.

Stella Ormai: pp. 187, 188, 190, 195, 202.

Blanche Sims: pp. 145, 147, 150, 153, 156, 269, 270, 275, 278, 280.

Krystyna Stasiak: pp. 304, 305.

George Ulrich: pp. 310–311.

Lane Yerkes: pp. 11, 13, 15, 19, 21, 23, 26, 52, 53, 55, 56, 58, 59, 62, 63, 64, 89, 91, 94, 95, 97, 101, 102, 122, 123, 127, 131, 132, 135, 209, 211, 212, 216, 218, 219, 245, 246, 248, 253, 254, 257, 260, 285, 286, 289, 290.

Handwriting by Chris Czernota and Mary Keefe.

Photography

Camilla Smith/Rainbow: p. 8; Elizabeth Crews: p. 30; David Smith: p. 45; Michael Philip Manheim/Photo Researchers: p. 50; Read Brugger/Picture Cube: p. 70; David Smith: p. 82; Carl Purcell/Photo Researchers: p. 86; Richard Choy/Peter Arnold: p. 108; Linda Moore/Rainbow: p. 120; Tom McCarthy/Image Bank: p. 140; Paul Fusco/Magnum: p. 143; Edith Haun/Stock, Boston: p. 158; Martha Cooper/EPA: p. 184; Runk/Schoenberger/Grant Heilman: p. 204; Gabe Palmer/Black Star: p. 206; Ivan Massar/Black Star: p. 224; Gus Gregory/After Image: p. 242; Ed Hof/Picture Cube: p. 264; Bradley Olman/Bruce Coleman: p. 282; Isaac Geib/Grant Heilman: p. 298; Grant Heilman: p. 308; Lou Jones: p. 312.